New Art Dealers Alliance

NADA ART FAIR MIAMI

2008
12.3–12.7

THE ICE PALACE
1400 NORTH MIAMI AVENUE

CORNER OF NORTH MIAMI AVENUE
AND NW 14TH STREET

PICTUREBOX, BROOKLYN

Mission Statement

Founded in 2002, New Art Dealers Alliance (NADA) is a not-for-profit collective of professionals working with contemporary art. Our mission is to create an open flow of information, support, and collaboration within our field and to develop a stronger sense of community among our constituency. We believe that the adversarial approach to exhibiting and selling art has run its course. We believe that change can be achieved through fostering constructive thought and dialogue between various points in the art industry from large galleries to small spaces, non-profit and commercial alike.

Our international group of members includes both galleries and individuals (art professionals, independent curators, and established gallery directors). The various perspectives and ideas offered by our diverse roster creates a network which, at its most basic, is a resource which people could contribute to and take as much (or as little) as they are inclined. The benefits for some may be a matter of business, for others a source of intellectual or aesthetic stimulation.

To date, our initiatives have succeeded on two fronts: making the contemporary arts more accessible for the general public, and creating opportunities that nurture the growth of emerging artists, curators, and galleries. Our events have included: artist talks/gallery walks with critics and curators; benefits in support of charitable institutions; members-only seminars to stimulate dedication and ethics in our profession; and an annual art fair in Miami, which is held in December and is free and open to the public.

The New Art Dealers Alliance is a not-for-profit organization, registered in the State of New York. Membership is by invitation only, following nomination by an existing member and approval by the executive and advisory boards.

For more information on the New Art Dealers Alliance (NADA), please visit our website www.newartdealers.org or email info@newartdealers.org.

Participants

Ancient & Modern London
Arquebuse Geneva
ATM Gallery New York
Laura Bartlett London
Bellwether Gallery New York
Joseé Bienvenu Gallery New York
Blanket Contemporary Art Inc. Vancouver
BolteLang Zurich
Brown London
Galerie Sandra Bürgel Berlin
Shane Campbell Gallery Chicago
Canada New York
Cardenas Bellanger Paris
Cerealart Philadelphia
Galerie Chez Valentin Paris
Cohan and Leslie New York
COMA Centre for Opinions in Music and Art Berlin
Lisa Cooley New York
Country Club Cincinnati
Czarna Galeria Warsaw
Elizabeth Dee Gallery New York
doggerfisher Edinburgh
ELASTIC Malmö
Galerie Frank Elbaz Paris
Eleven Rivington New York
Derek Eller Gallery New York
Evergreene Geneva
Figge Von Rosen Galerie Cologne
Fruit and Flower Deli New York
James Fuentes New York
Galerie Laurent Godin Paris
Green on Red Gallery Dublin
Greener Pastures Contemporary Art Toronto
ANDREAS GRIMM Munich/New York
Guild & Greyshkul New York
Kavi Gupta Gallery Chicago/Leipzig
Jack Hanley Gallery San Francisco/New York
Hudson Franklin New York
Hunt Kastner Prague
IBID PROJECTS London
Jancar Jones Gallery San Francisco
Parker Jones Gallery Los Angeles
Galerie Juliette Jongma Amsterdam
Karma International Zurich
Galerie Ben Kaufmann Berlin
Rowley Kennerk Gallery Chicago
Parisa Kind Frankfurt Am Main
Nicole Klagsbrun Gallery New York

Klaus von Nichtssagend Gallery Brooklyn
Klemm's Berlin
KLERKX Milan
Layr Wüestenhagen Contemporary Vienna
Kim Light/Light Box Los Angeles
Lokal_30 Warsaw
Linn Lühn Cologne
Andreiana Mihail Gallery Bucharest
Francesca Minini Milan
MISAKO & ROSEN Tokyo
Monitor Video & Contemporary Art Rome
Mother's Tankstation Dublin
Murray Guy New York
Museum 52 London/New York
Myto Mexico City
Neue Alte Brücke Frankfurt Am Main
Mihai Nicodim Gallery Los Angeles
Office Baroque Gallery Antwerp
Overduin and Kite Los Angeles
Simon Preston Gallery New York
Ratio 3 San Francisco
Roebling Hall New York
Sister Los Angeles
Small A Projects New York
gallery.sora. Tokyo
Jacky Strenz Frankfurt Am Main
Studio Voltaire London
SUNDAY L.E.S. New York
Take Ninagawa Tokyo
Thierry Goldberg Projects New York
Triple Base Gallery San Francisco
Upstream Amsterdam
Van Horn Düsseldorf
Martin Van Zomeren/gmvz Amsterdam
Wallspace New York
Galerie Jan Wentrup Berlin
Western Exhibitions Chicago
White Columns New York
Workplace Gallery Gateshead
ZieherSmith New York

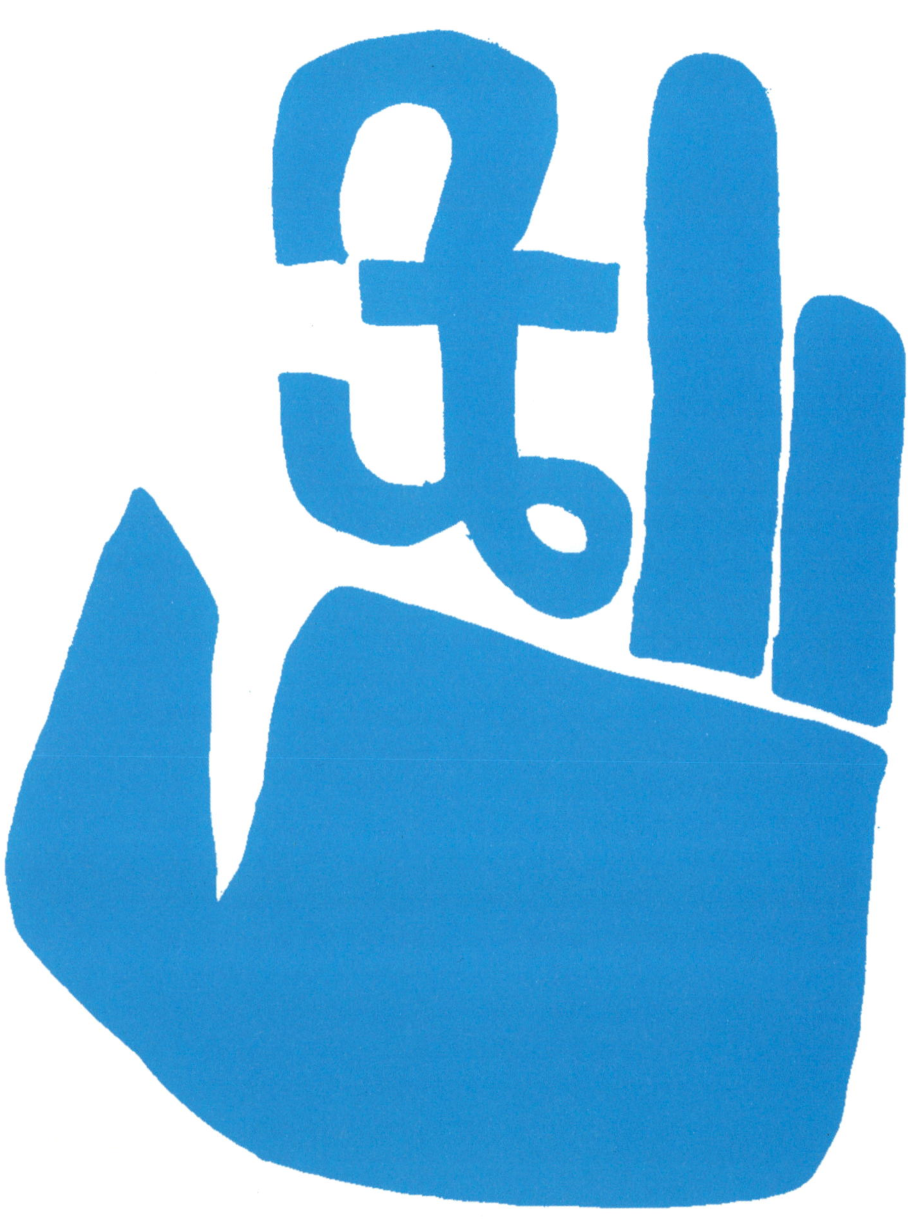

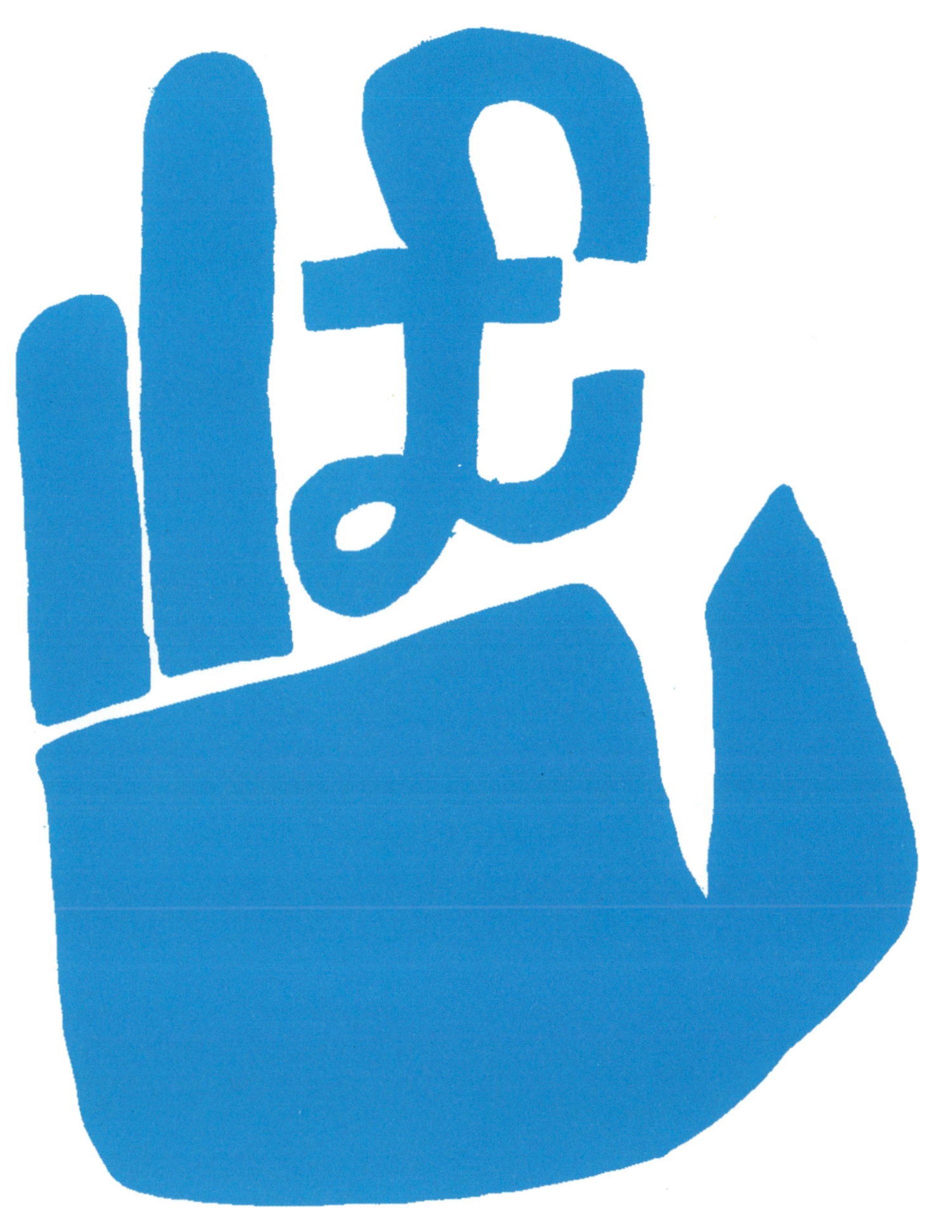

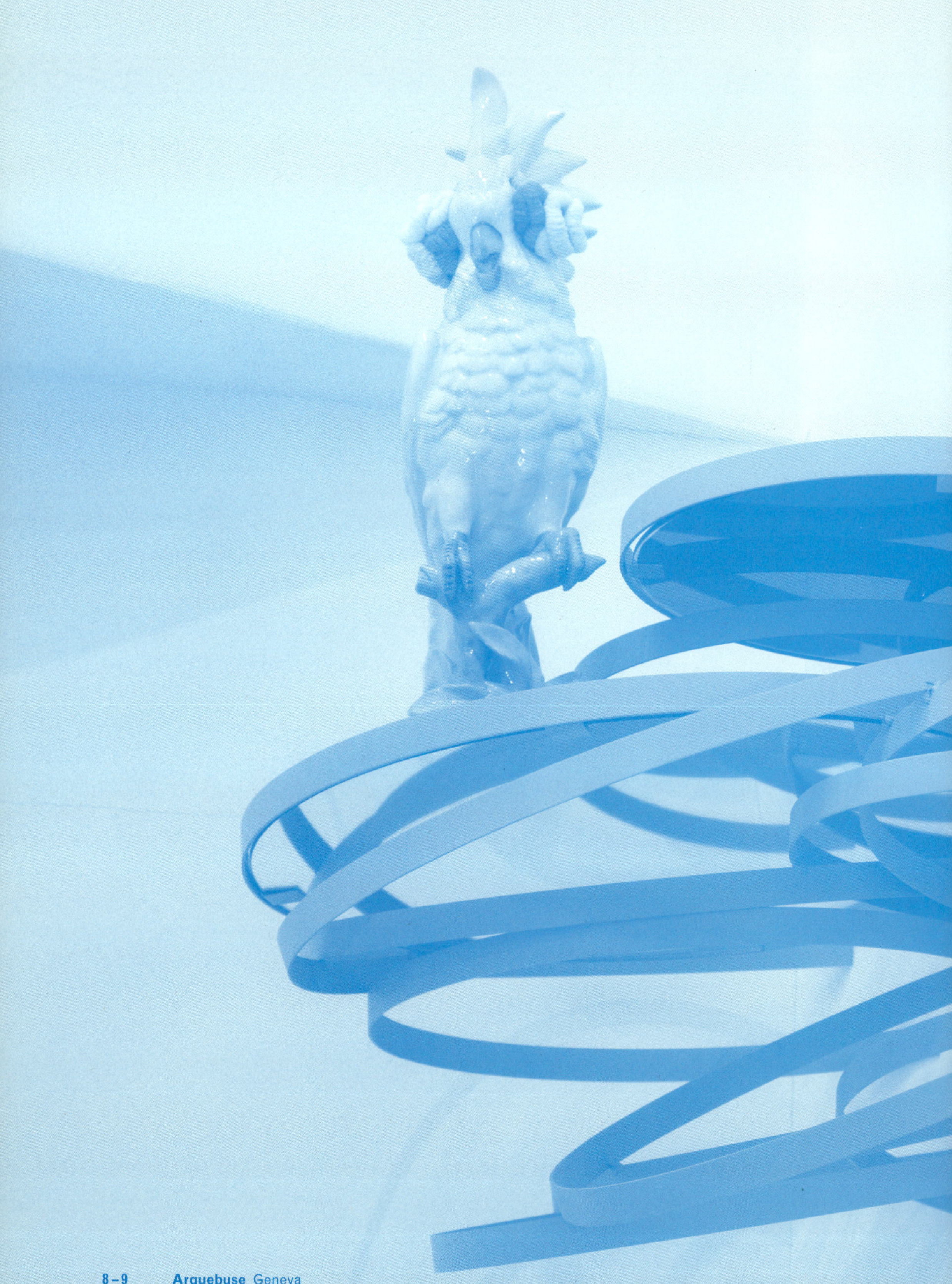

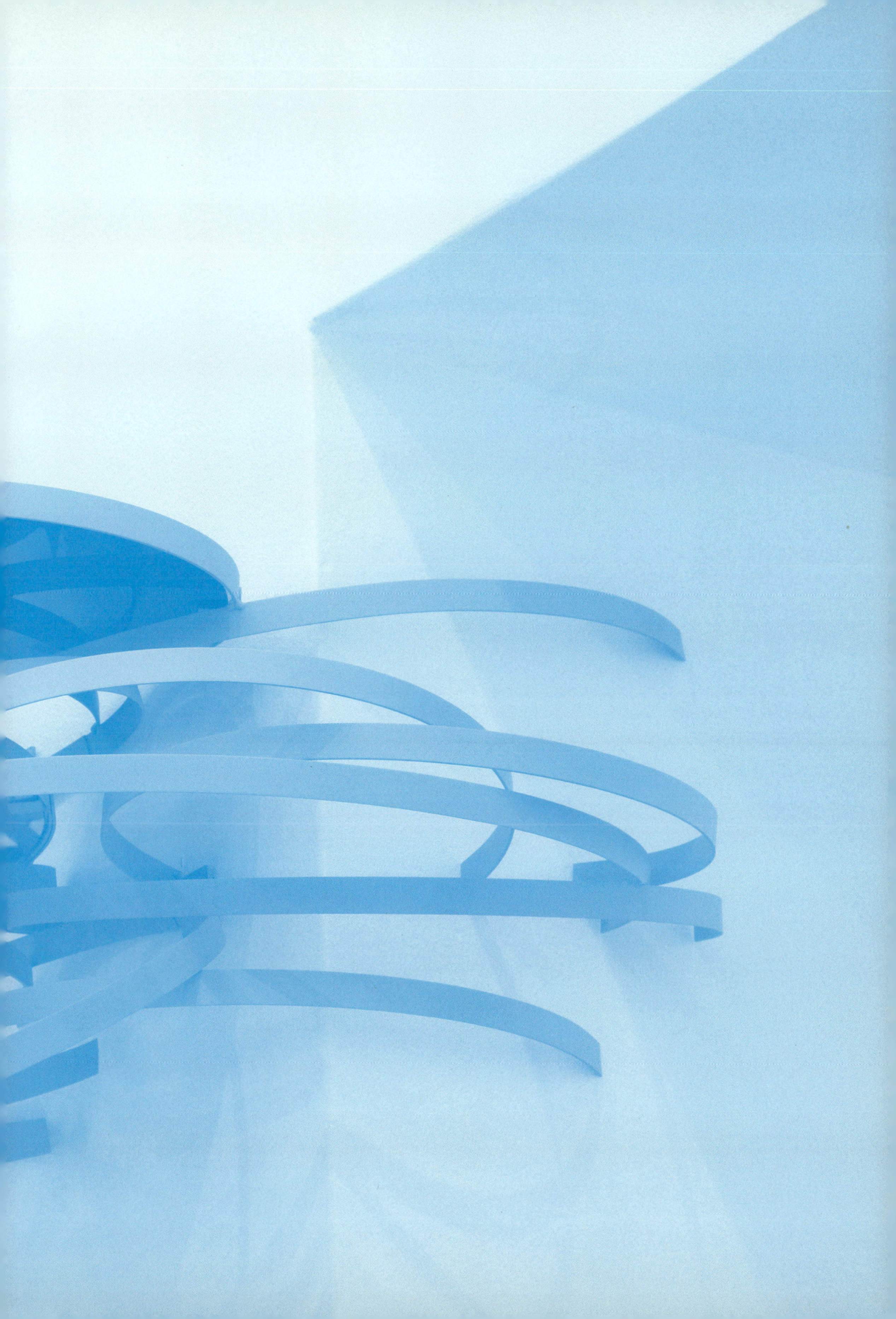

atm gallery

atmgallery

atm gallery

atmgallery

atmgallery

atmgallery

atmgallery

atmgallery

atm gallery
atm gallery
atm gallery
atm gallery
atm gallery
atm gallery
atm gallery

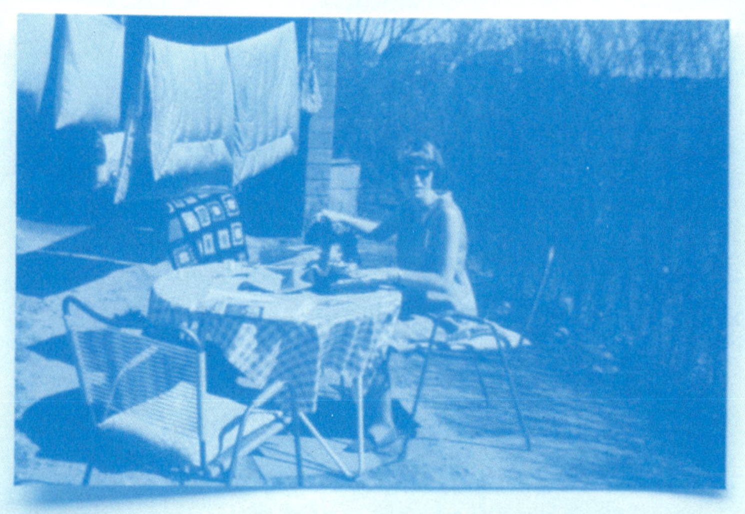

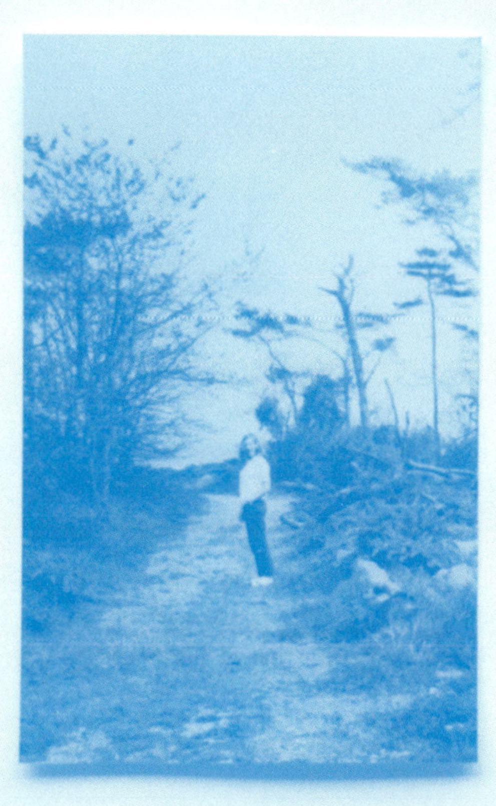

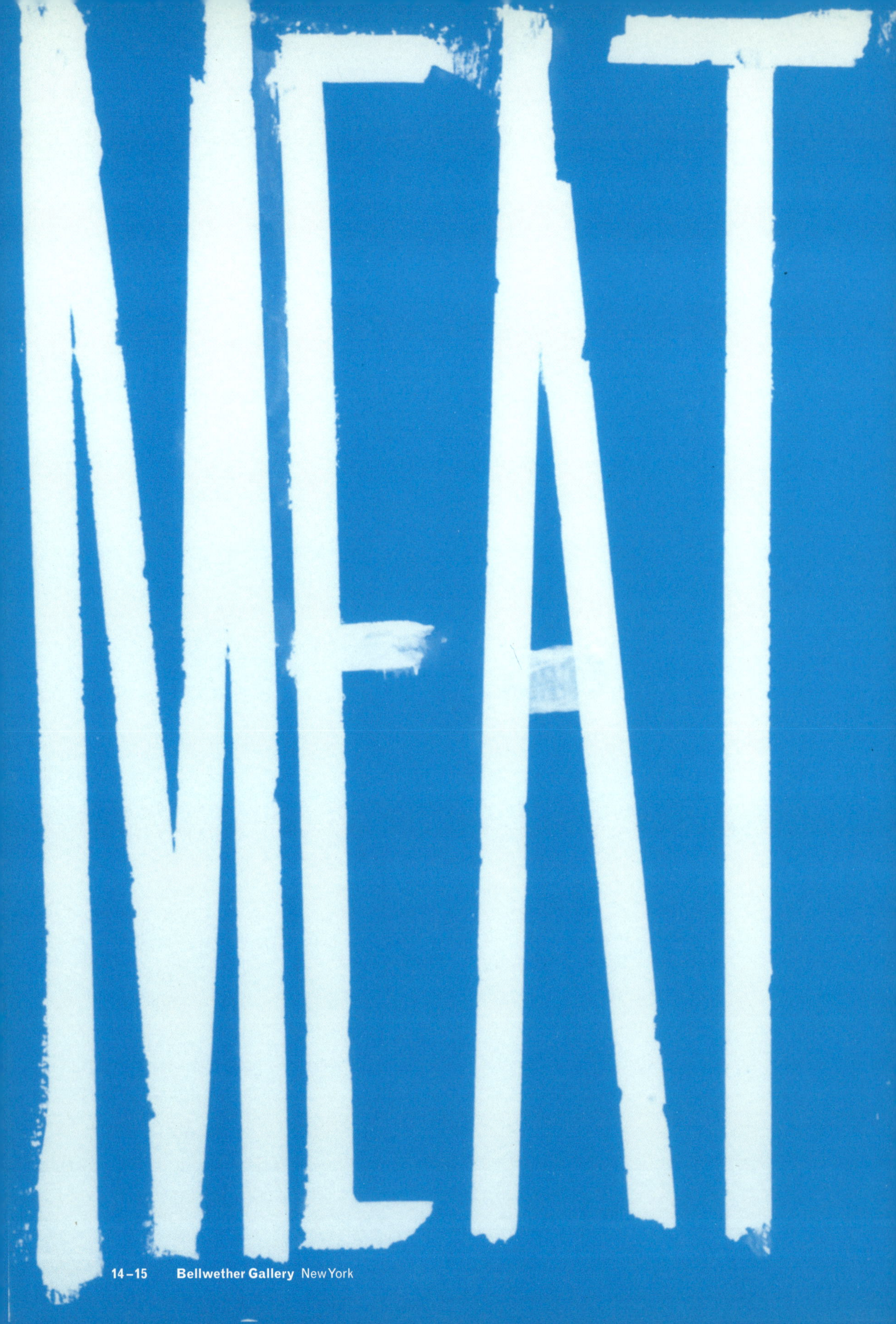
MEAT
14–15   Bellwether Gallery New York

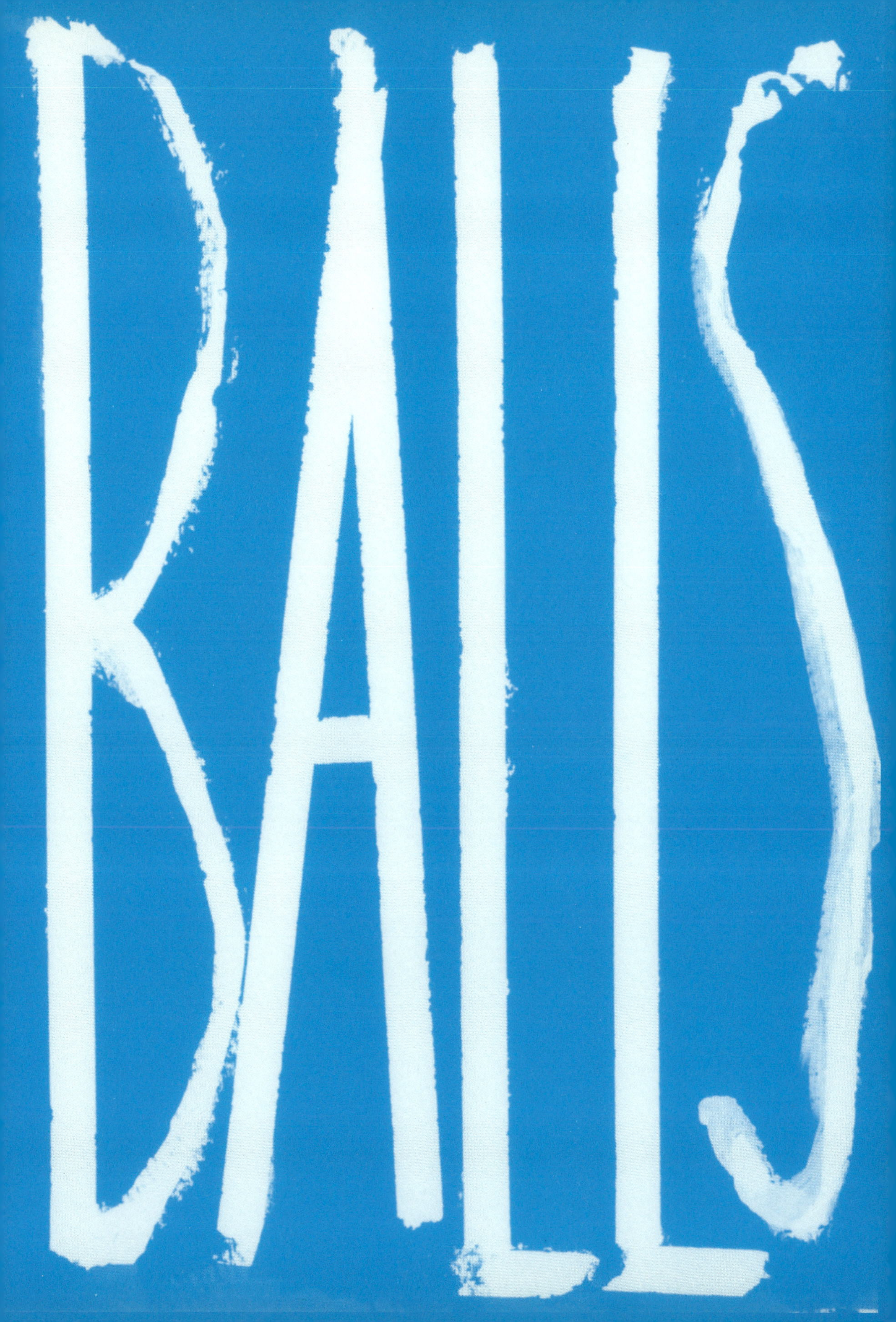
BALLS

William Astor Baitigan

Lucinda Butt

Alita Bush

Asof Dwight Cawk

Caymen Cider

Ollie Chout

Anita Lotta Dick

I.B. Doffalott

Imen Dowd

P. Sonya Face

Heath Gaye

Phin Gurrin-Nass

Ike Haim

Ulf Hucka Sr.

Anita Hummer

Katia Jerkinov

Jen Tyler Joo

Agatha Klapp

Don Keedick

I. Scott Krabbs

Fay Korgazzim

Kay Minner

Jen Nittlewartz

Maya Rection

Yuri Tardid

Olive Tiffuck

Shea Vior-Busch

Amadou Yurrass

Alger Q. Woff

Essie Yecks

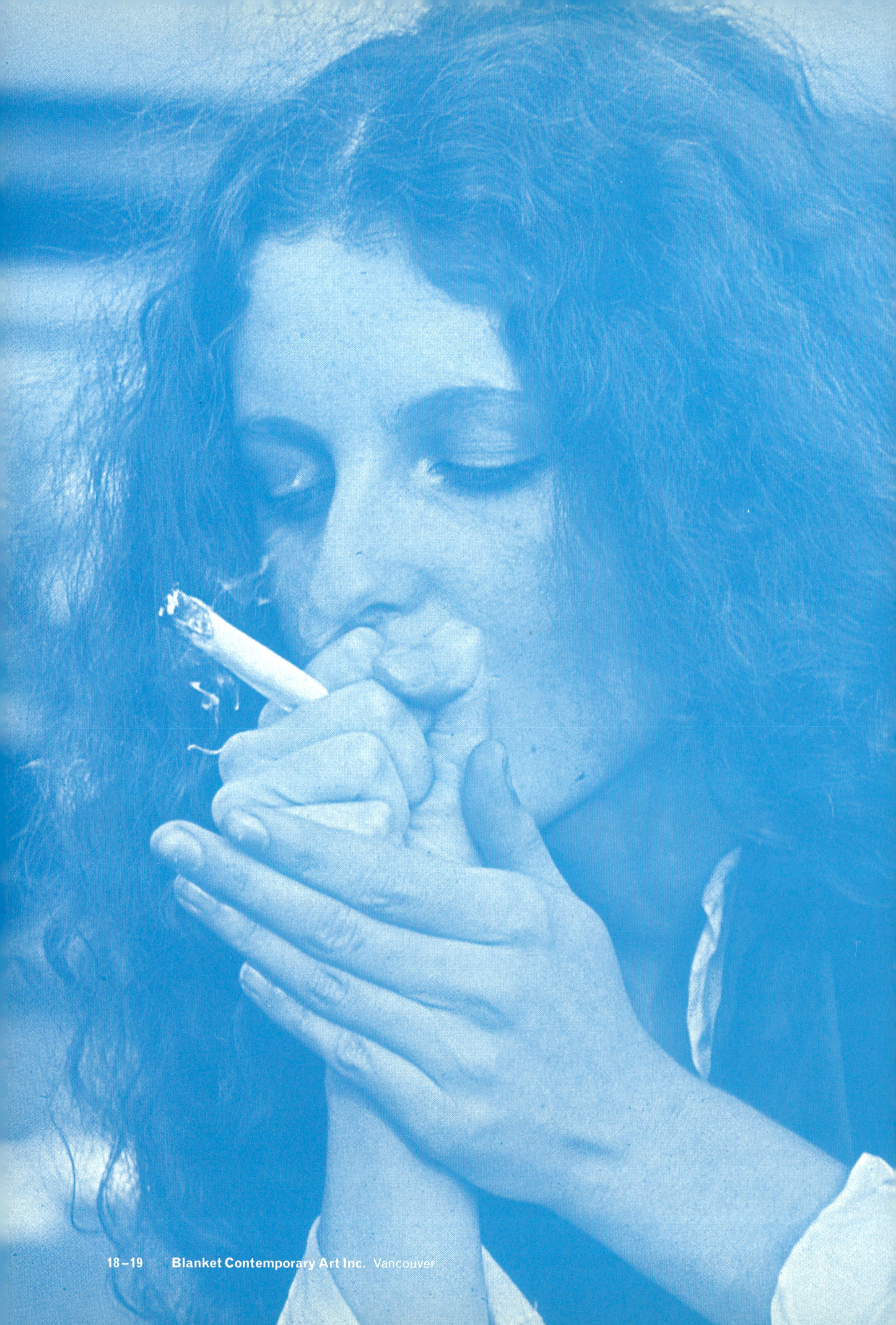

 Blanket Contemporary Art Inc. Vancouver

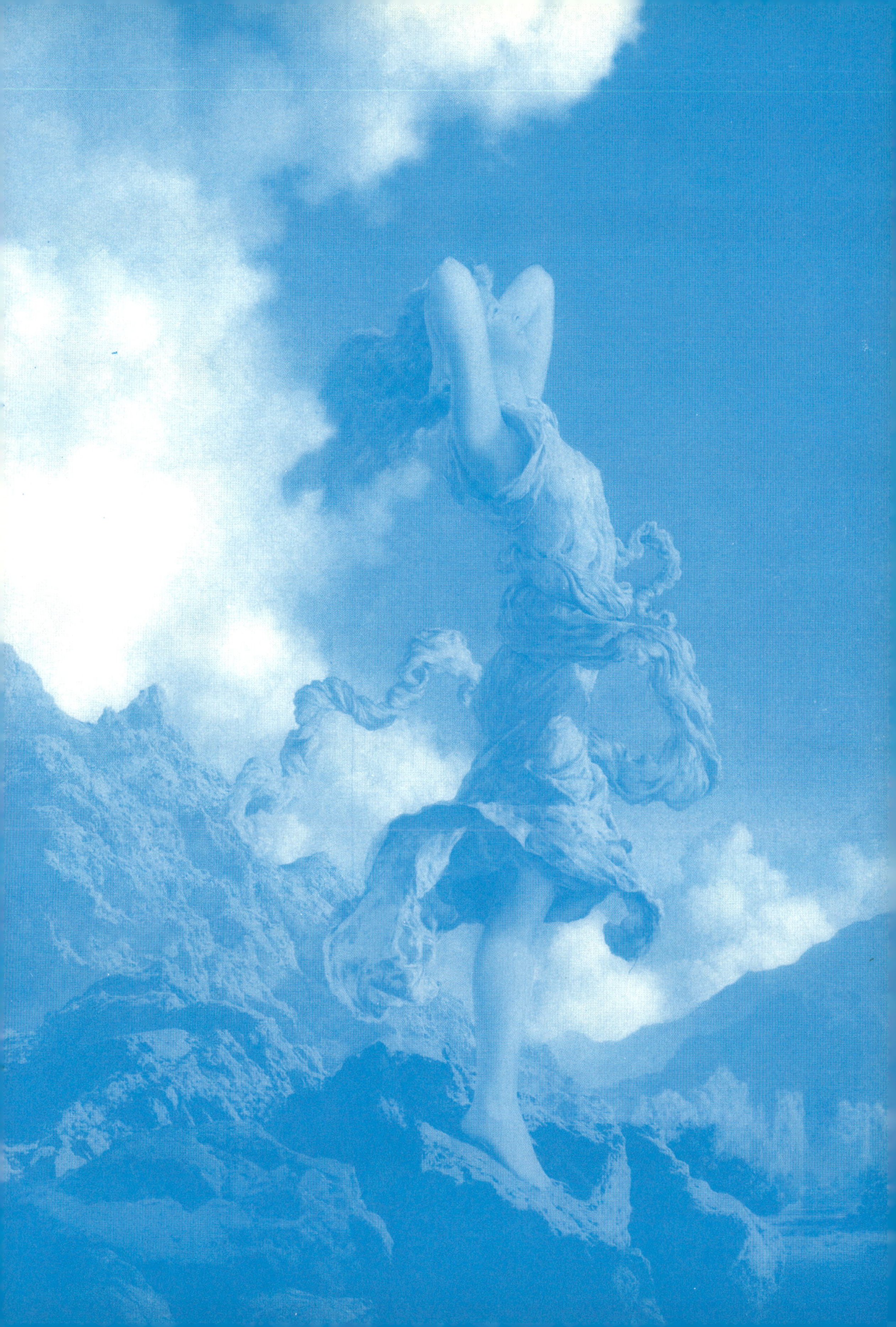

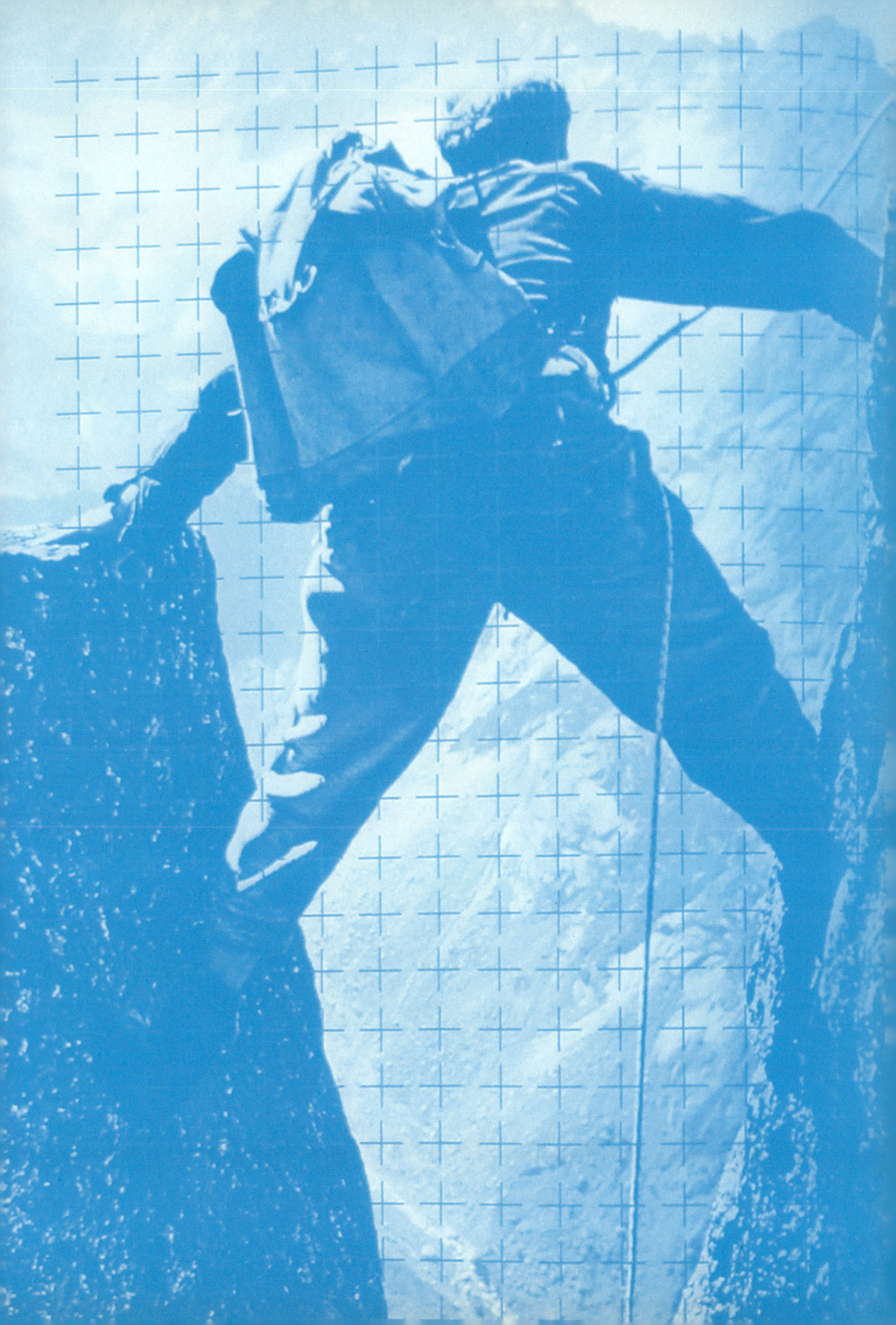

OK
ALRIGHT
UH HUH

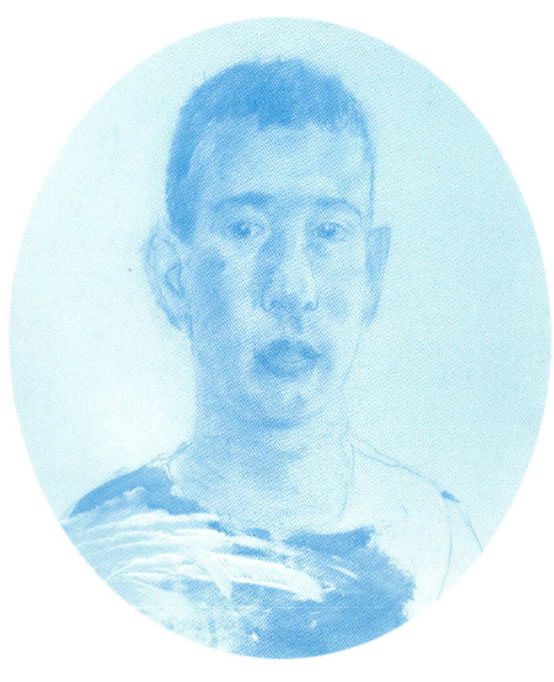

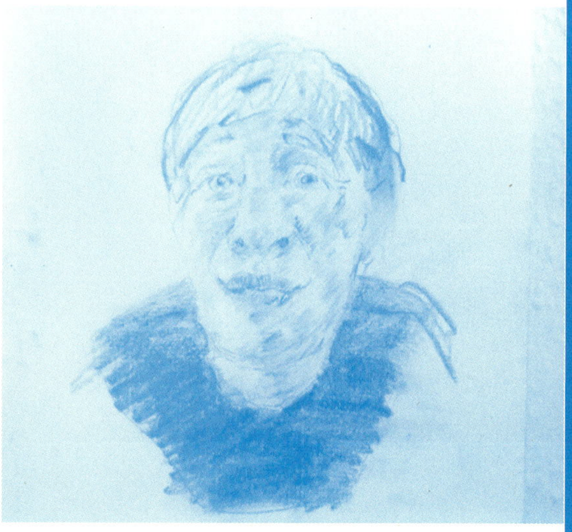

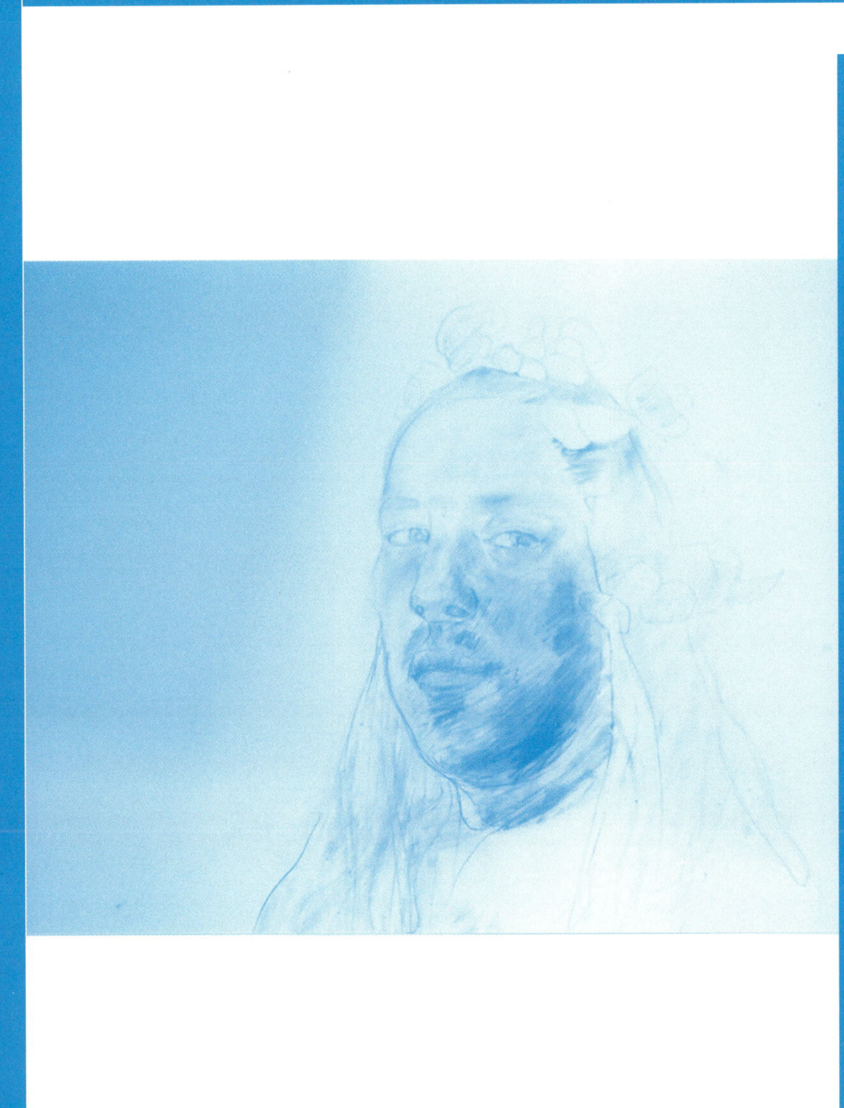

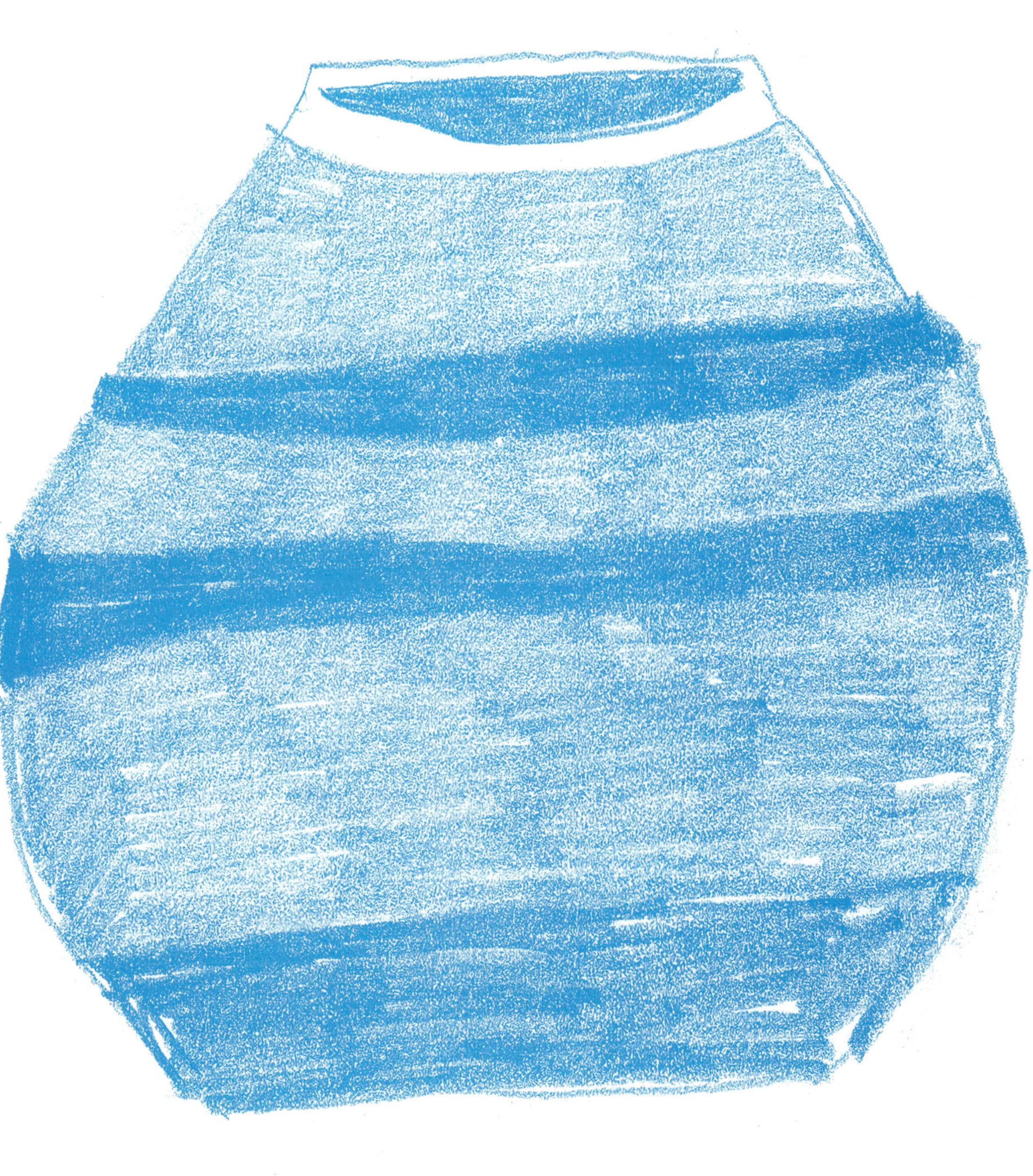

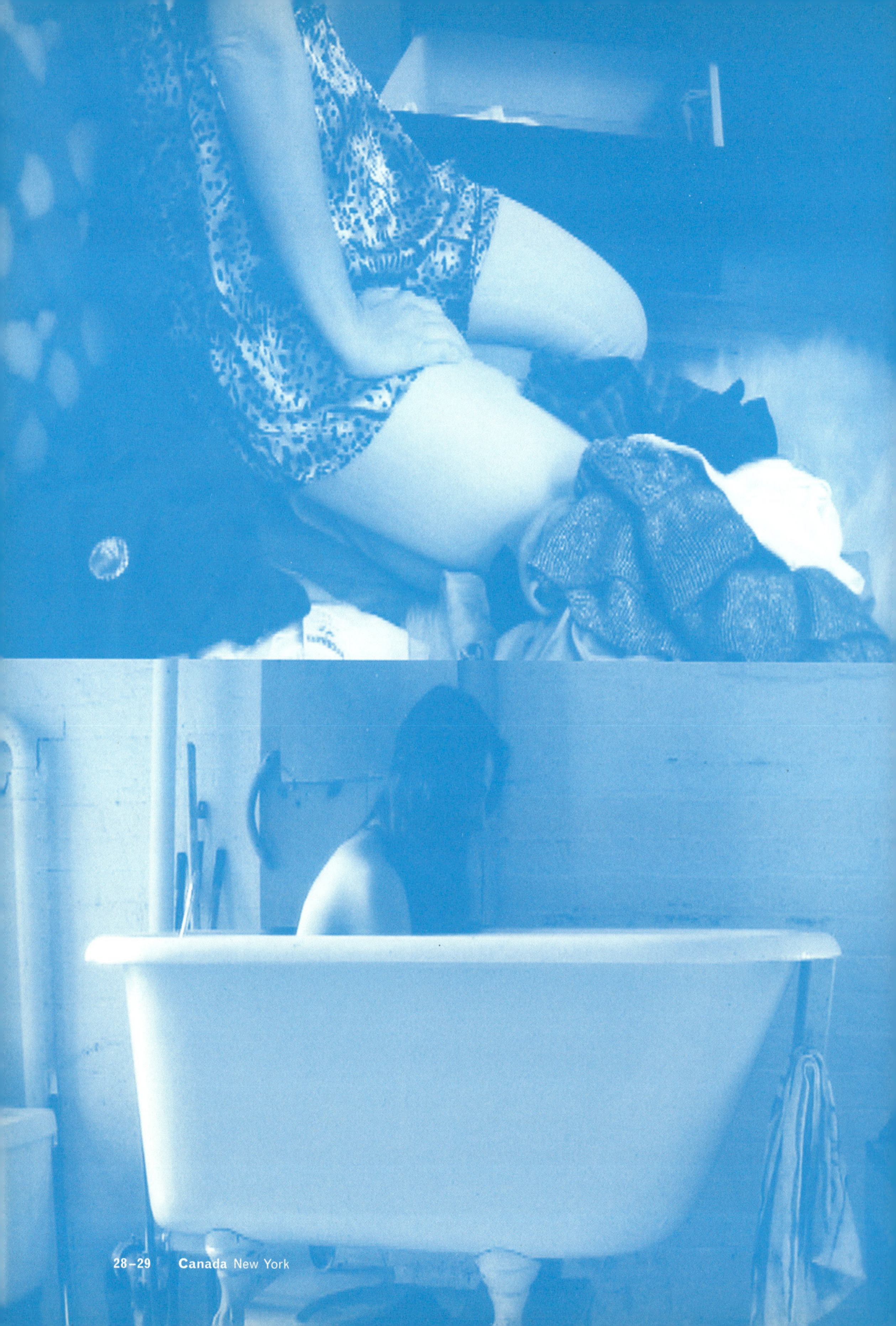

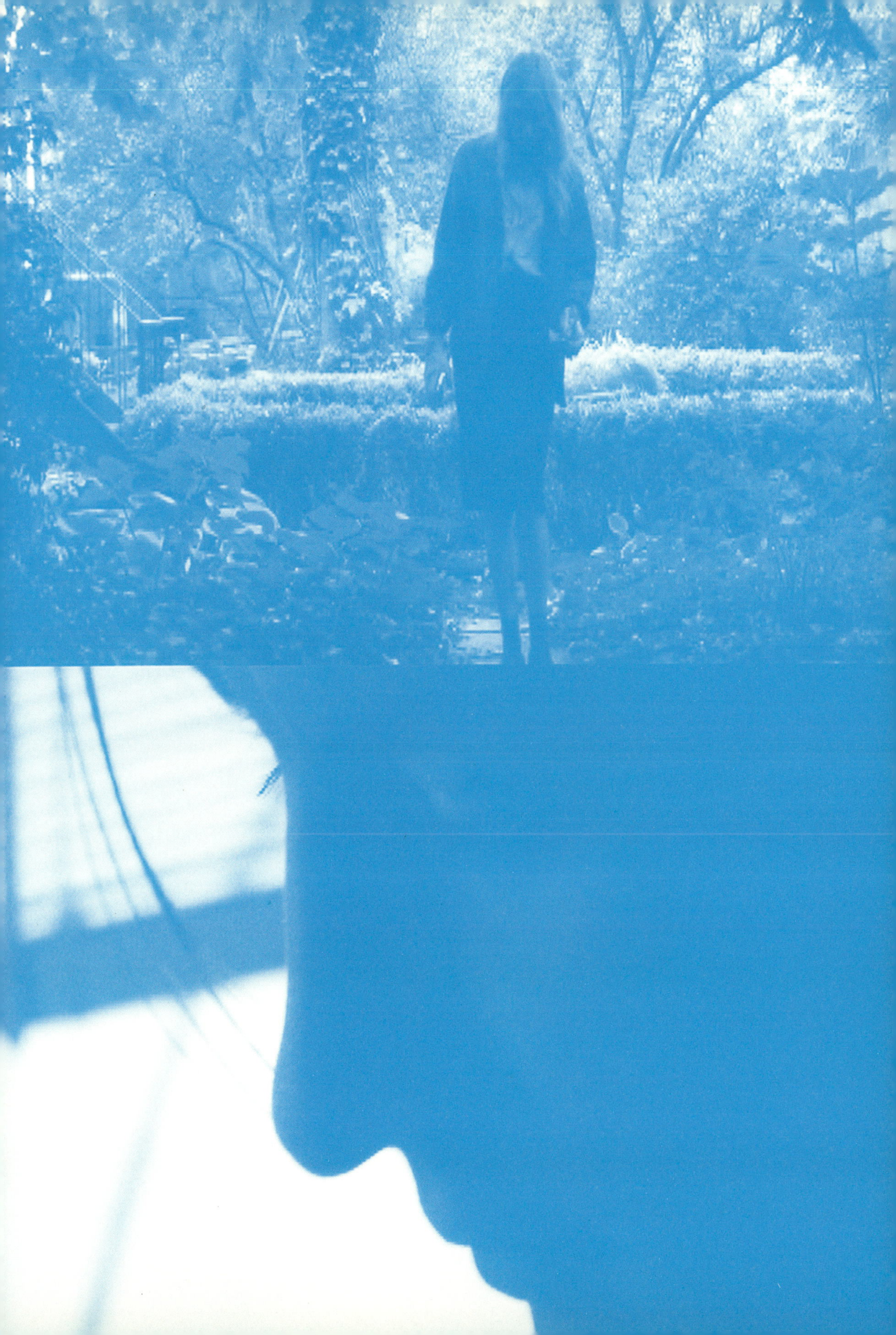

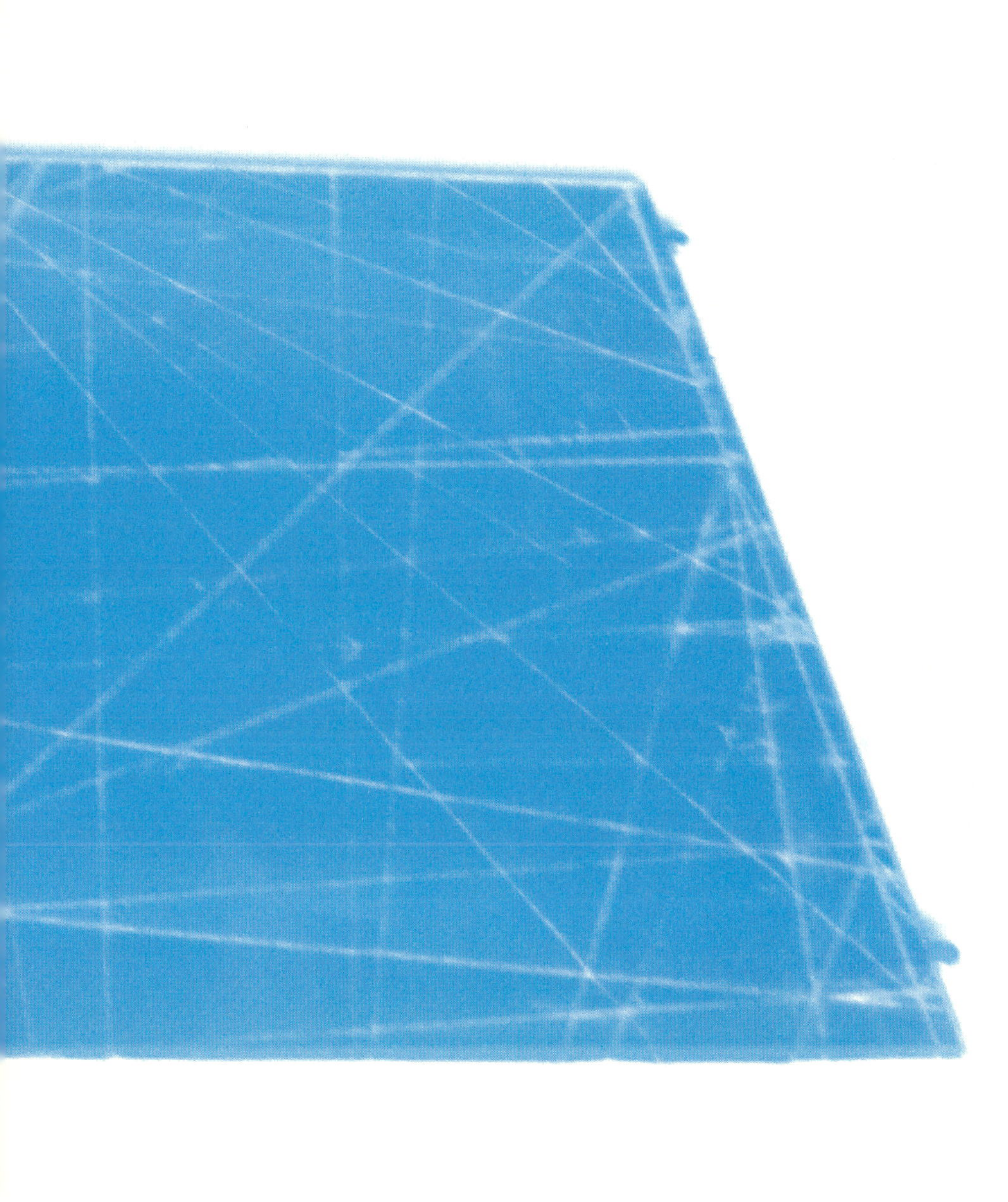

 Cerealart Philadelphia

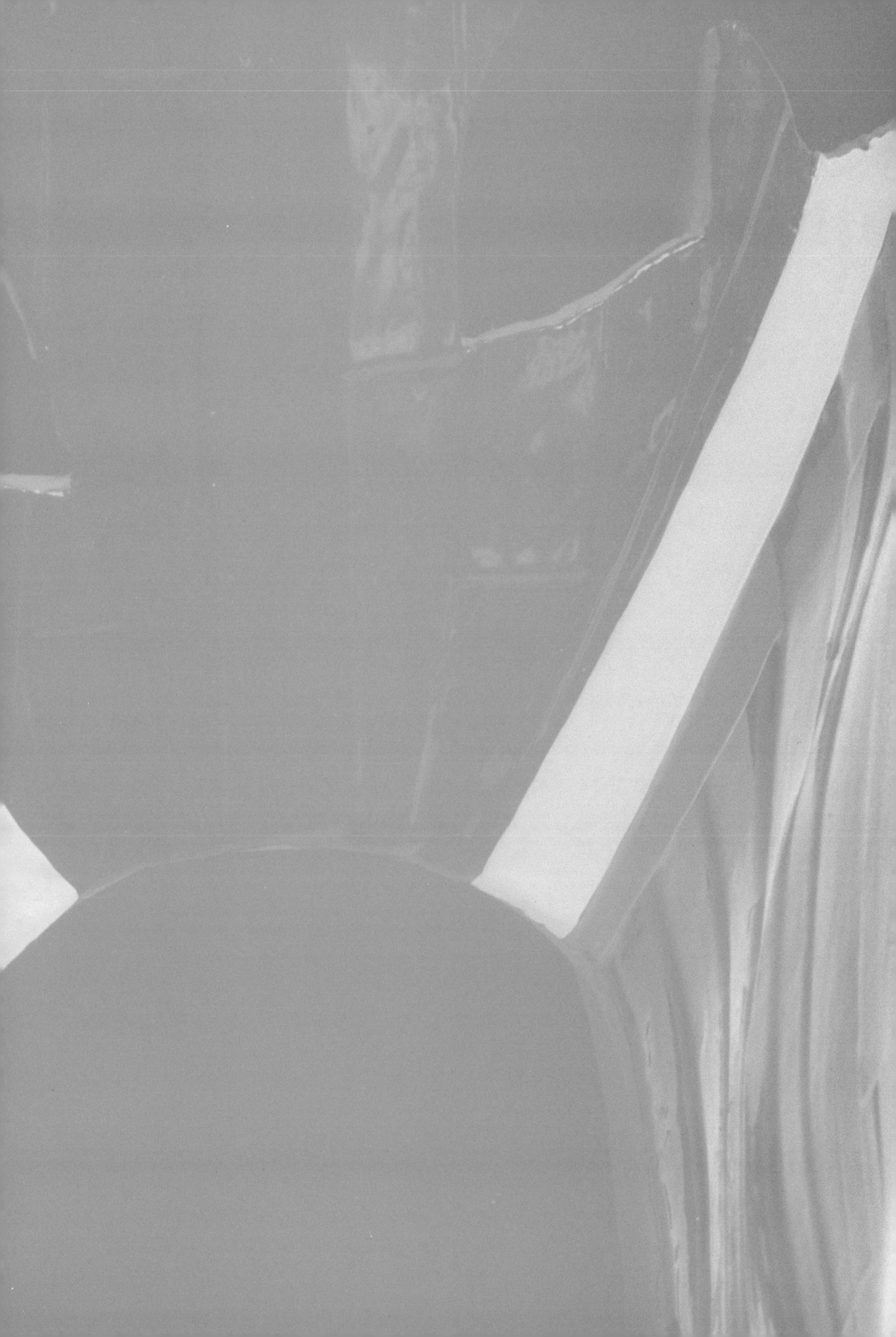

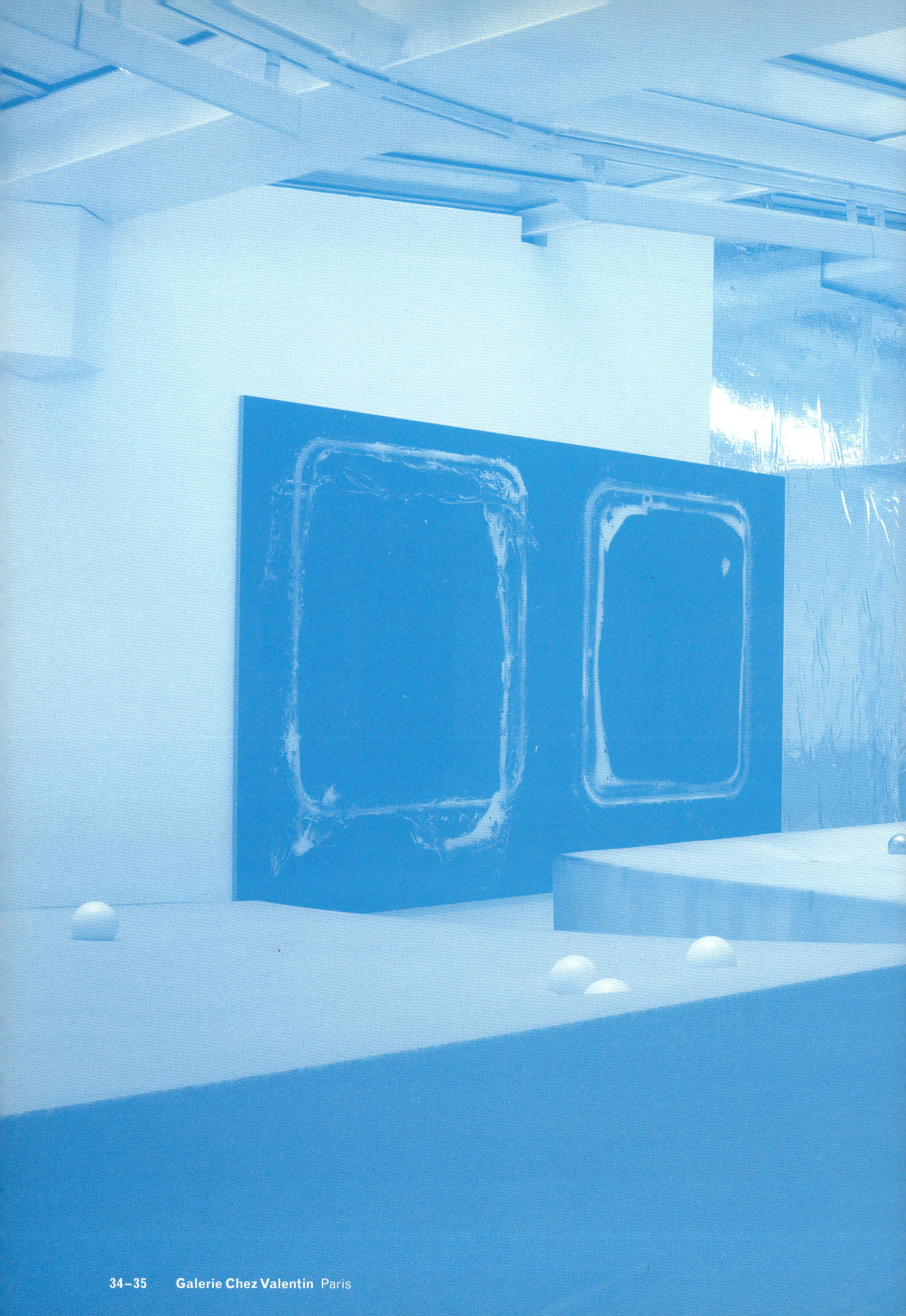

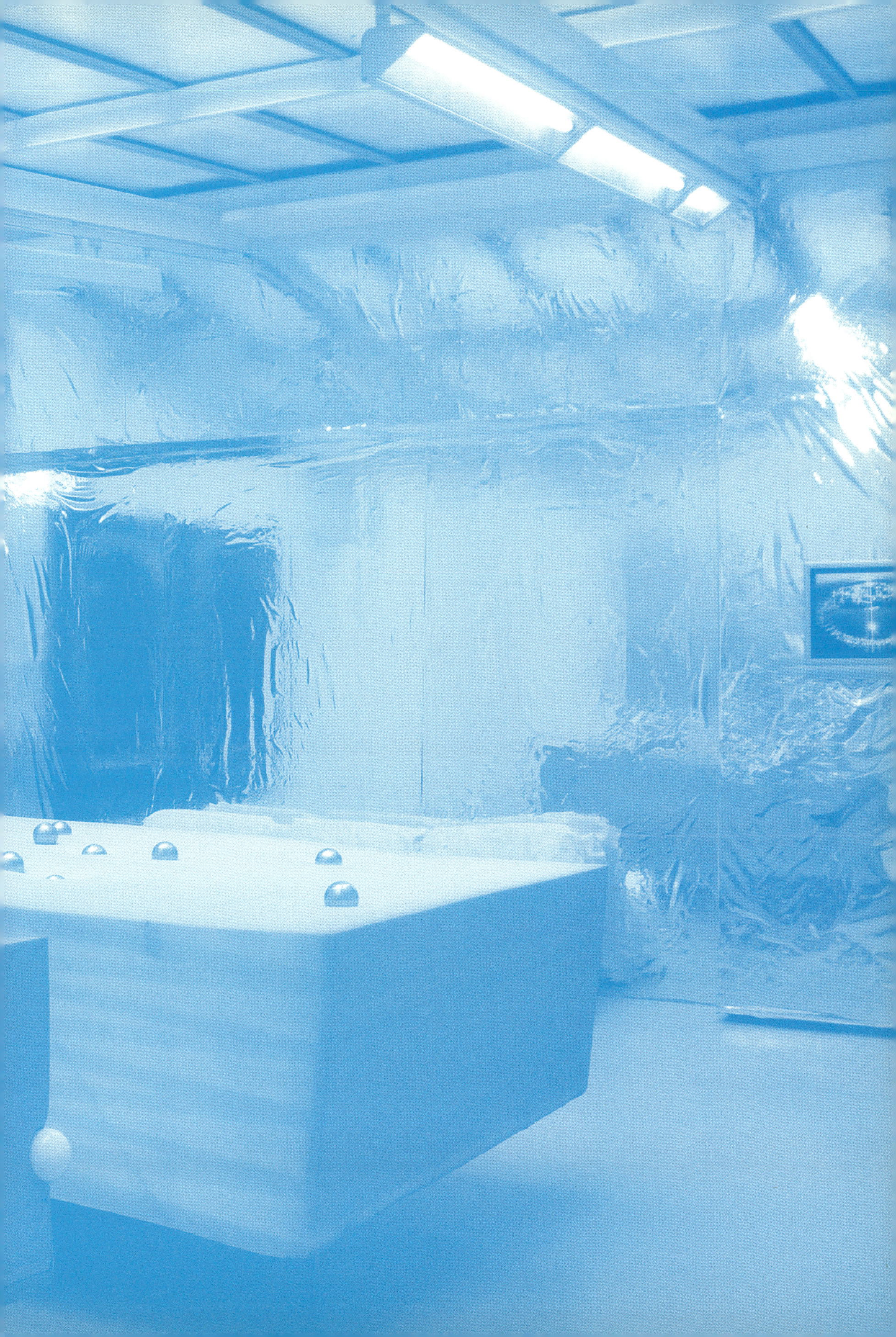

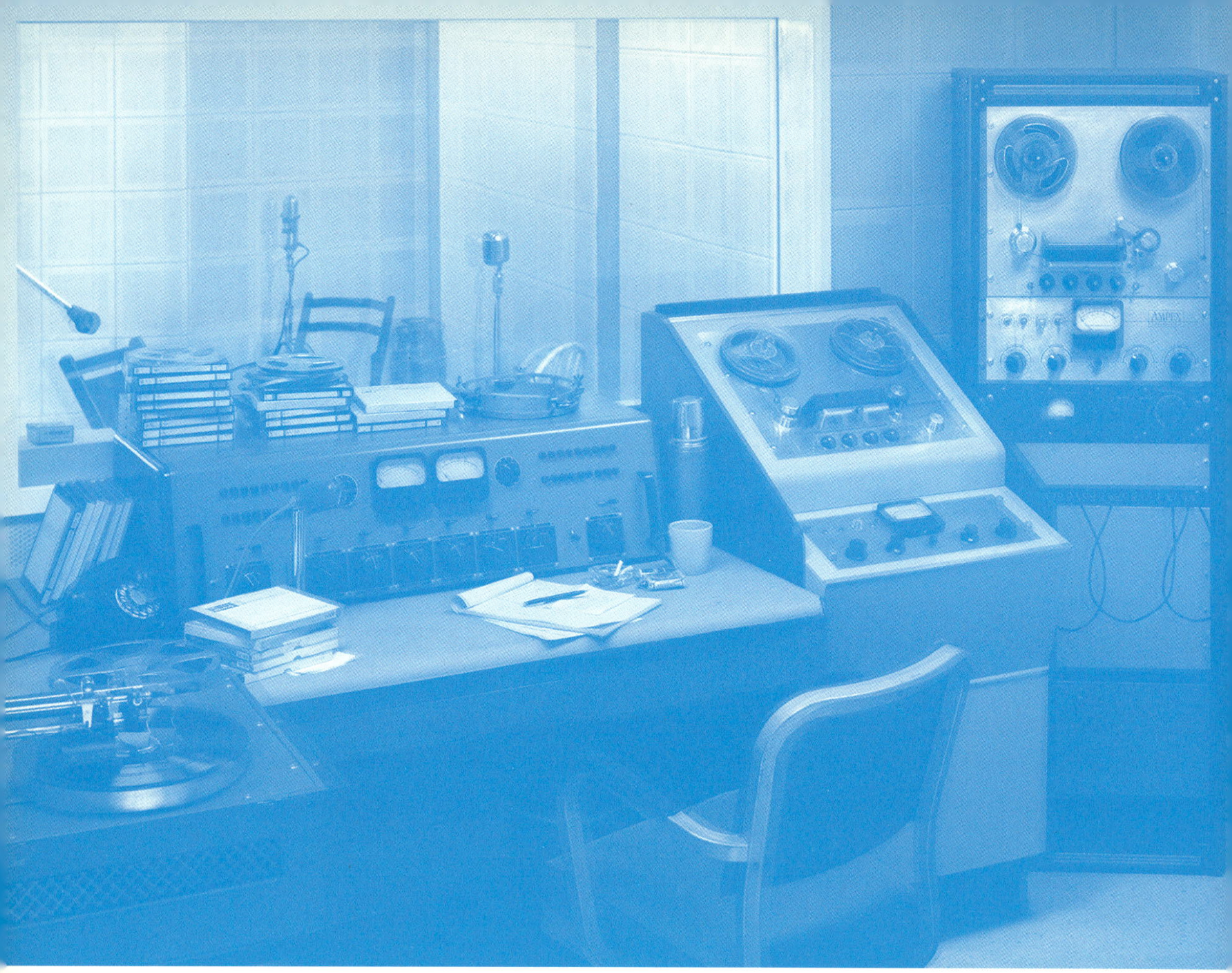

36–37   **Cohan and Leslie** New York

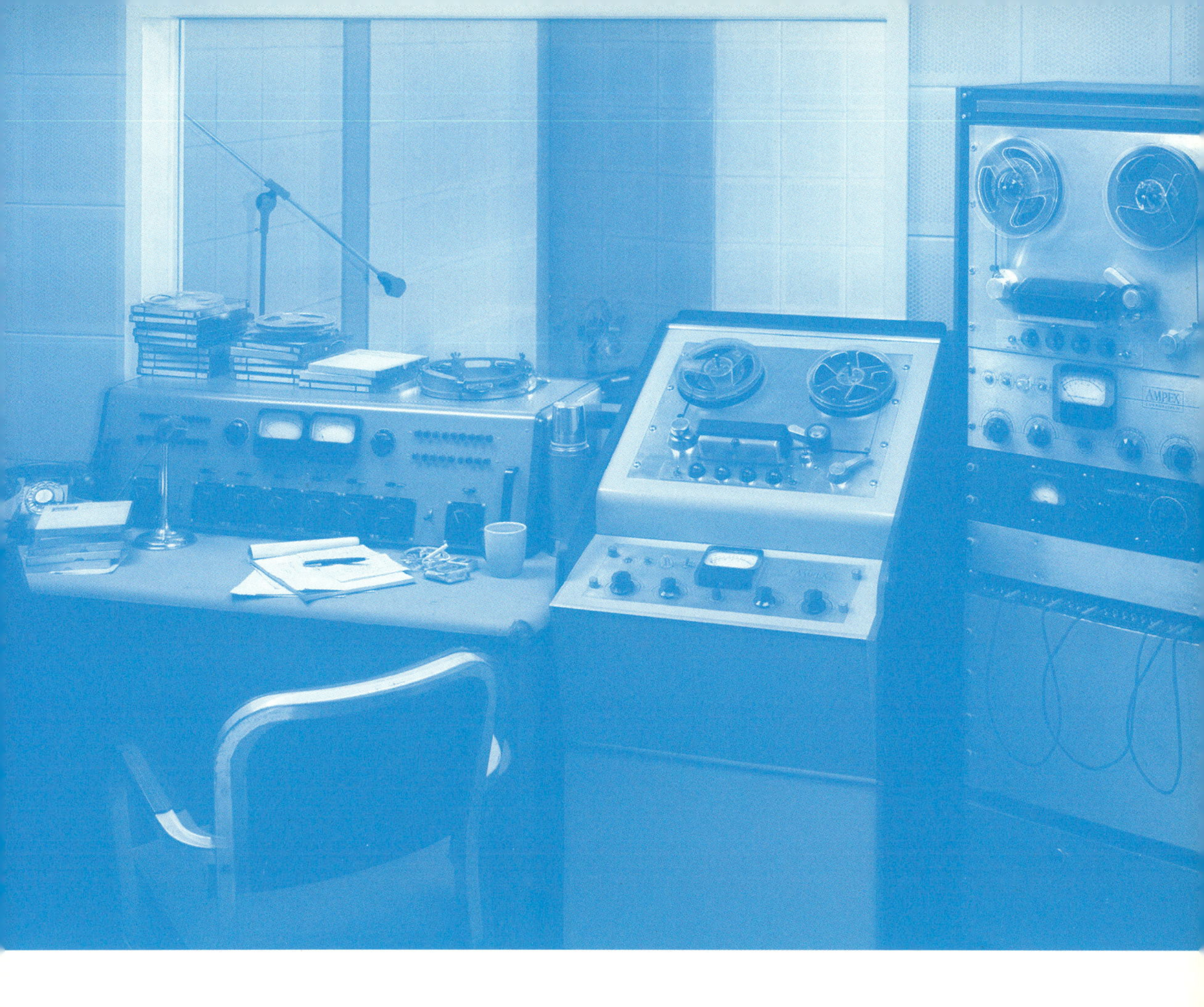

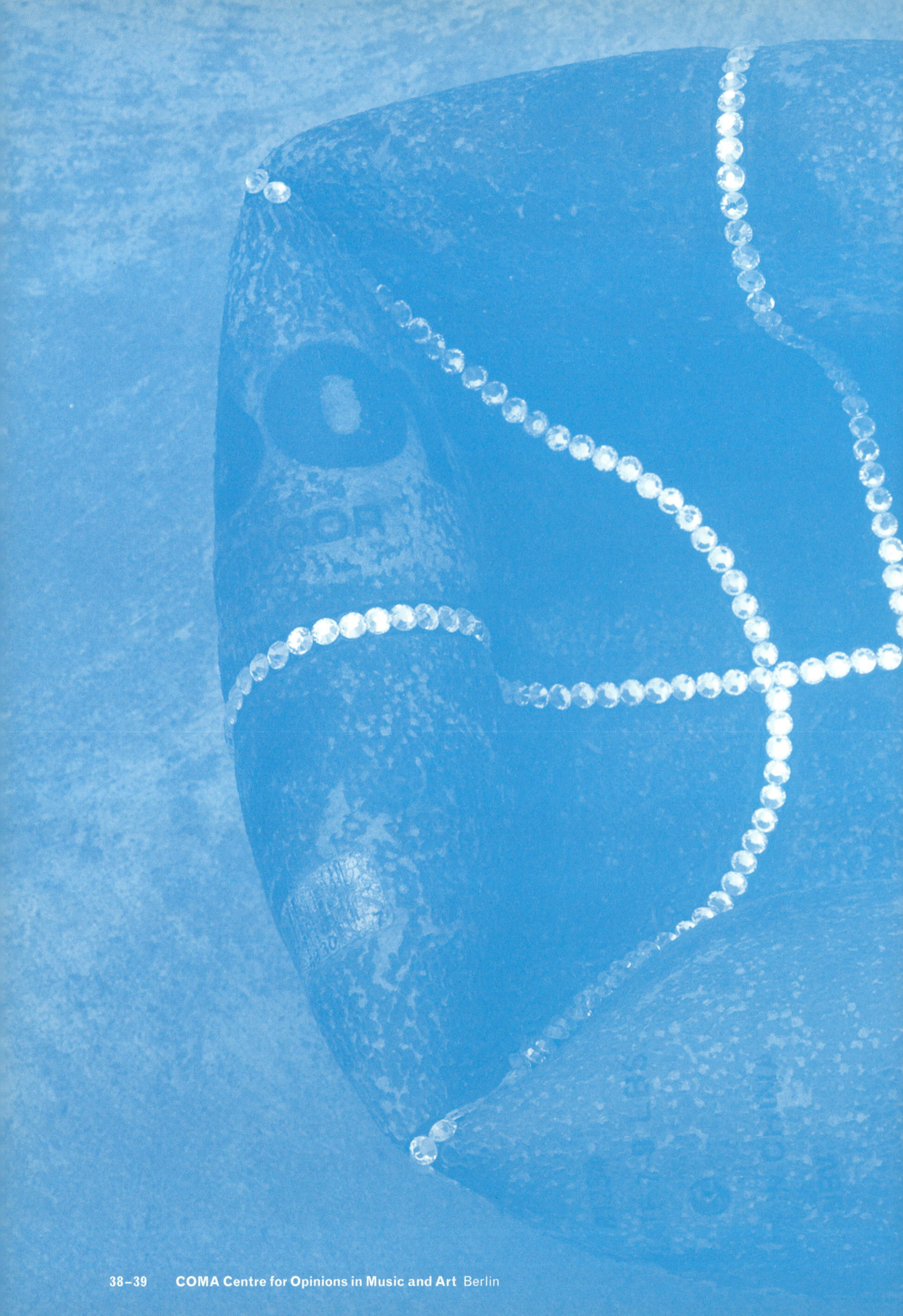

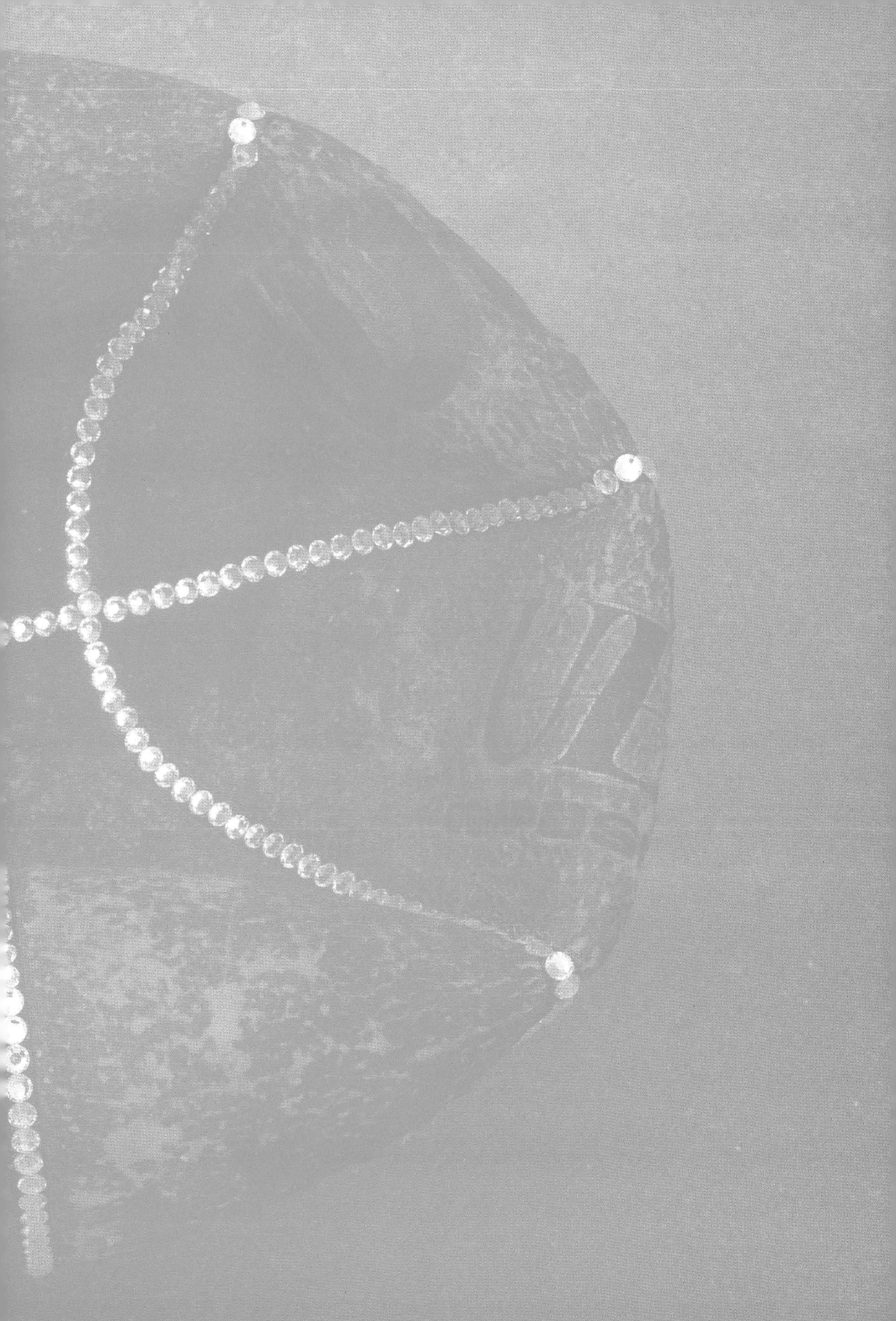

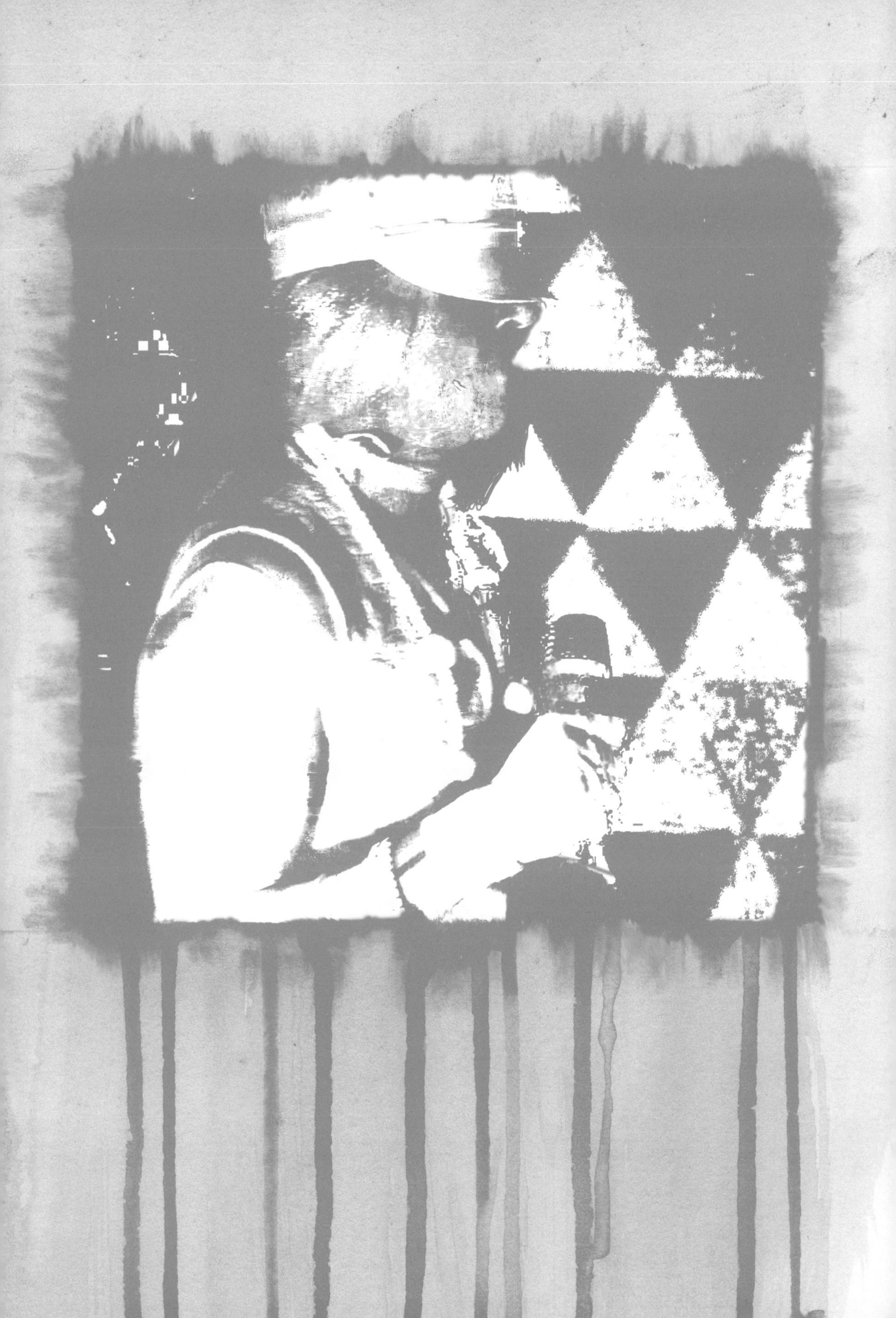

TESSELLATION

To form of small squares or blocks. To arrange in a checkered or mosaic pattern.

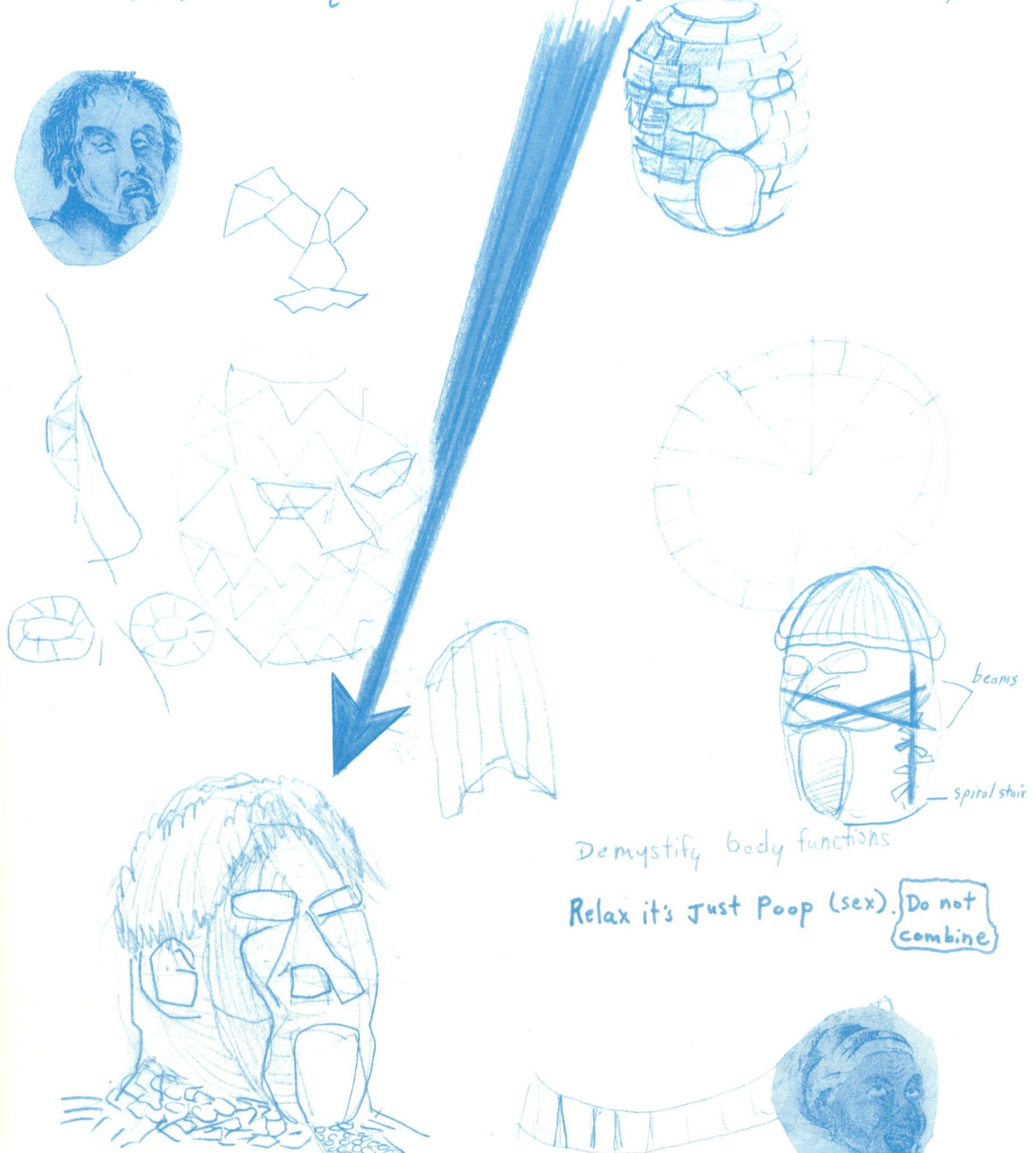

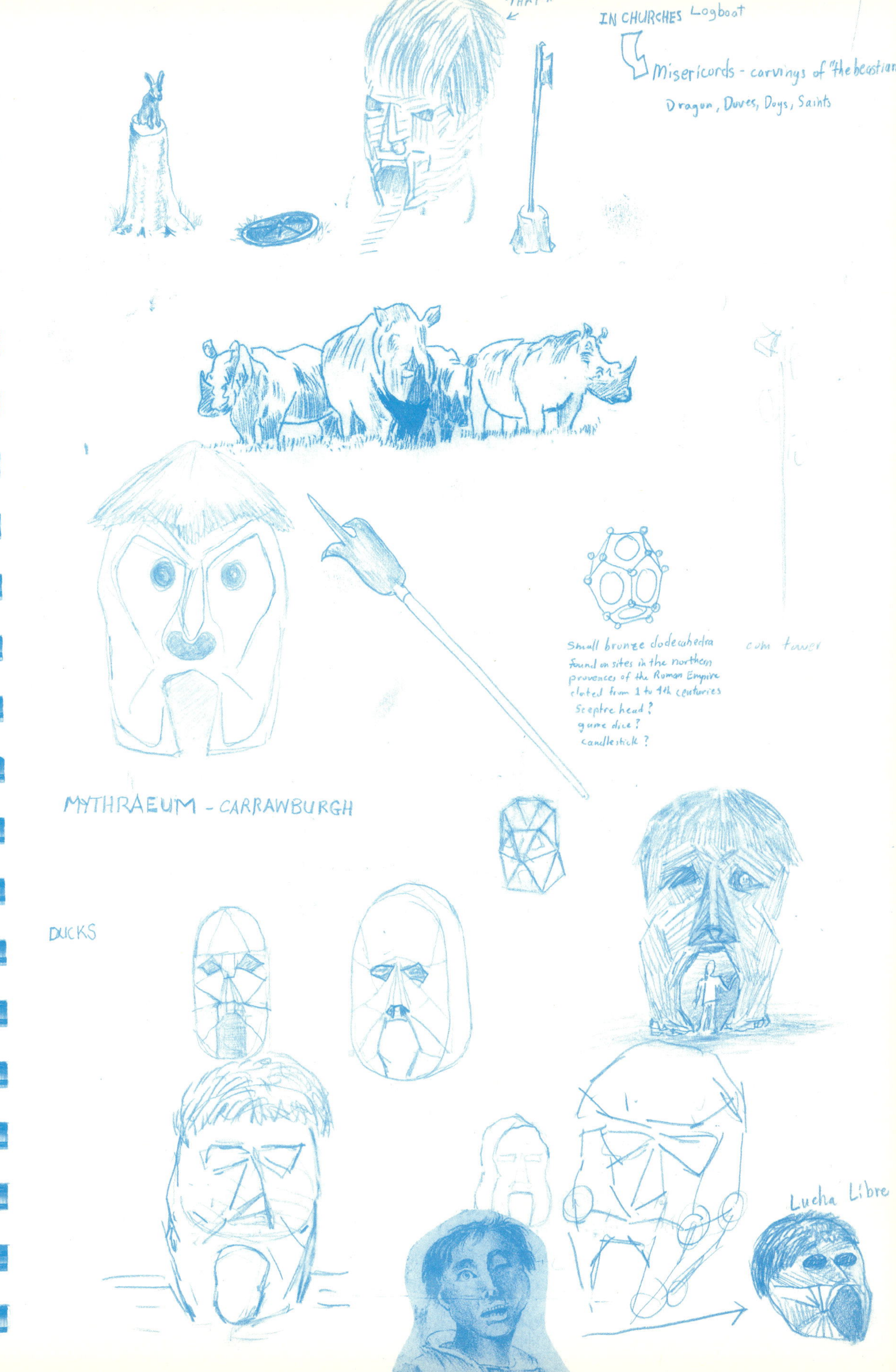
IN CHURCHES Logboat
Misericords - carvings of the bestiary
Dragon, Doves, Dogs, Saints
Small bronze dodecahedra
found on sites in the northern
provences of the Roman Empire
dated from 1 to 4th centuries
Sceptre head?
game dice?
candlestick?
cow tower
MYTHRAEUM - CARRAWBURGH
DUCKS
Luchia Libre

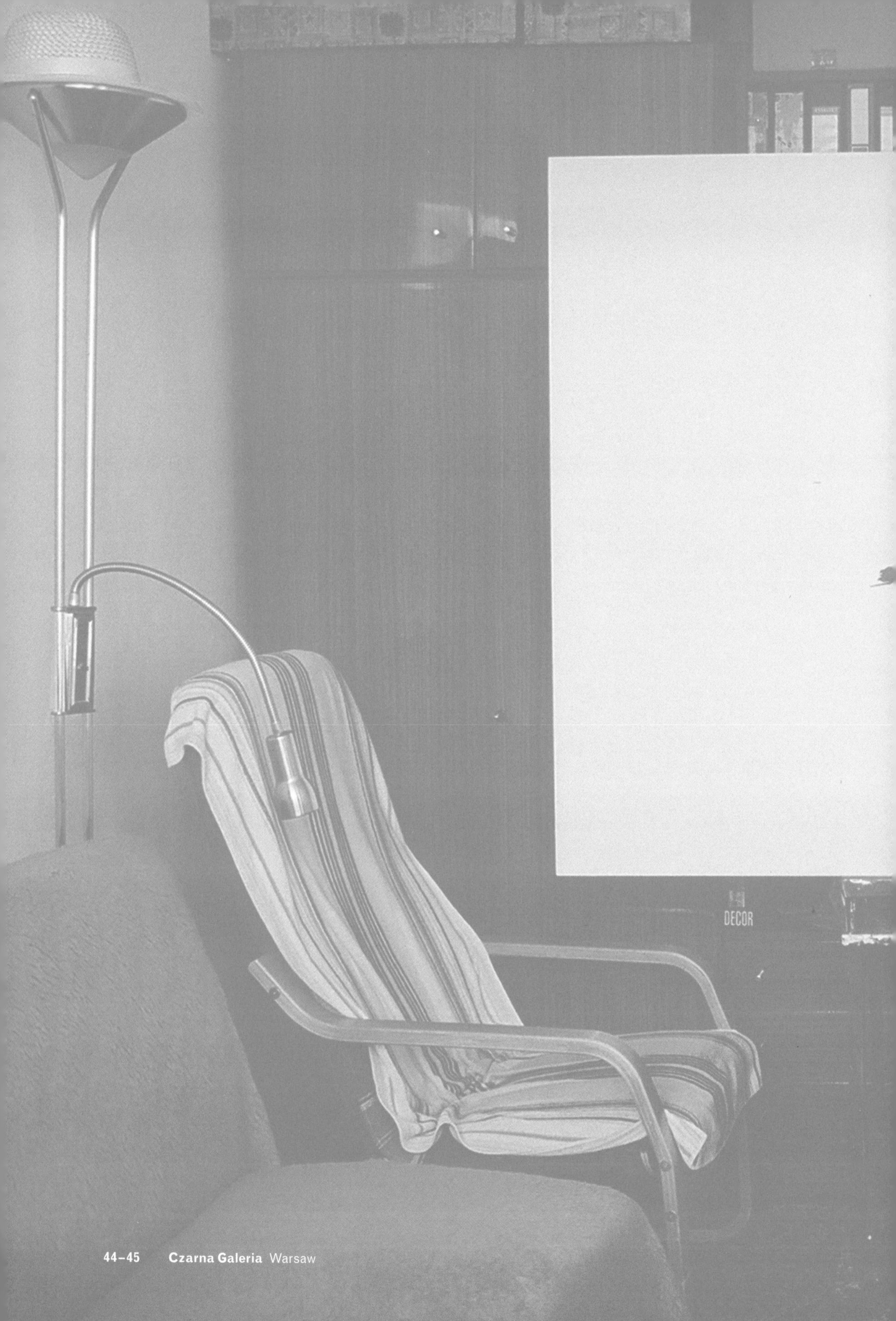
DECOR

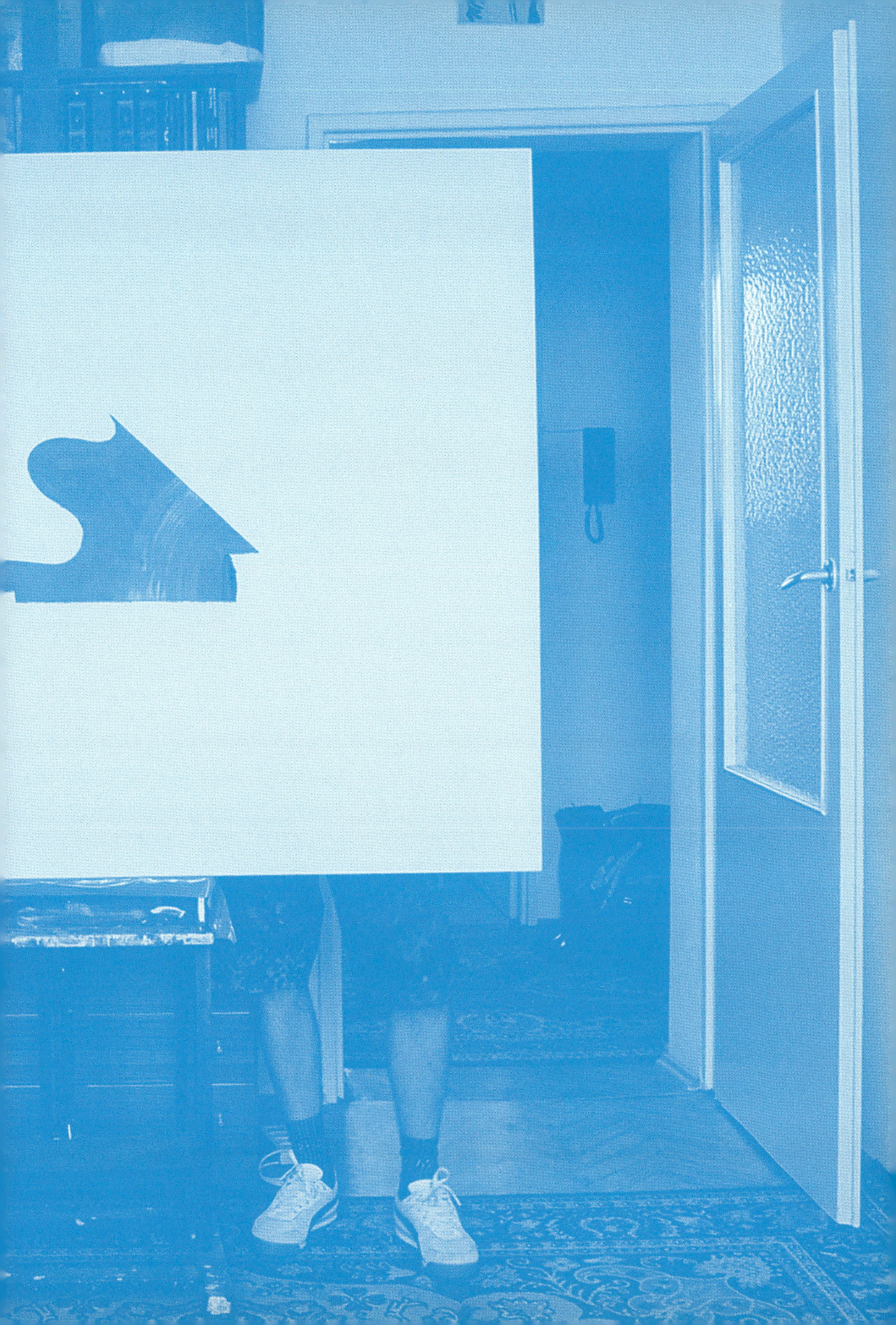

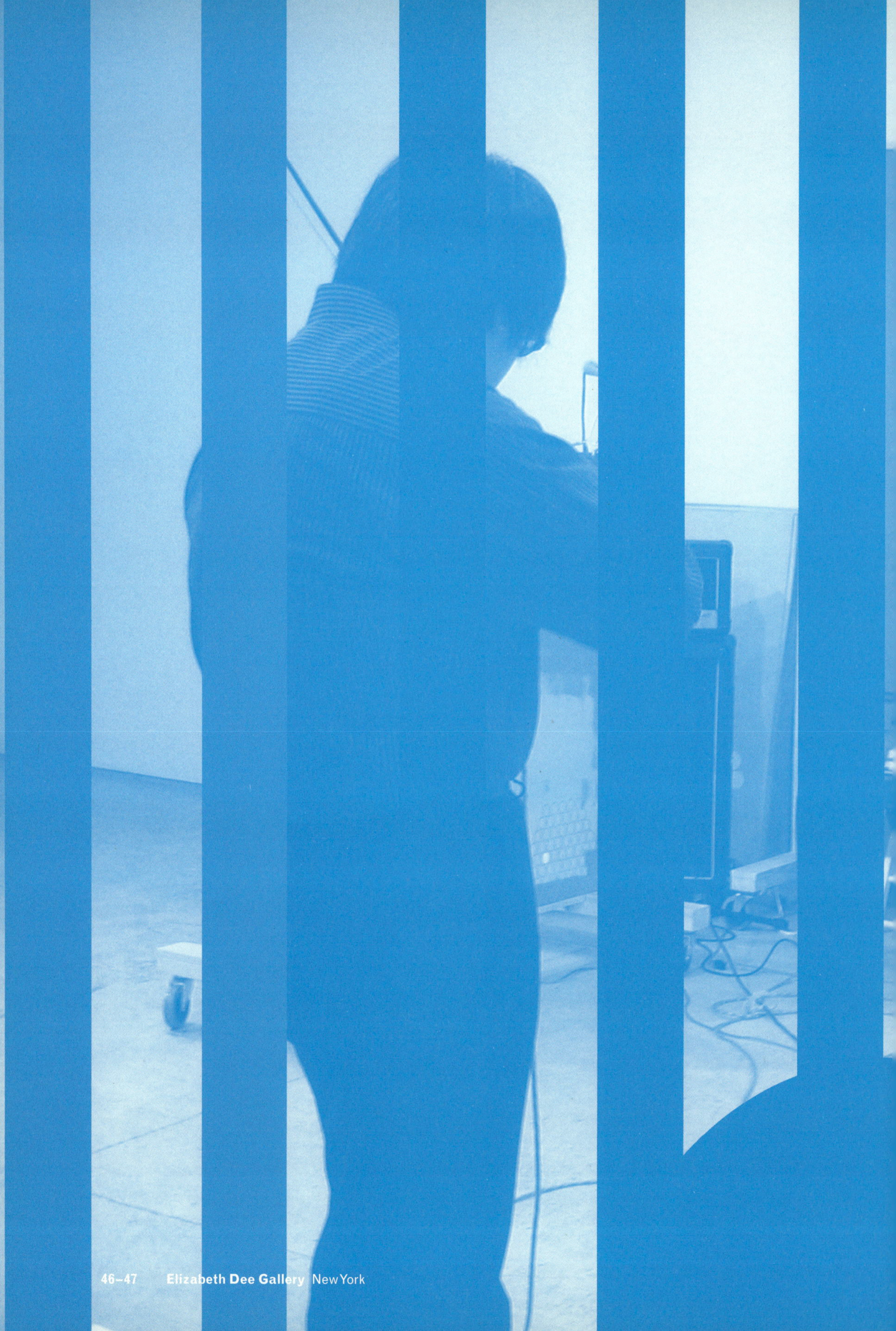

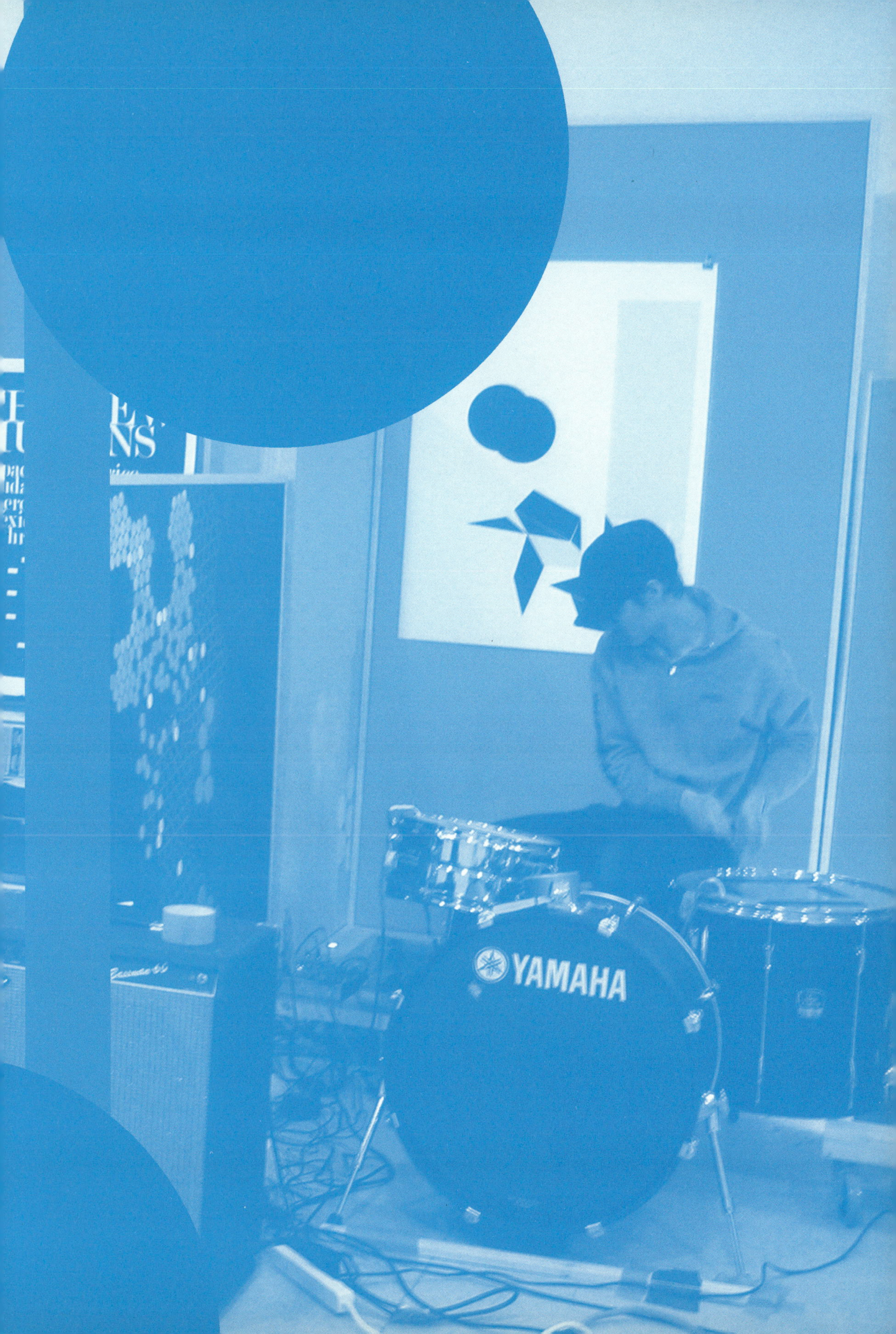

YAMAHA

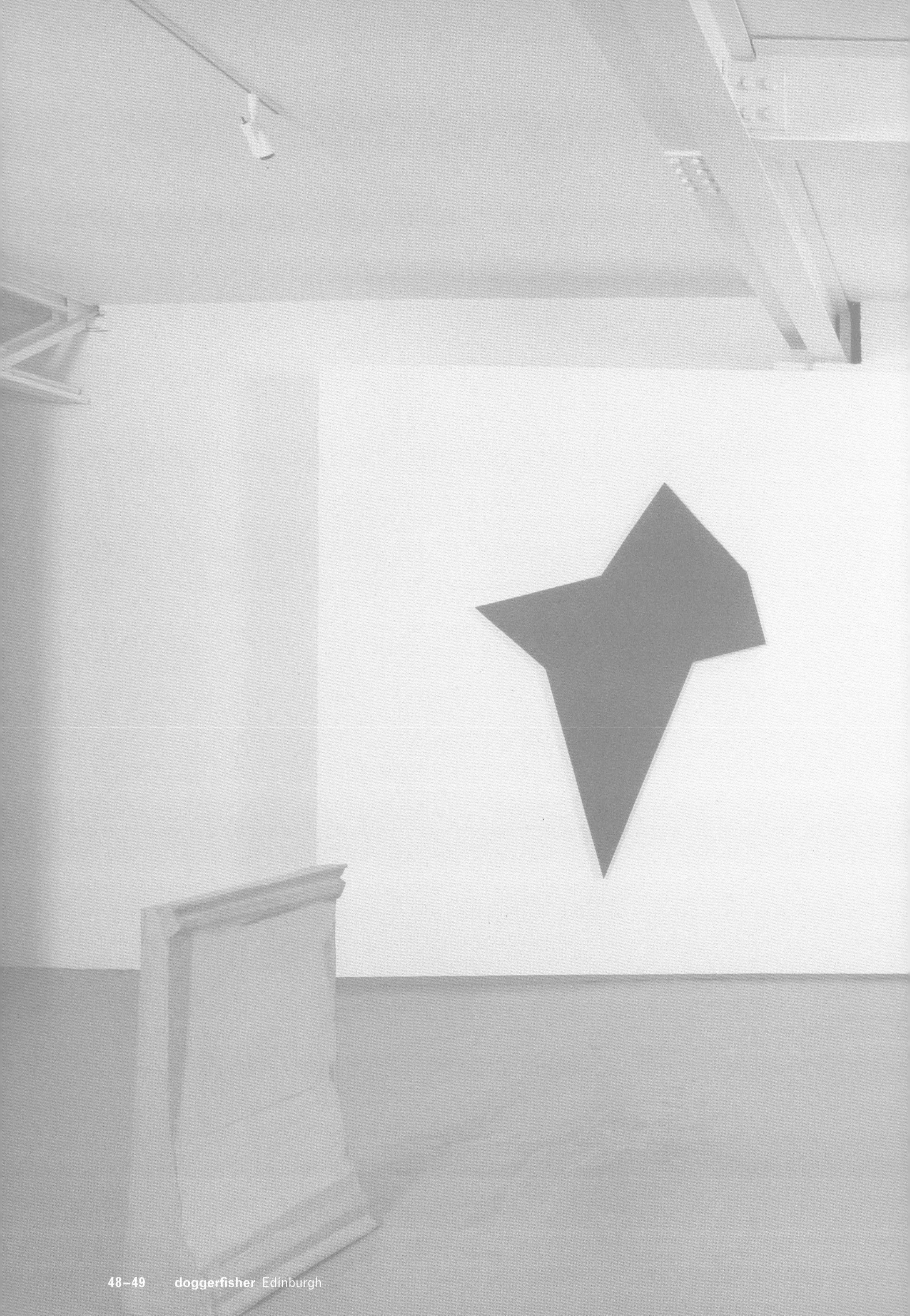

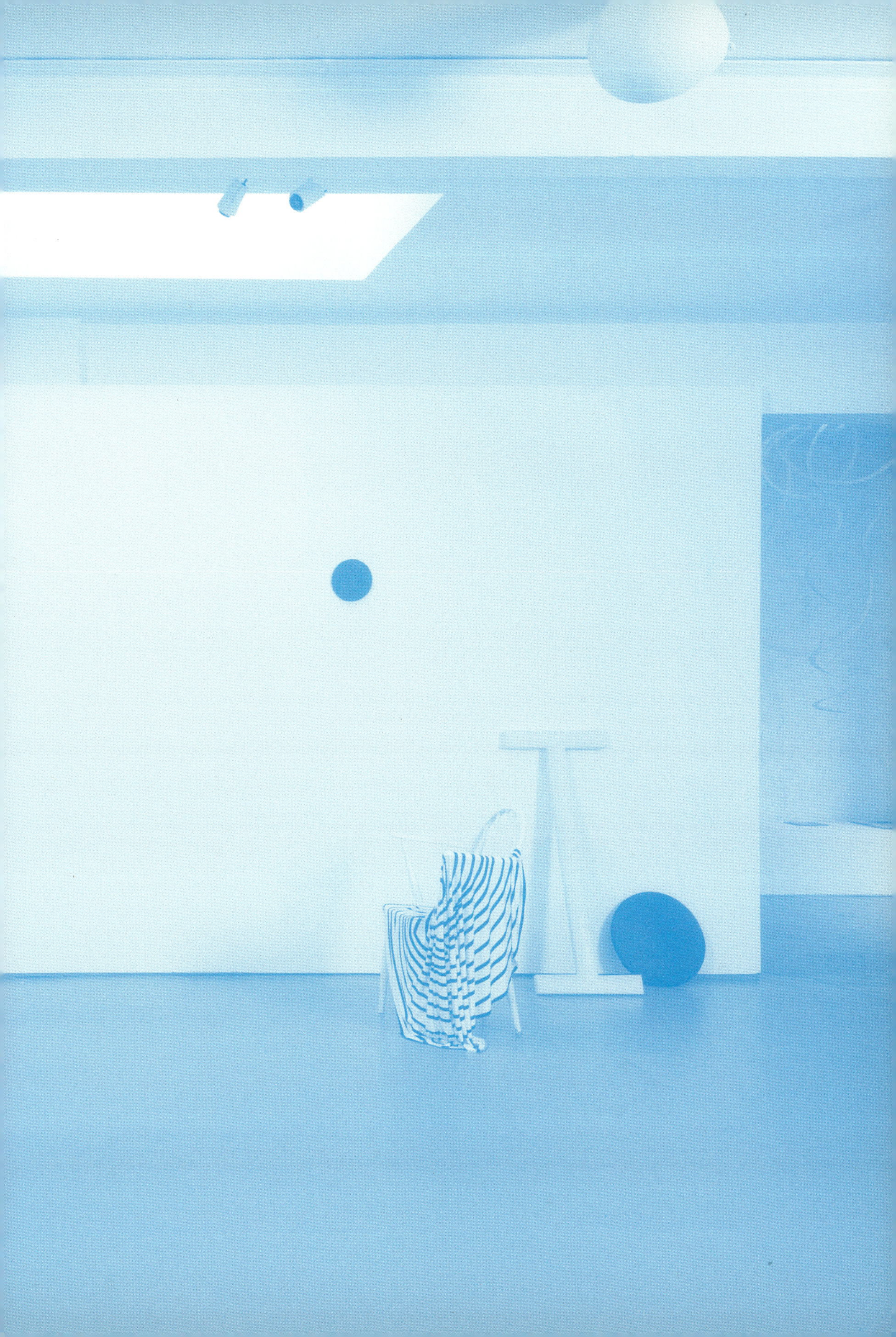

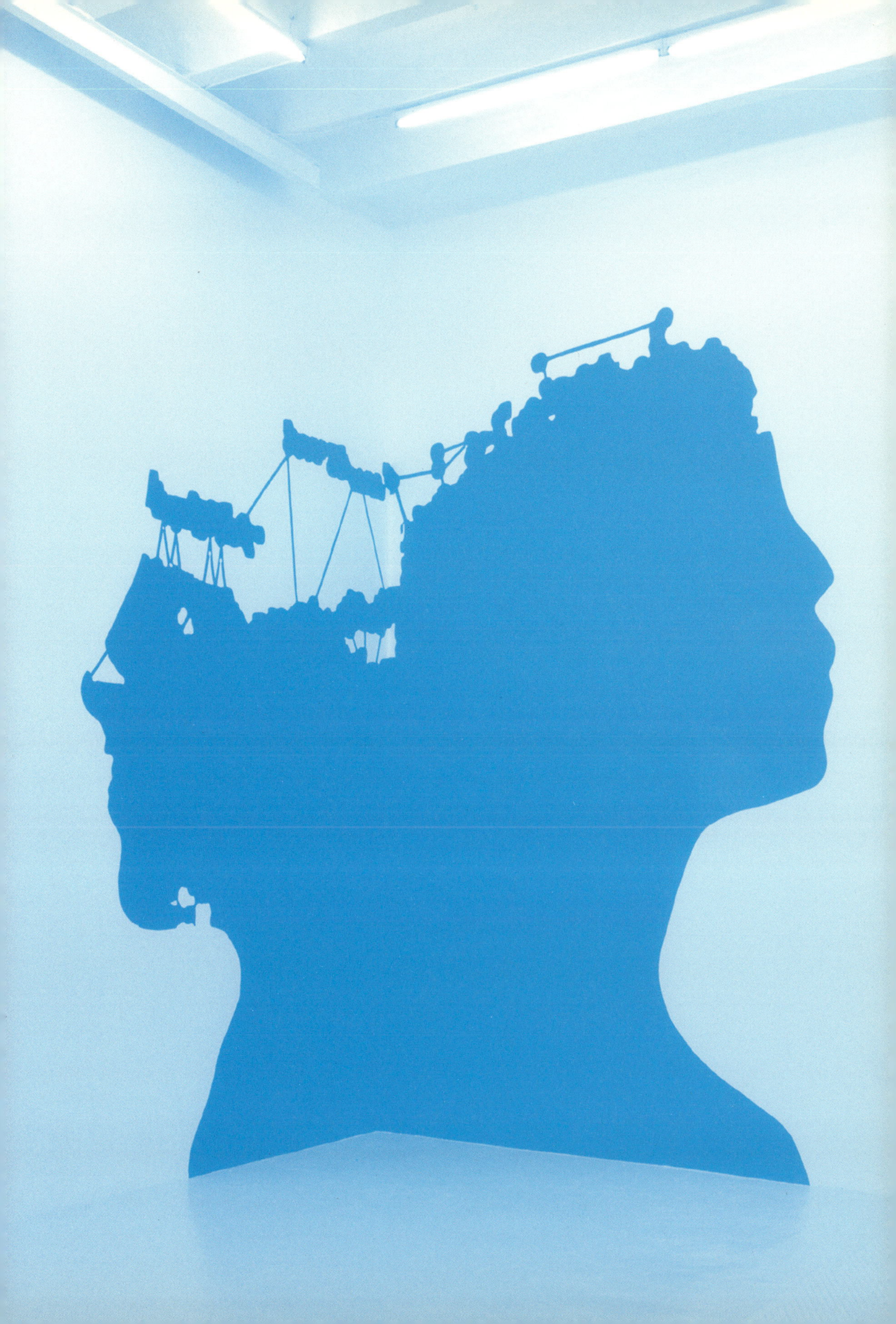

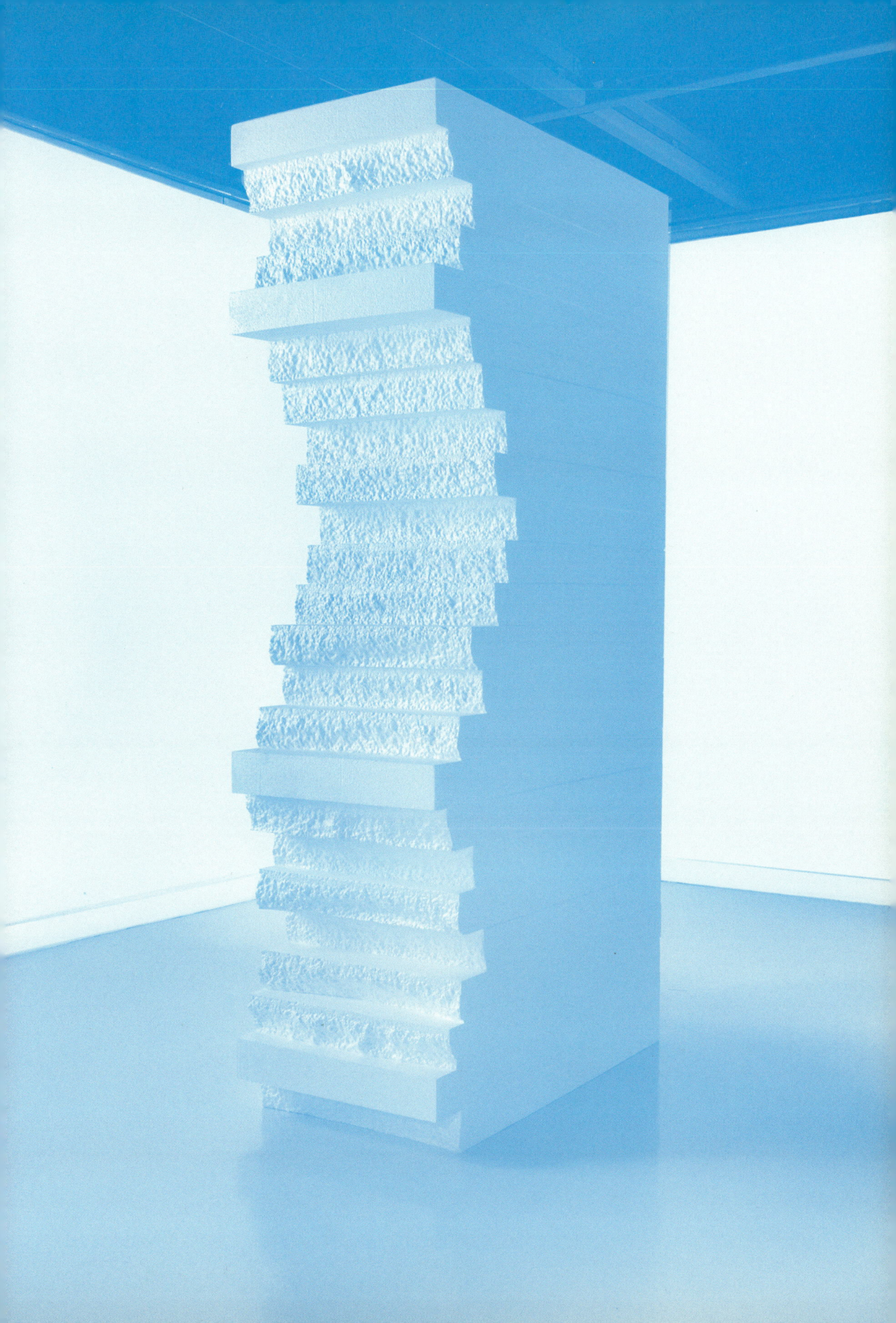

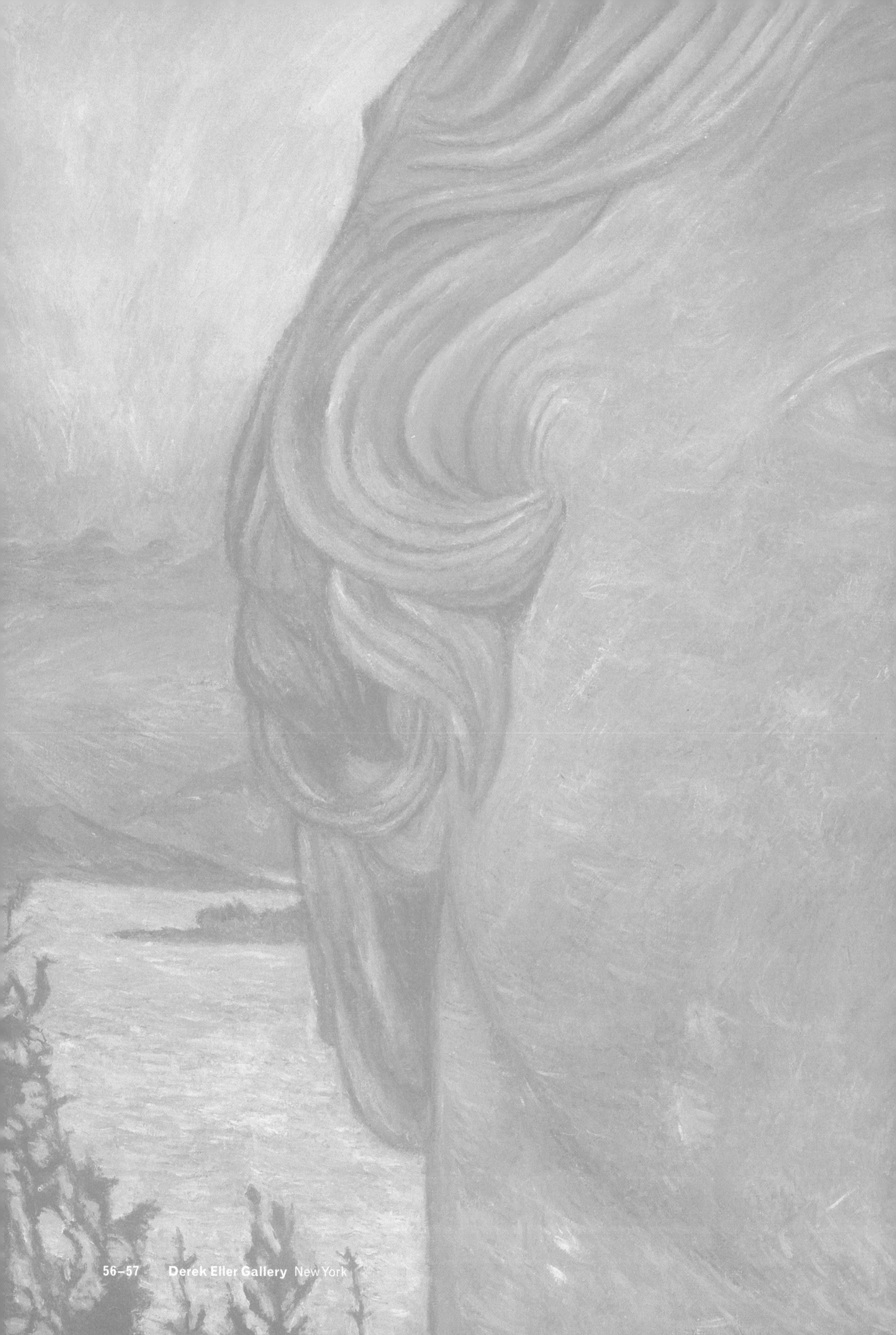
 Derek Eller Gallery New York

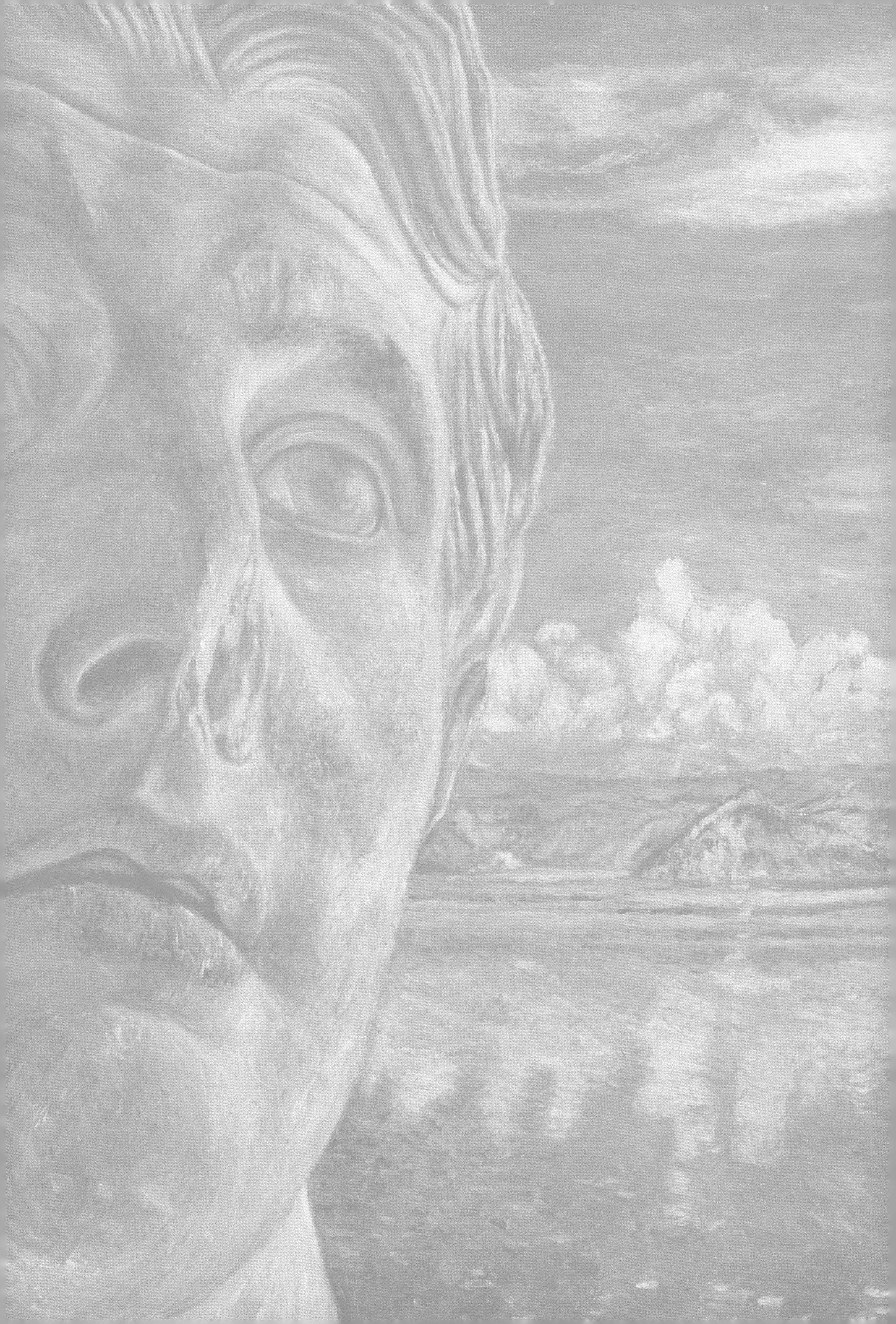

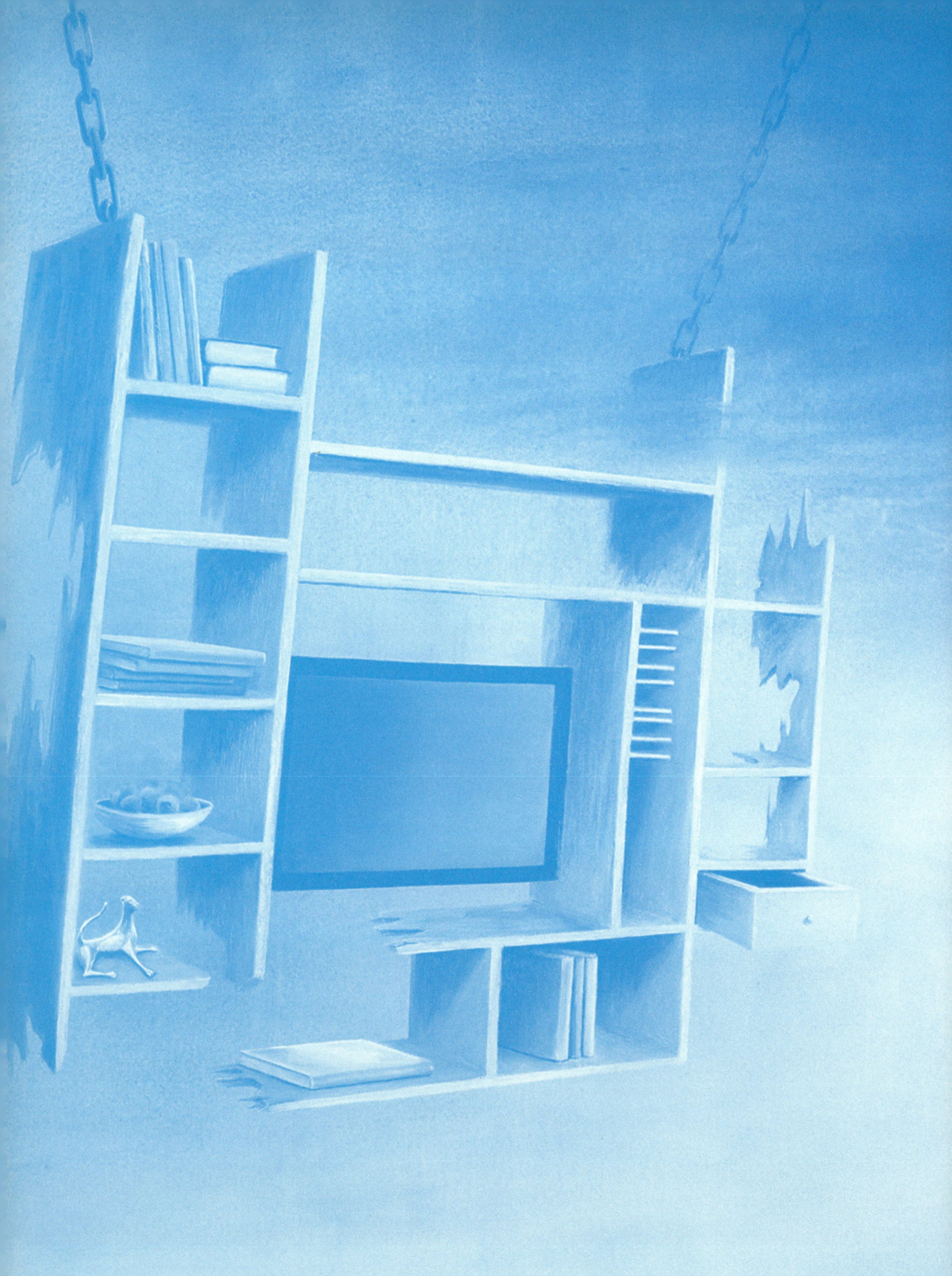

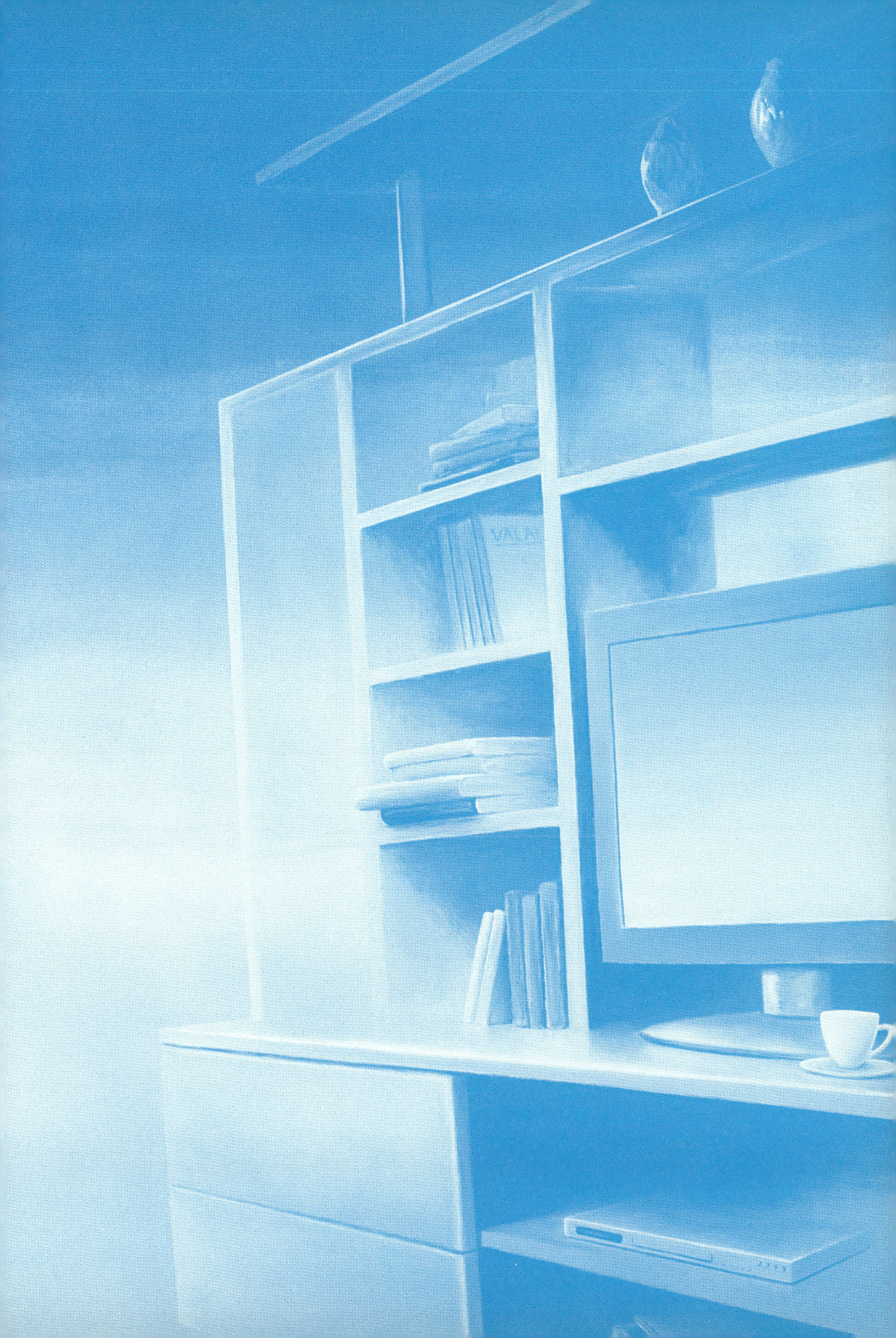

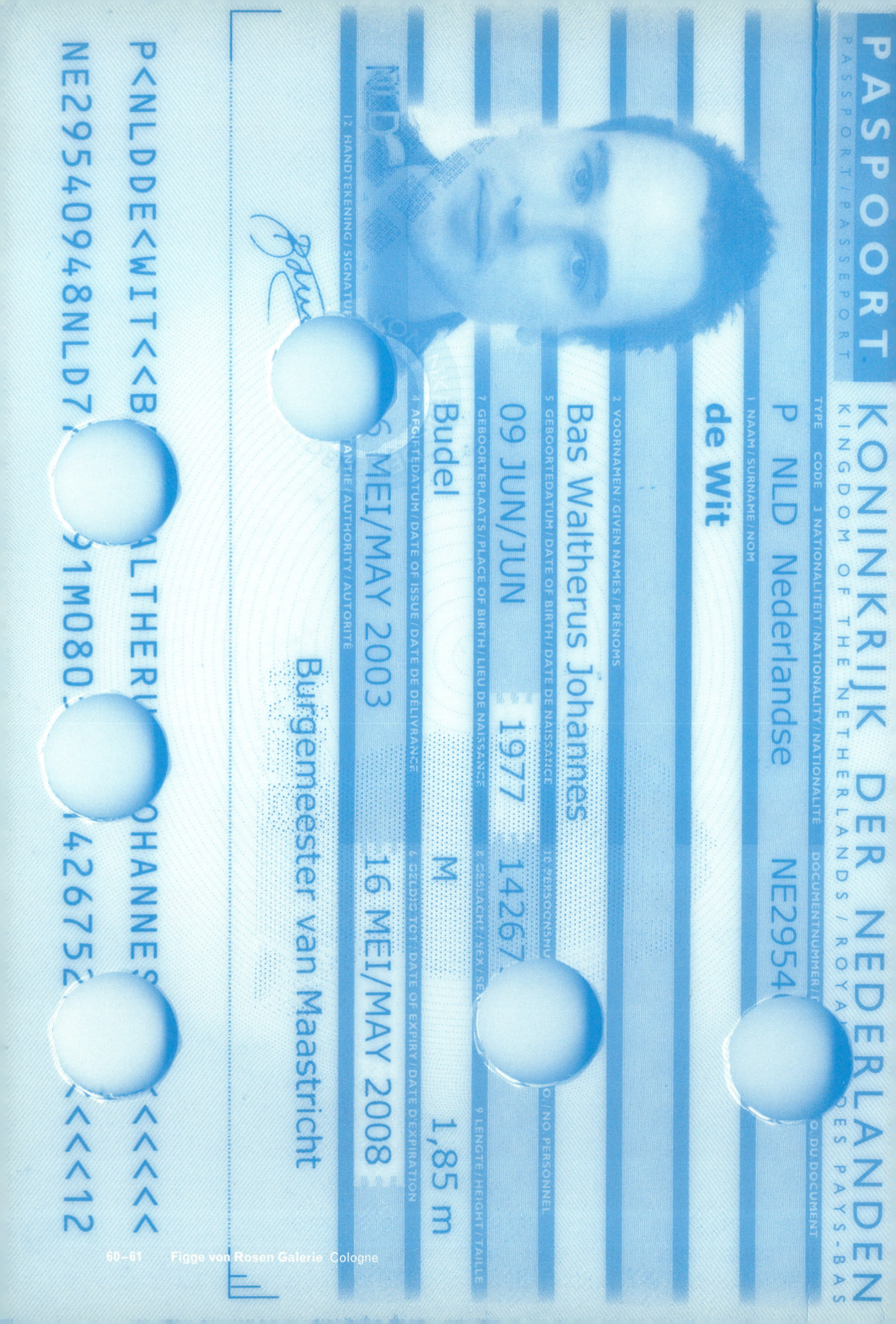

PASPOORT.
PASSPORT / PASSEPORT

KONINKRIJK DER NEDERLANDEN
KINGDOM OF THE NETHERLANDS / ROYAUME DES PAYS-BAS

TYPE   CODE   3 NATIONALITEIT / NATIONALITY / NATIONALITÉ   DOCUMENTNUMMER / O. DU DOCUMENT
P   NLD   Nederlandse   NE29540

1 NAAM / SURNAME / NOM
de Wit

2 VOORNAMEN / GIVEN NAMES / PRÉNOMS
Bas Waltherus Johannes

5 GEBOORTEDATUM / DATE OF BIRTH / DATE DE NAISSANCE   10 PERSOONSNU... / NO. PERSONNEL
09 JUN/JUN   1977   14267

7 GEBOORTEPLAATS / PLACE OF BIRTH / LIEU DE NAISSANCE   8 GESLACHT / SEX / SEX   9 LENGTE / HEIGHT / TAILLE
Budel   M   1,85 m

4 AFGIFTEDATUM / DATE OF ISSUE / DATE DE DELIVRANCE   6 GELDIG TOT / DATE OF EXPIRY / DATE D'EXPIRATION
16 MEI/MAY 2003   16 MEI/MAY 2008

12 HANDTEKENING / SIGNATURE   ...ANTIE / AUTHORITY / AUTORITÉ
Burgemeester van Maastricht

P<NLDDE<WIT<<BAS<WALTHERUS<JOHANNES<<<<<<<
NE29540948NLD77...91M080...142675...<<<<12

GELDIG VOOR ALLE LANDEN

Valid for all countries / Valable pour tous les pays

OPMERKINGEN VAN BEVOEGDE INSTANTIES

Page reserved for issuing authorities / Page réservée aux autorités
compétentes pour délivrer le passeport (14)

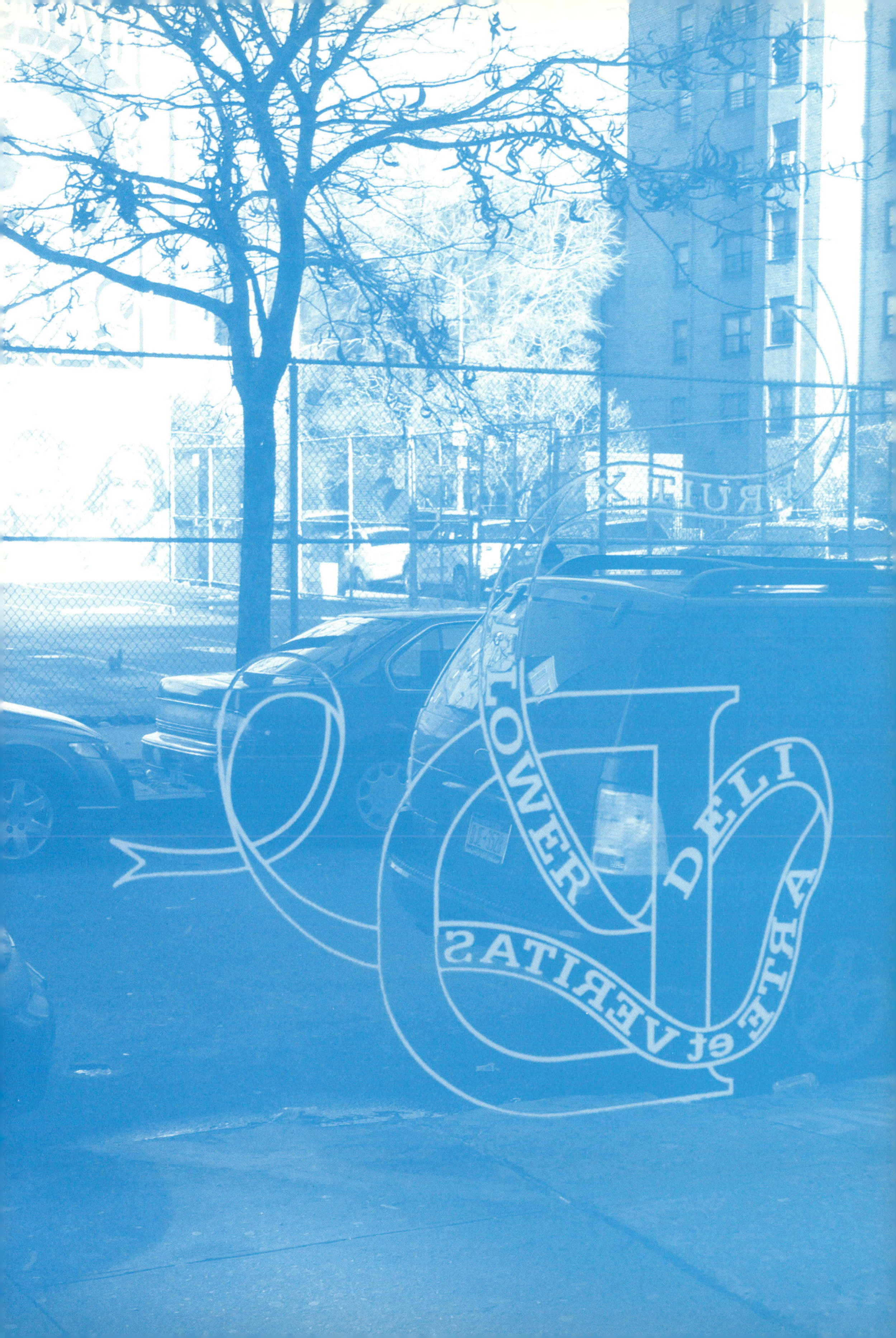
LOWER
DELI
ARTE et VERITAS

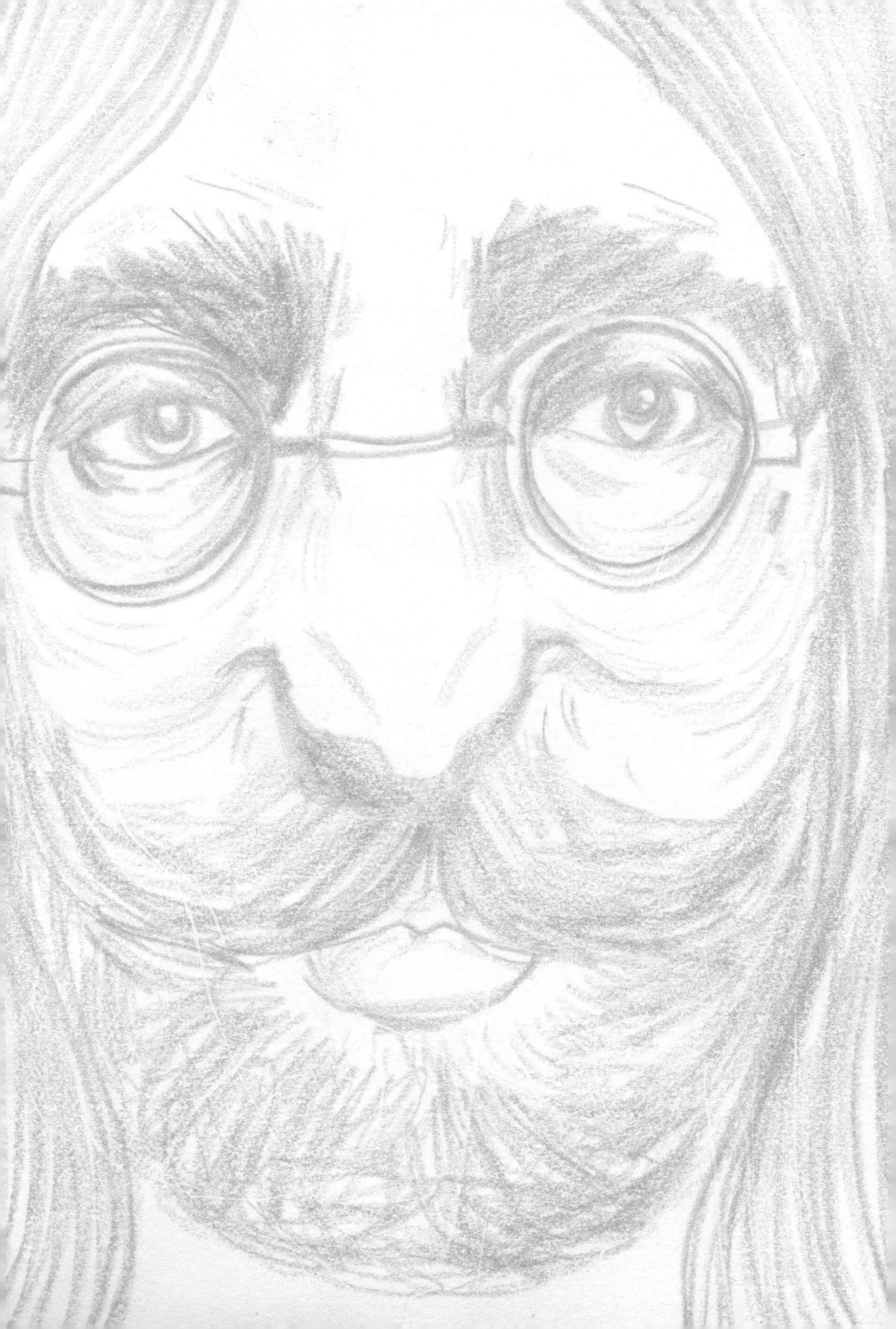

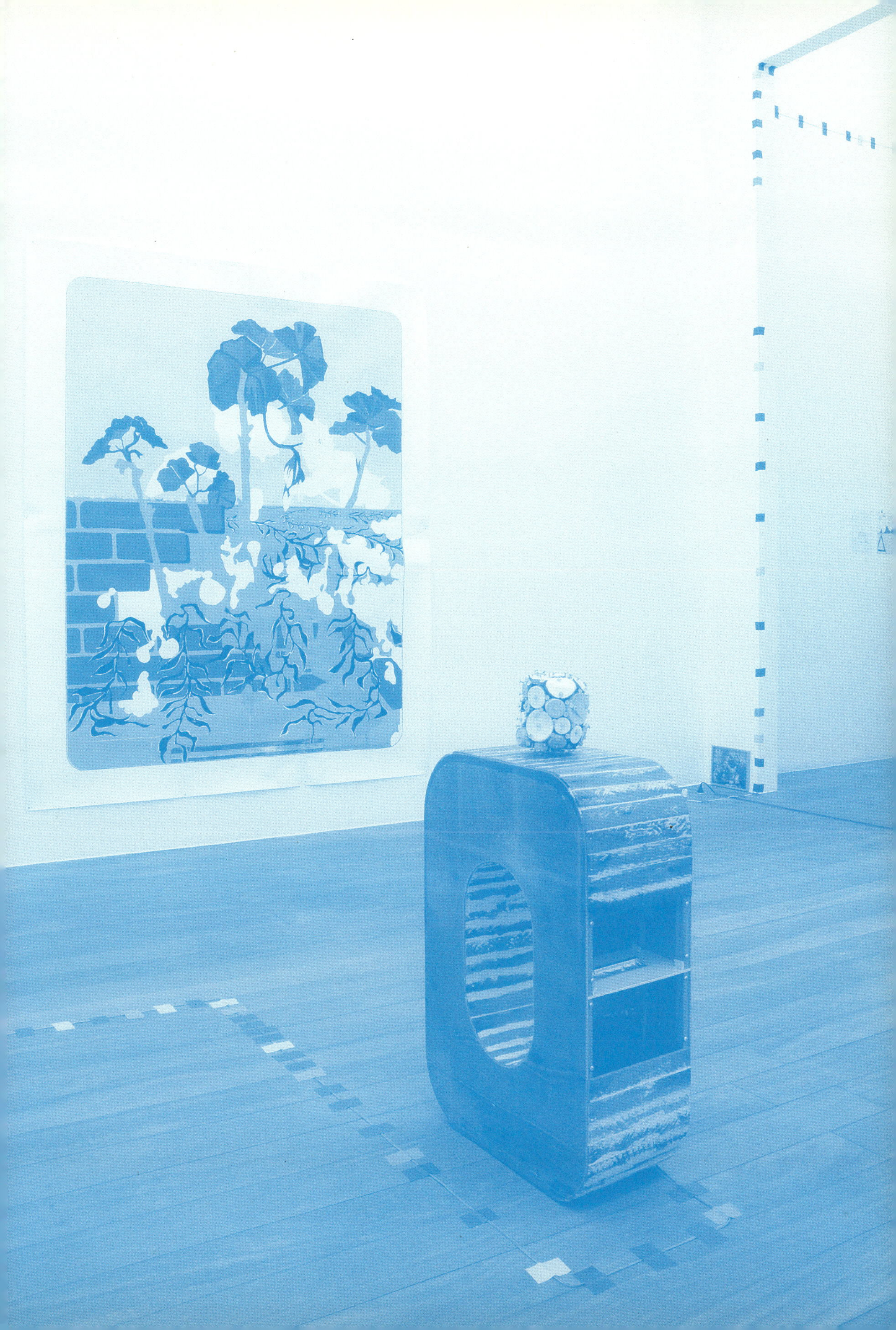

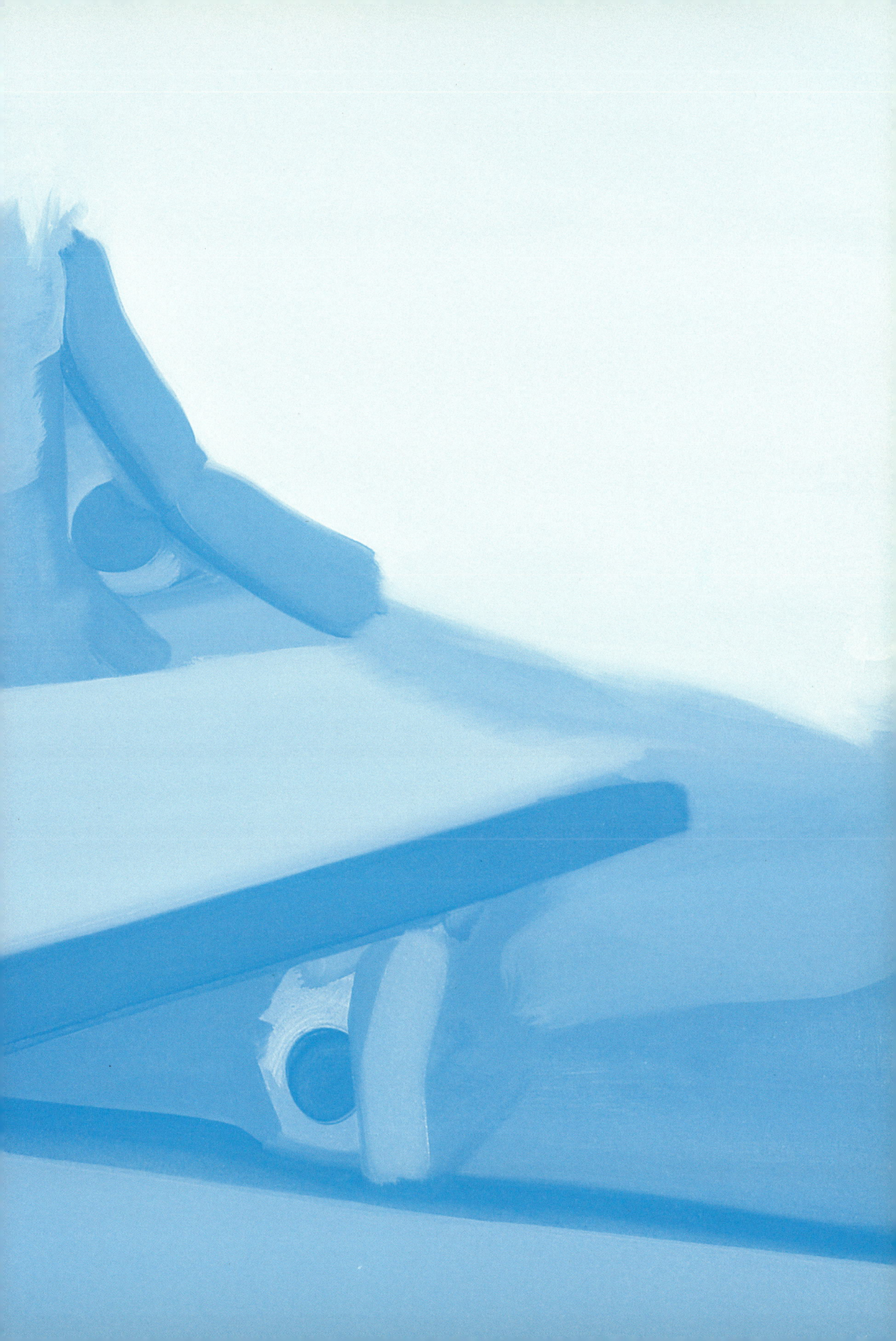

COLDARGAN

© G. GETREUER
2008

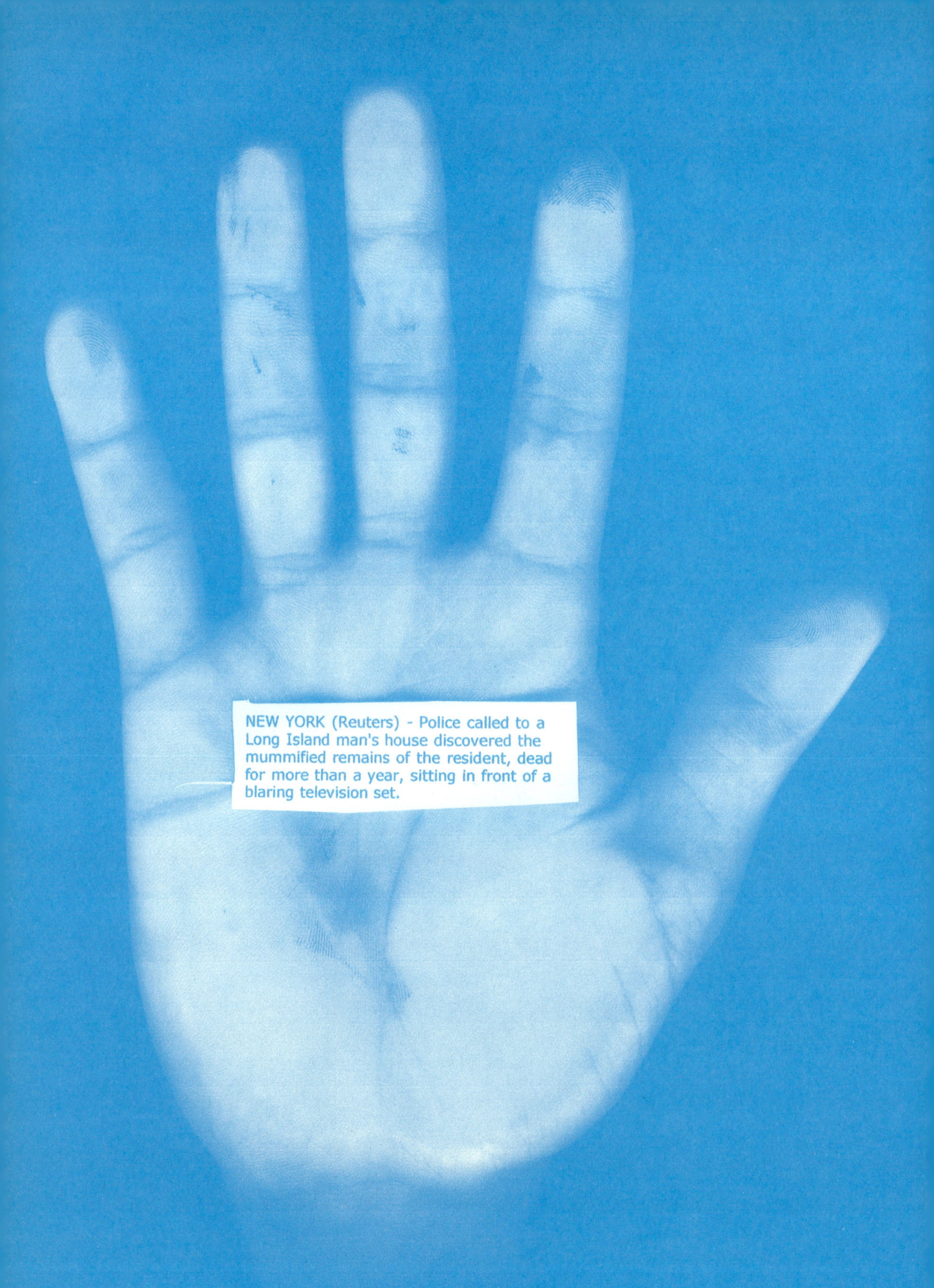

NEW YORK (Reuters) - Police called to a
Long Island man's house discovered the
mummified remains of the resident, dead
for more than a year, sitting in front of a
blaring television set.

Ryan Johnson
Guild & Greyshkul

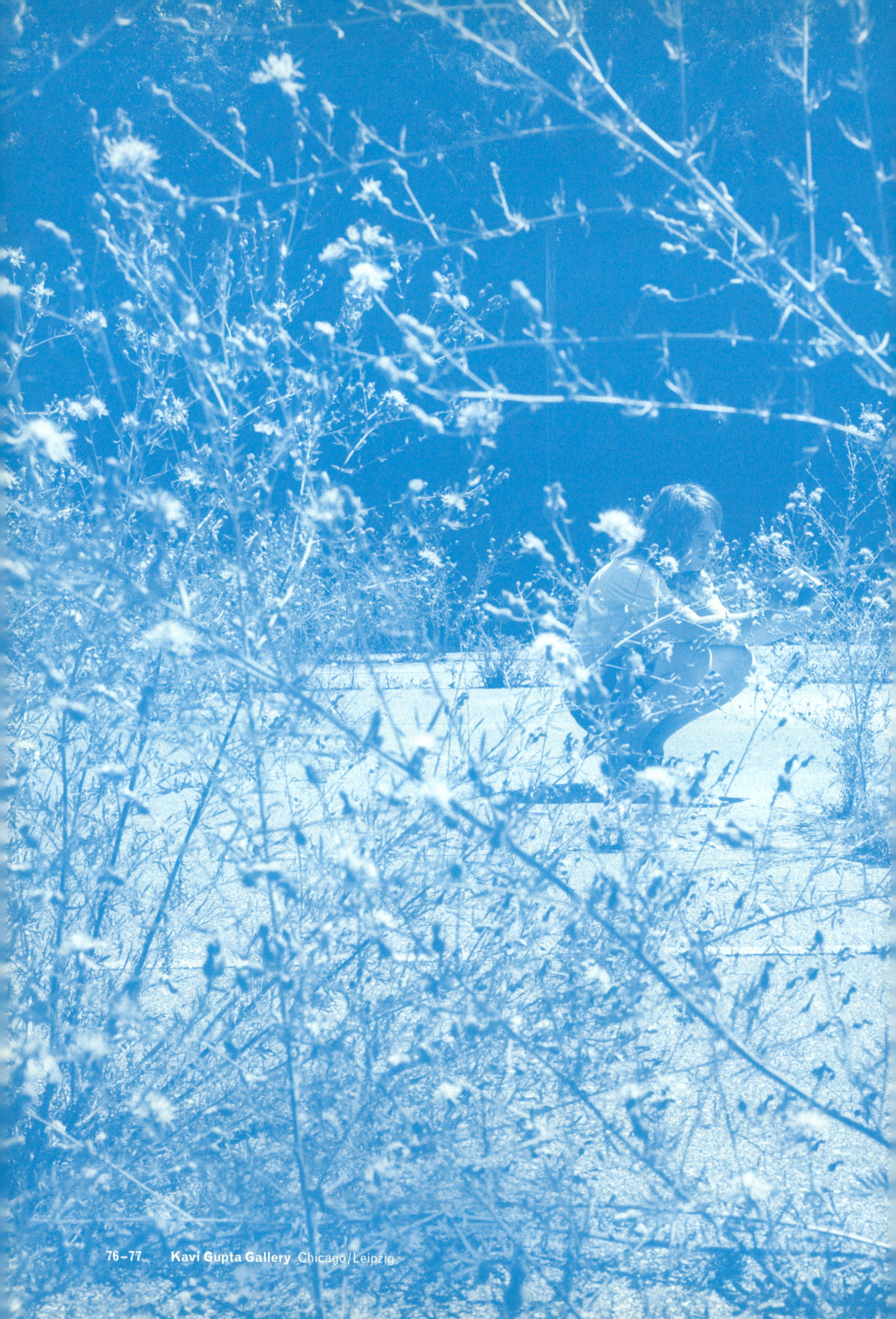

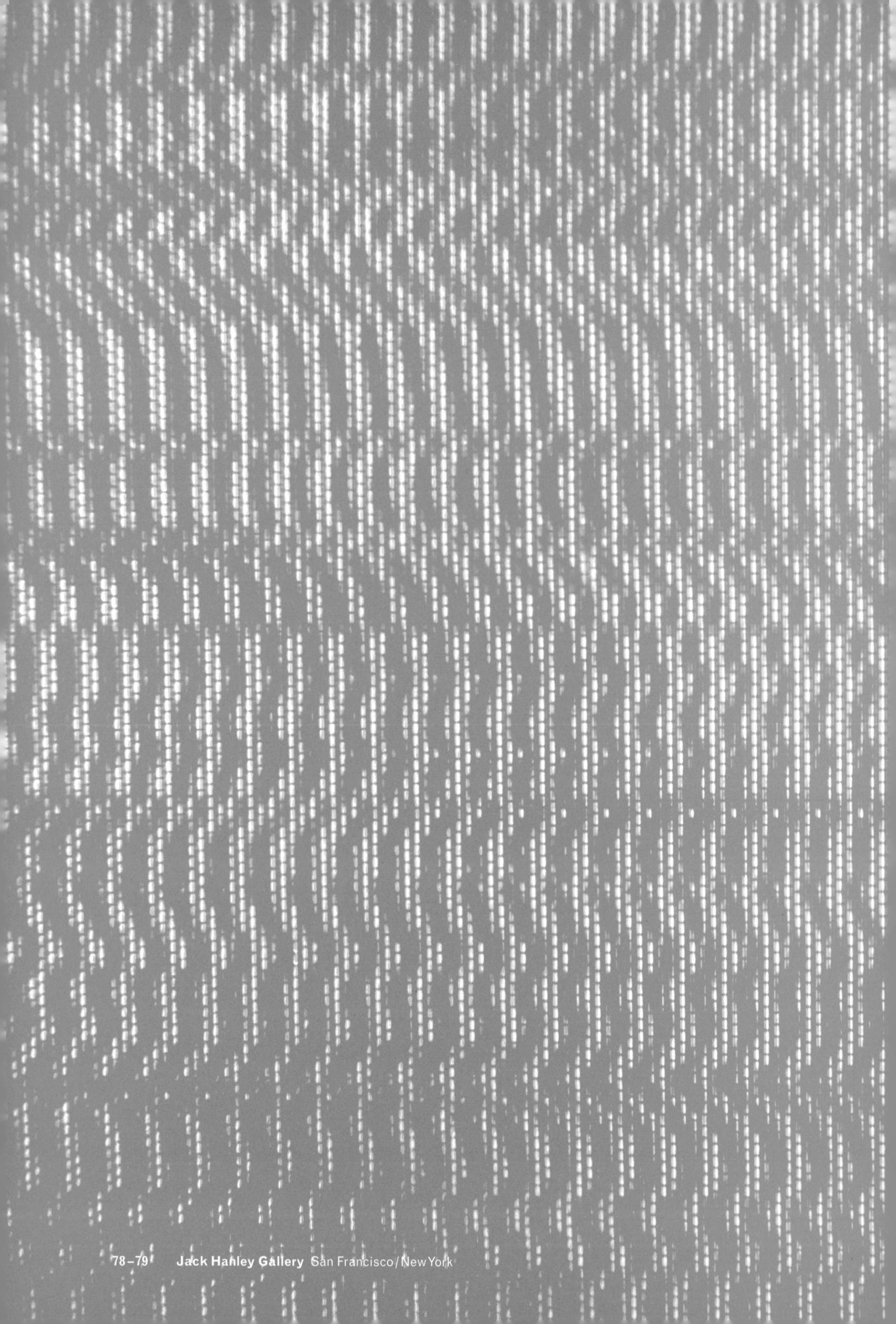

 Jack Hanley Gallery San Francisco / New York

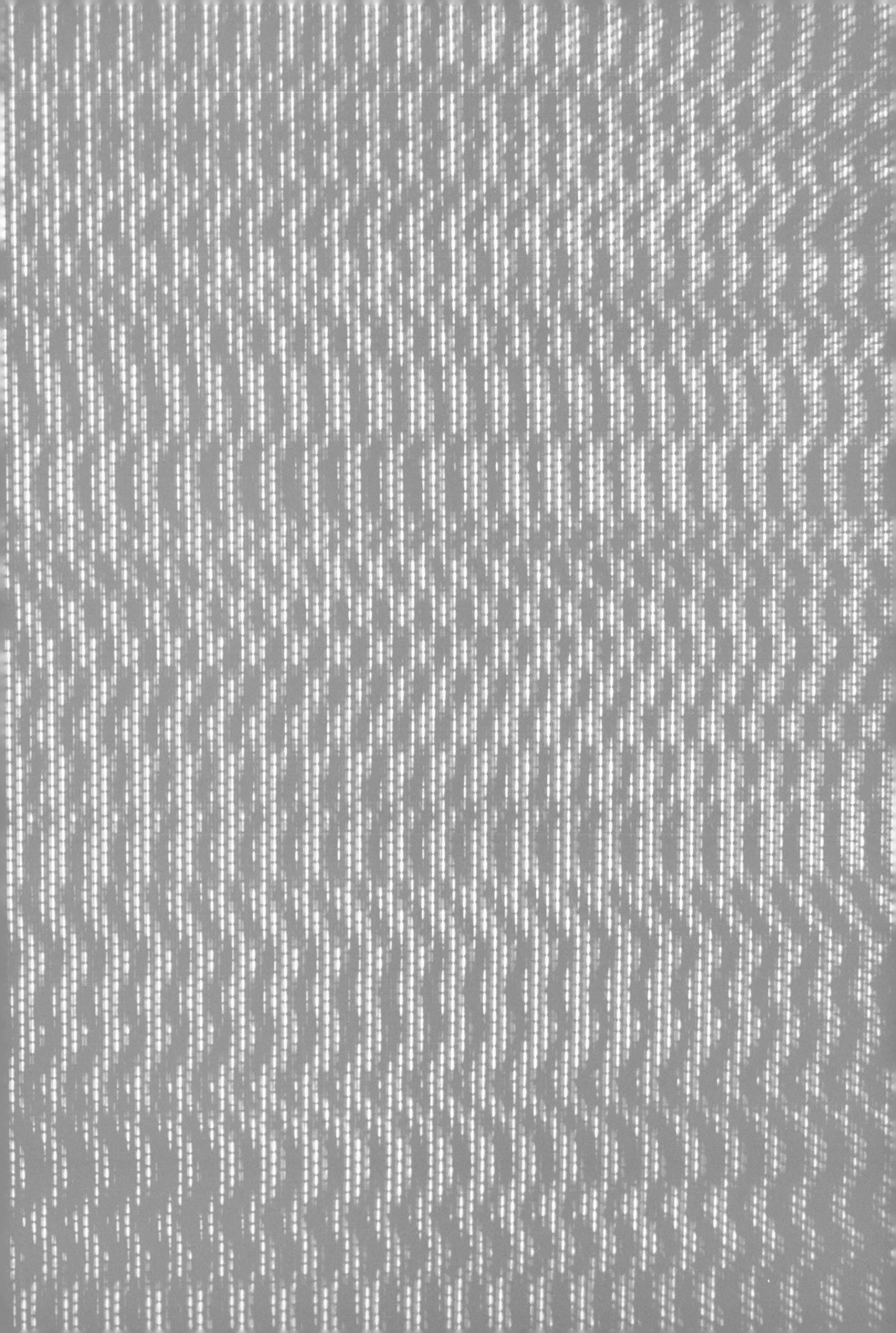

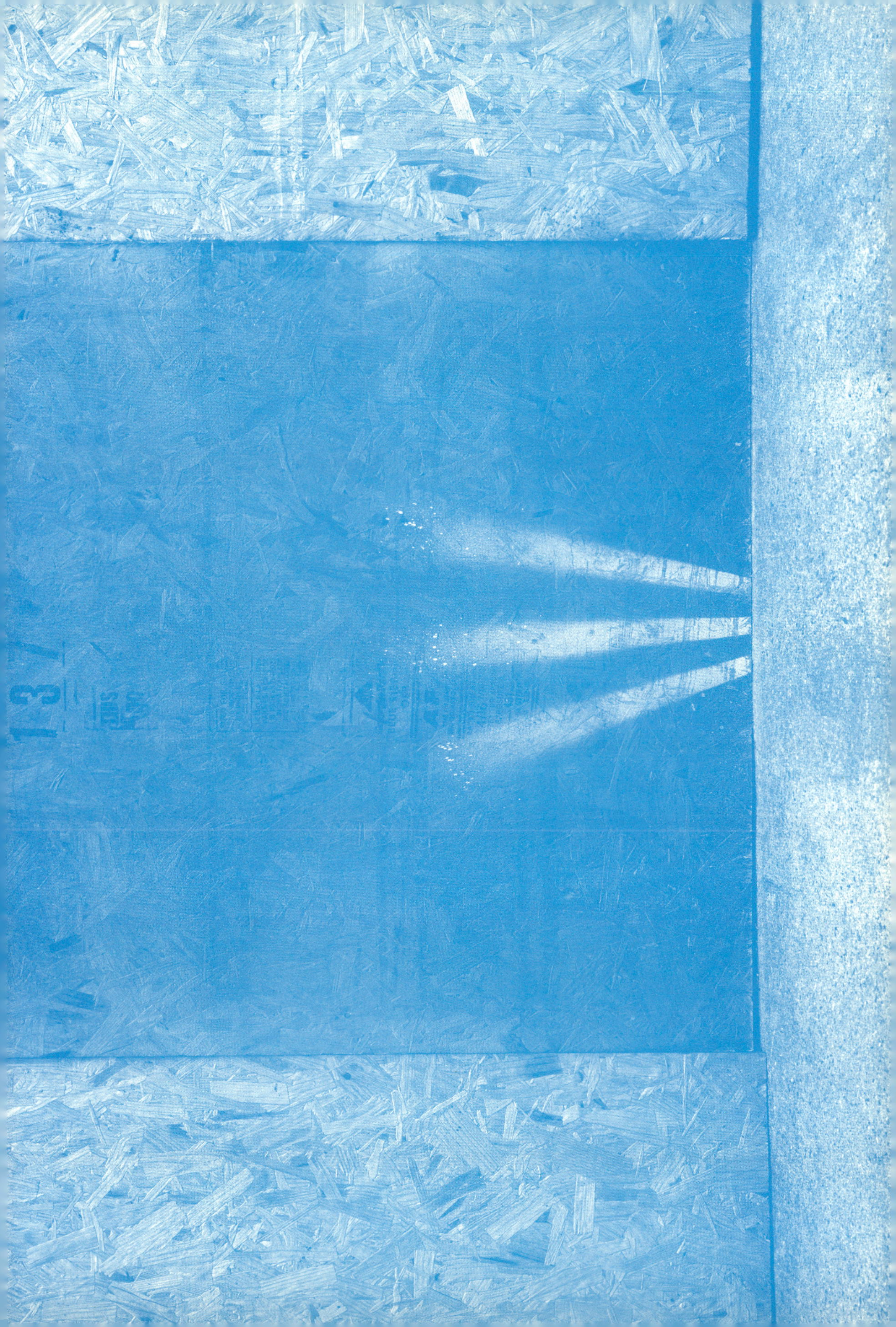

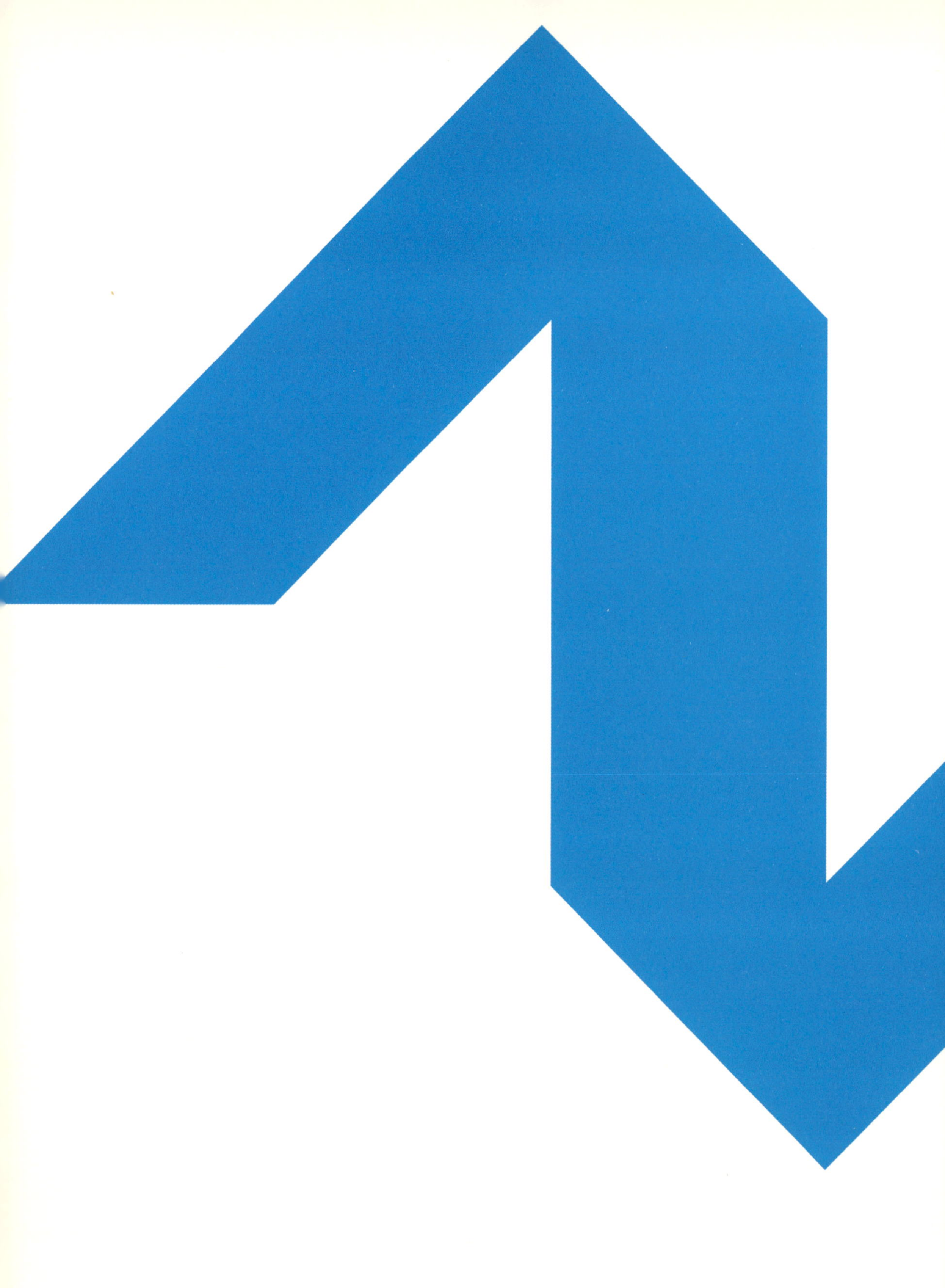

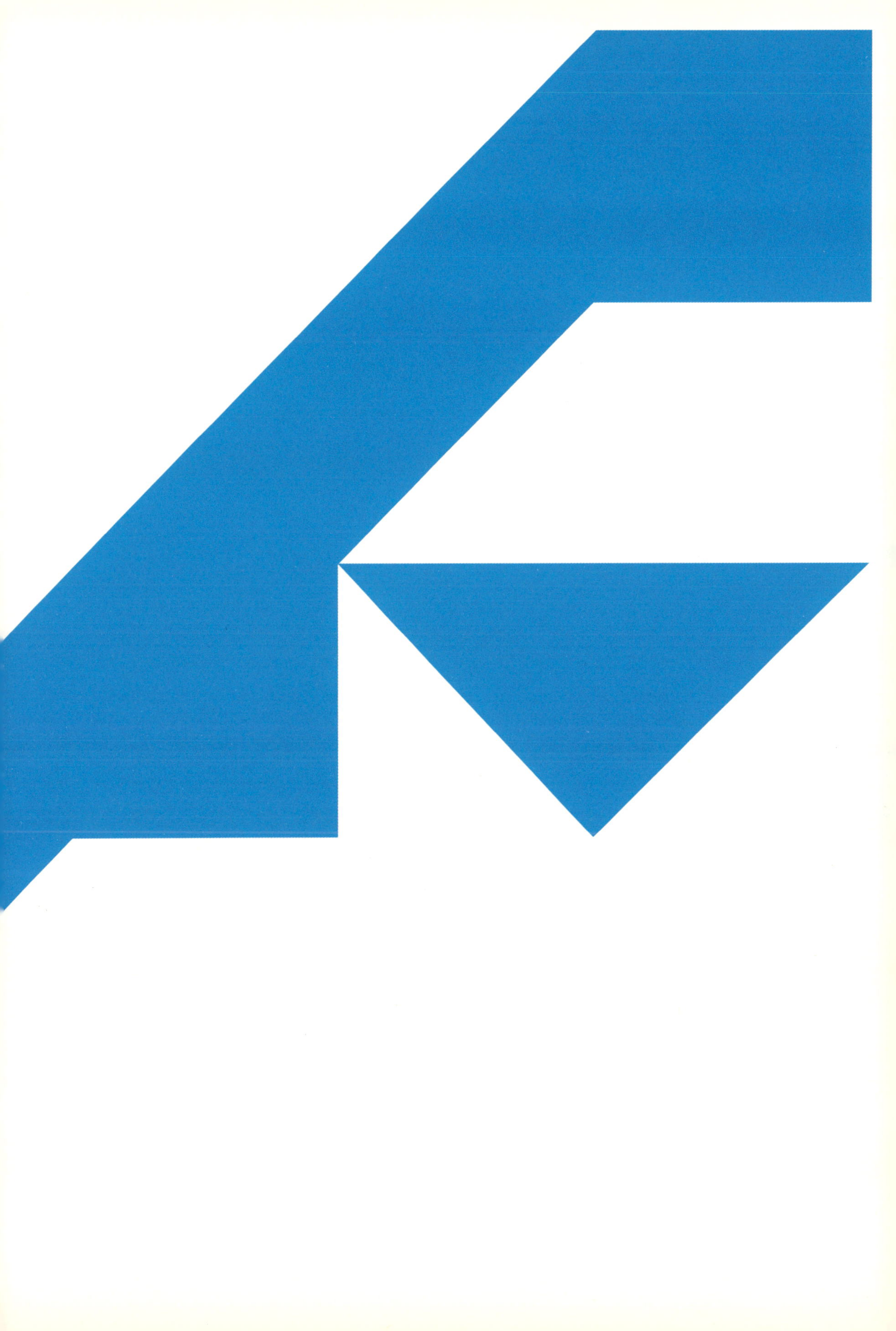

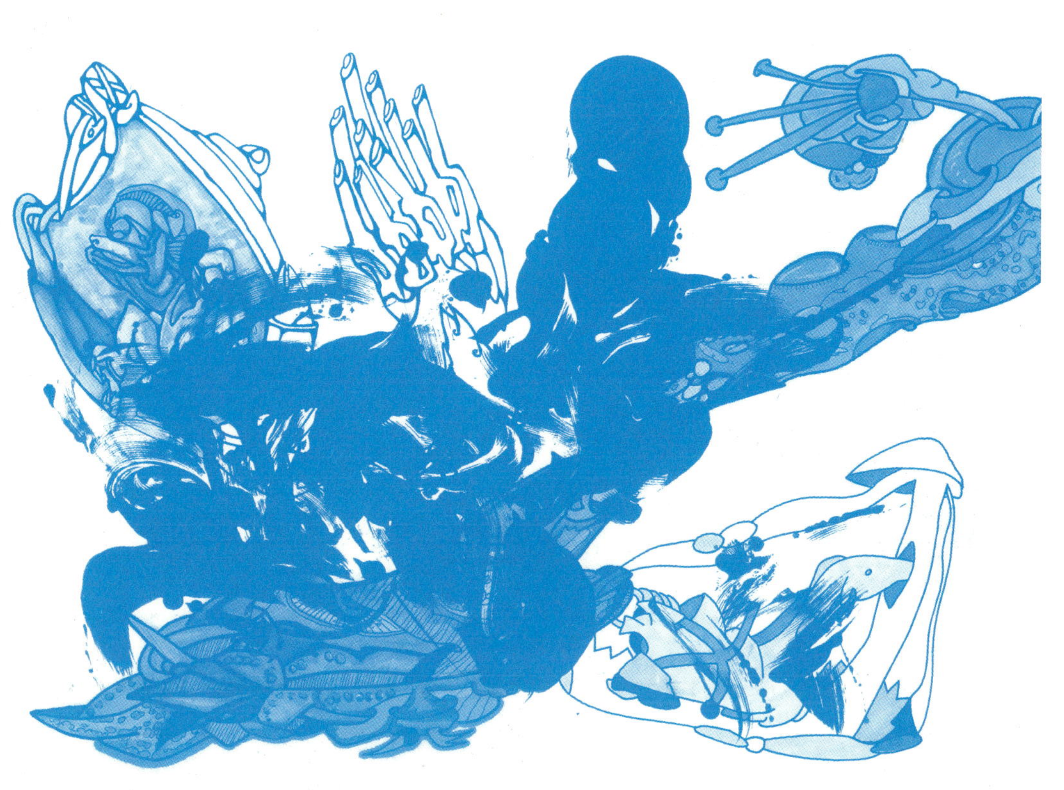

ALTERNATIVE HEALING INSTITUTE

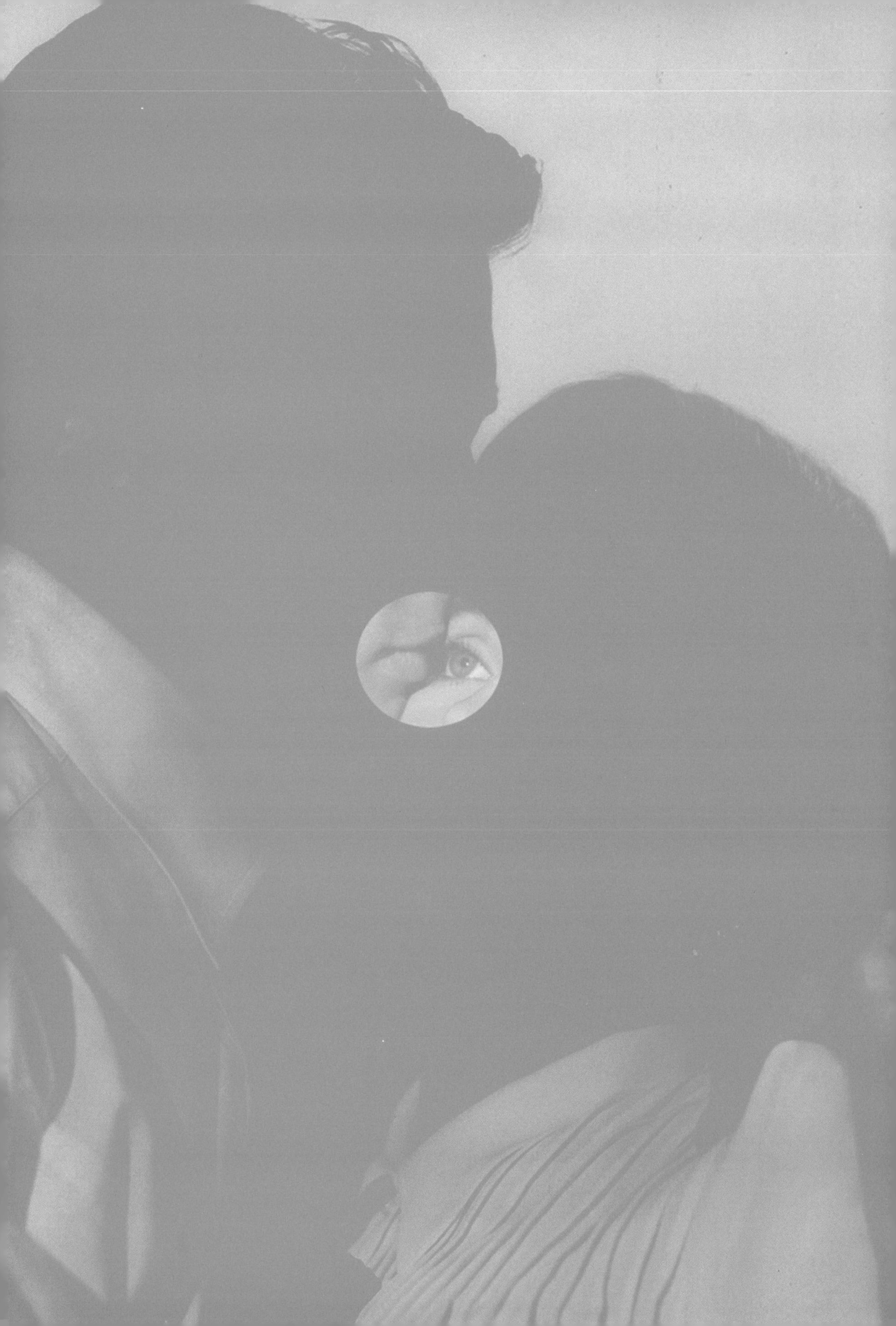

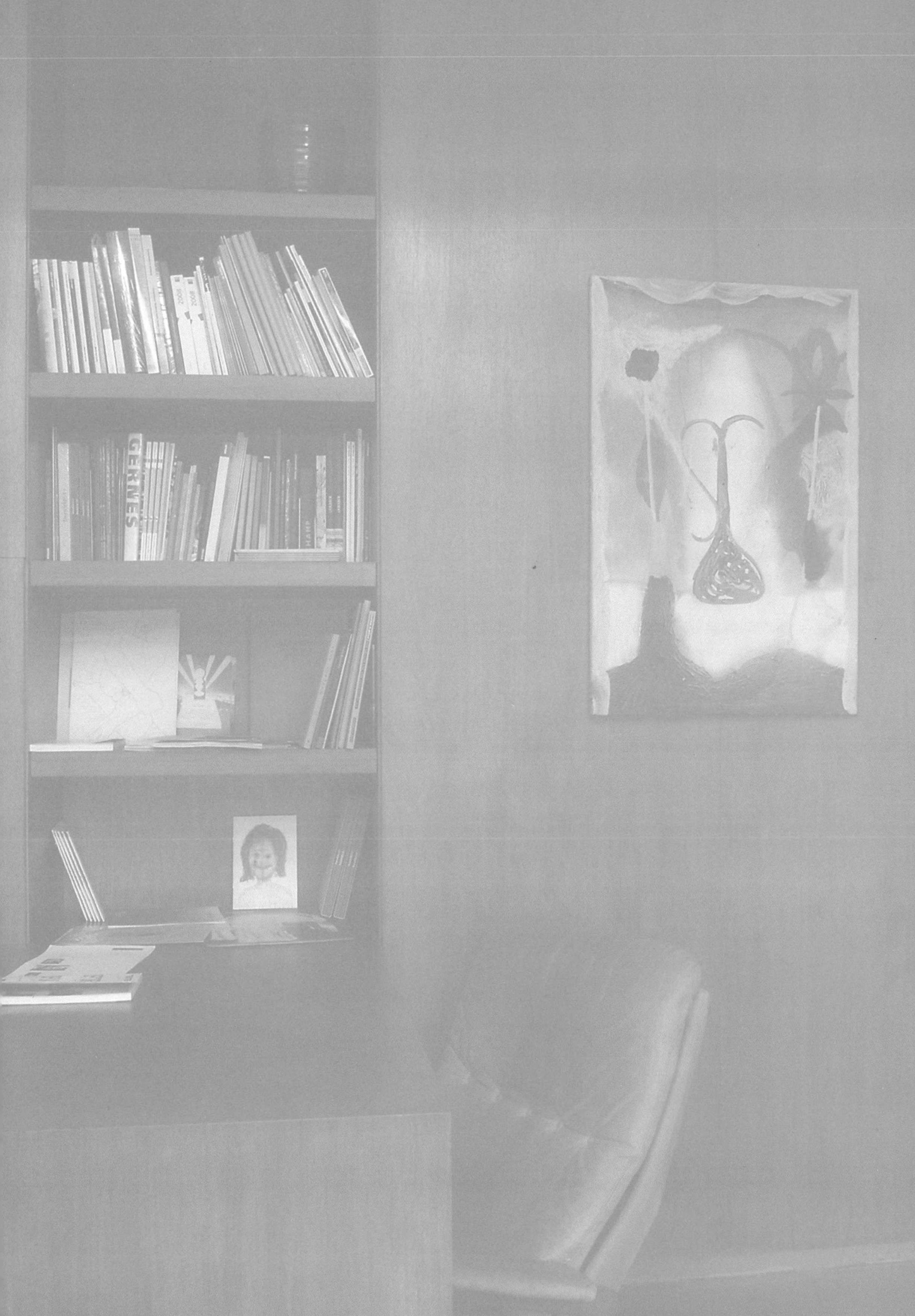

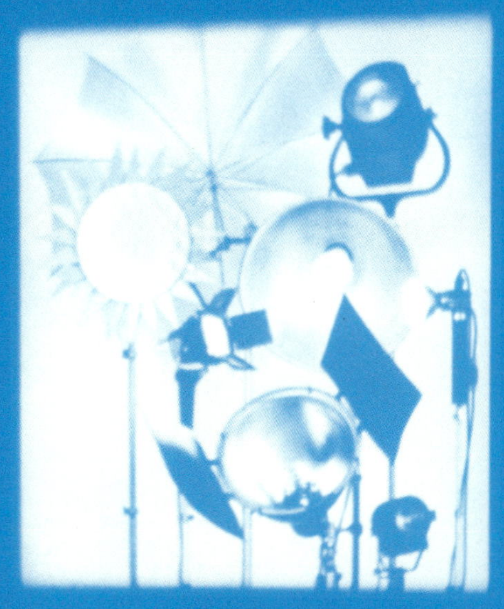

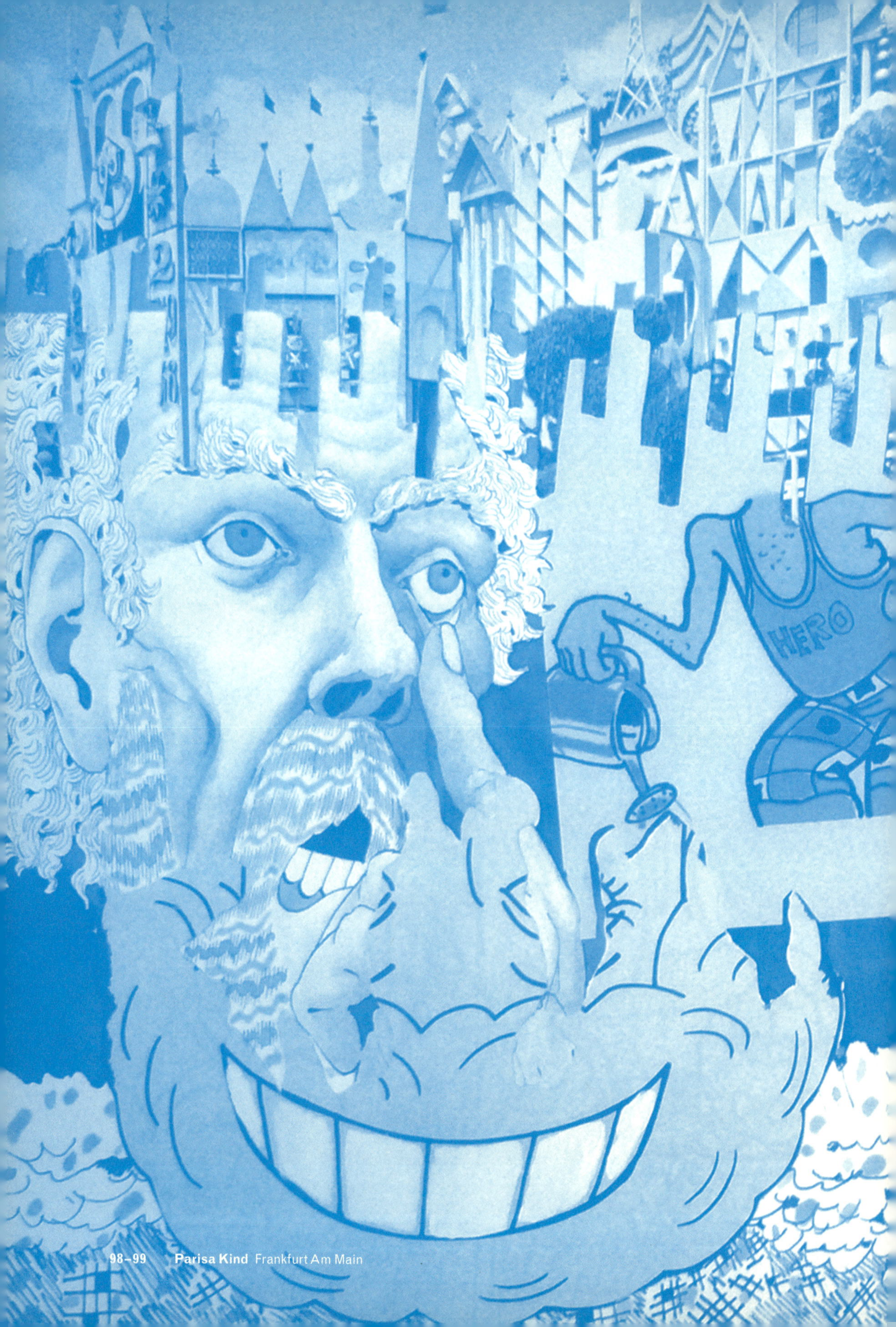

 Parisa Kind Frankfurt Am Main

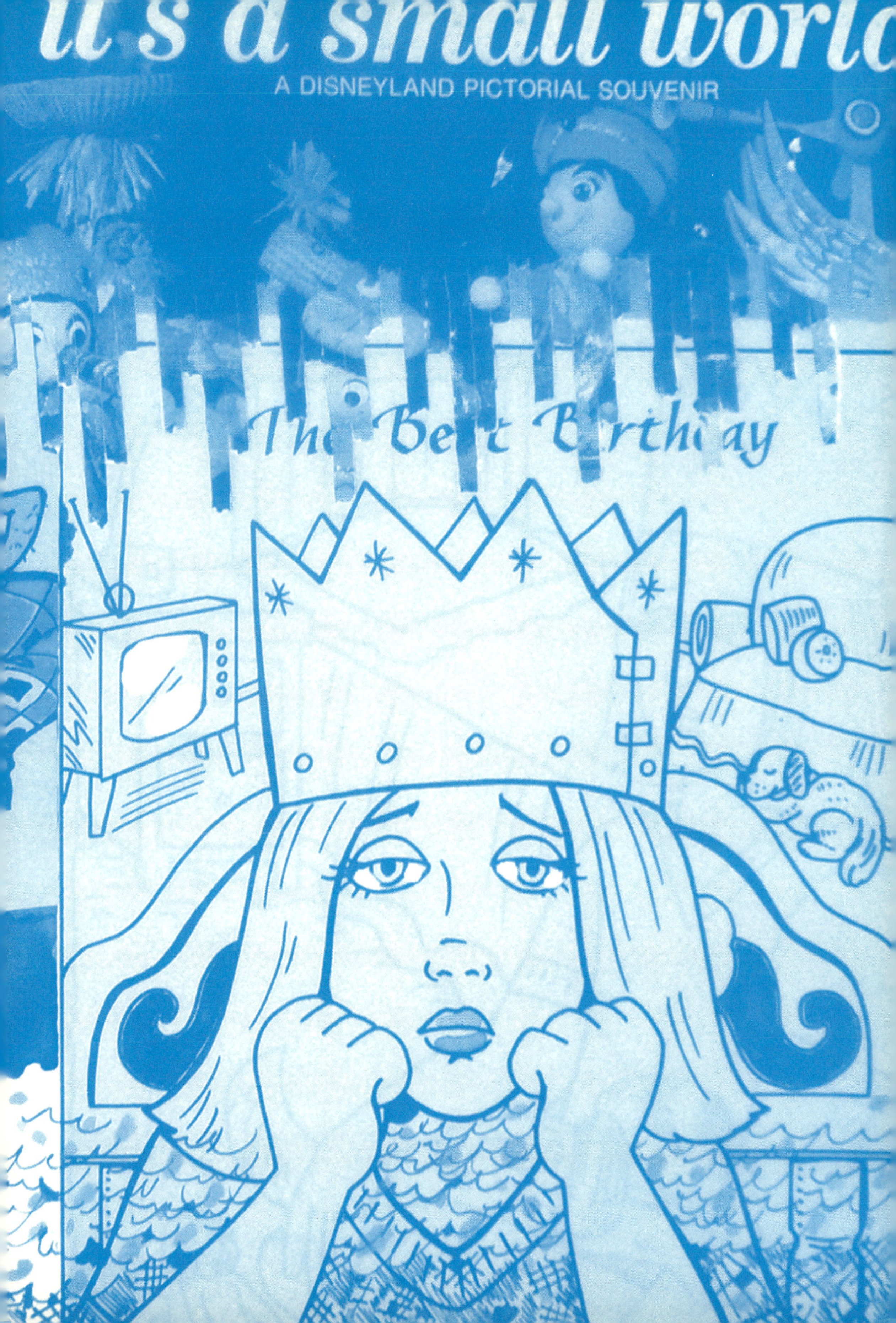
it's a small world
A DISNEYLAND PICTORIAL SOUVENIR
The Best Birthday

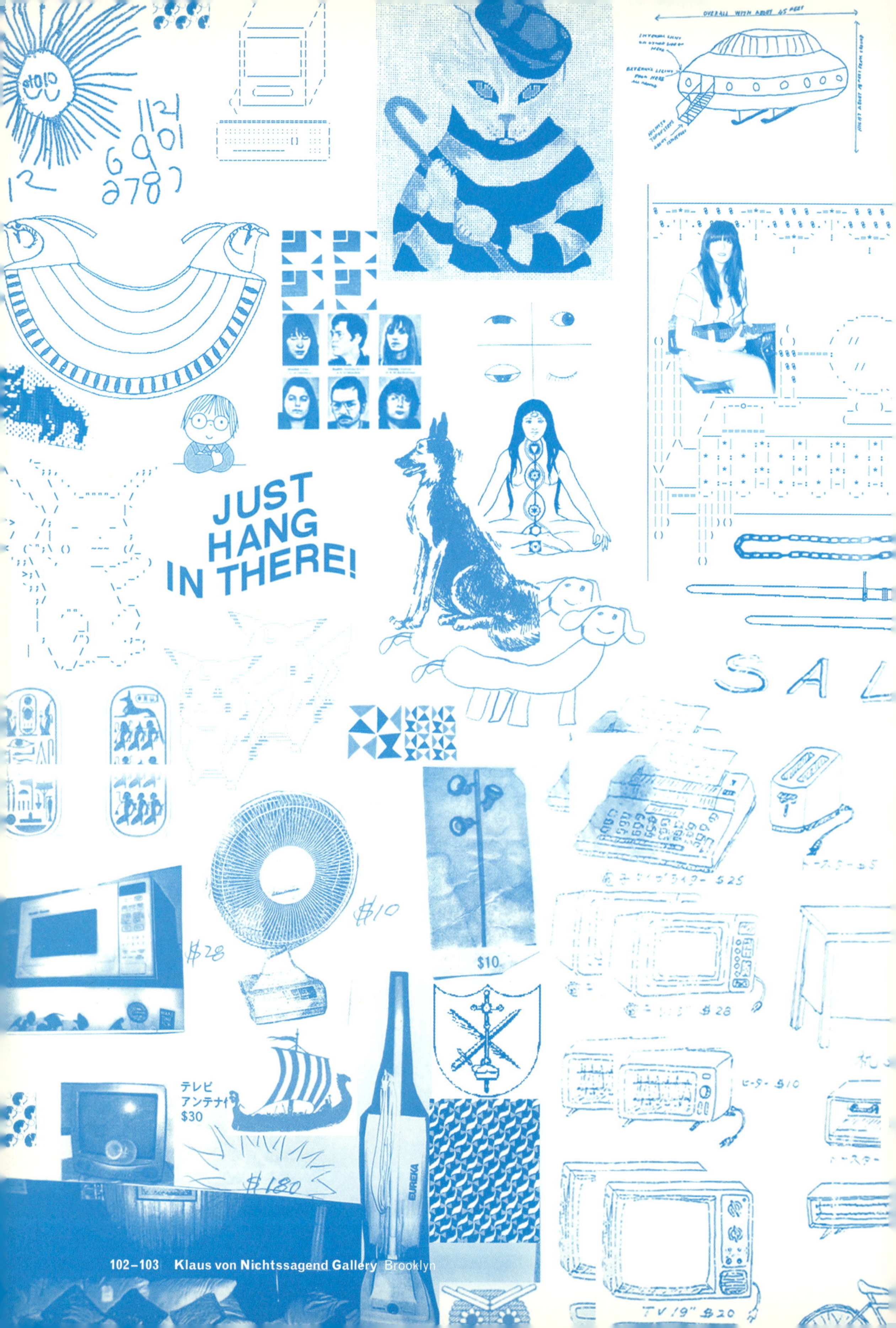

JUST
HANG
IN THERE!

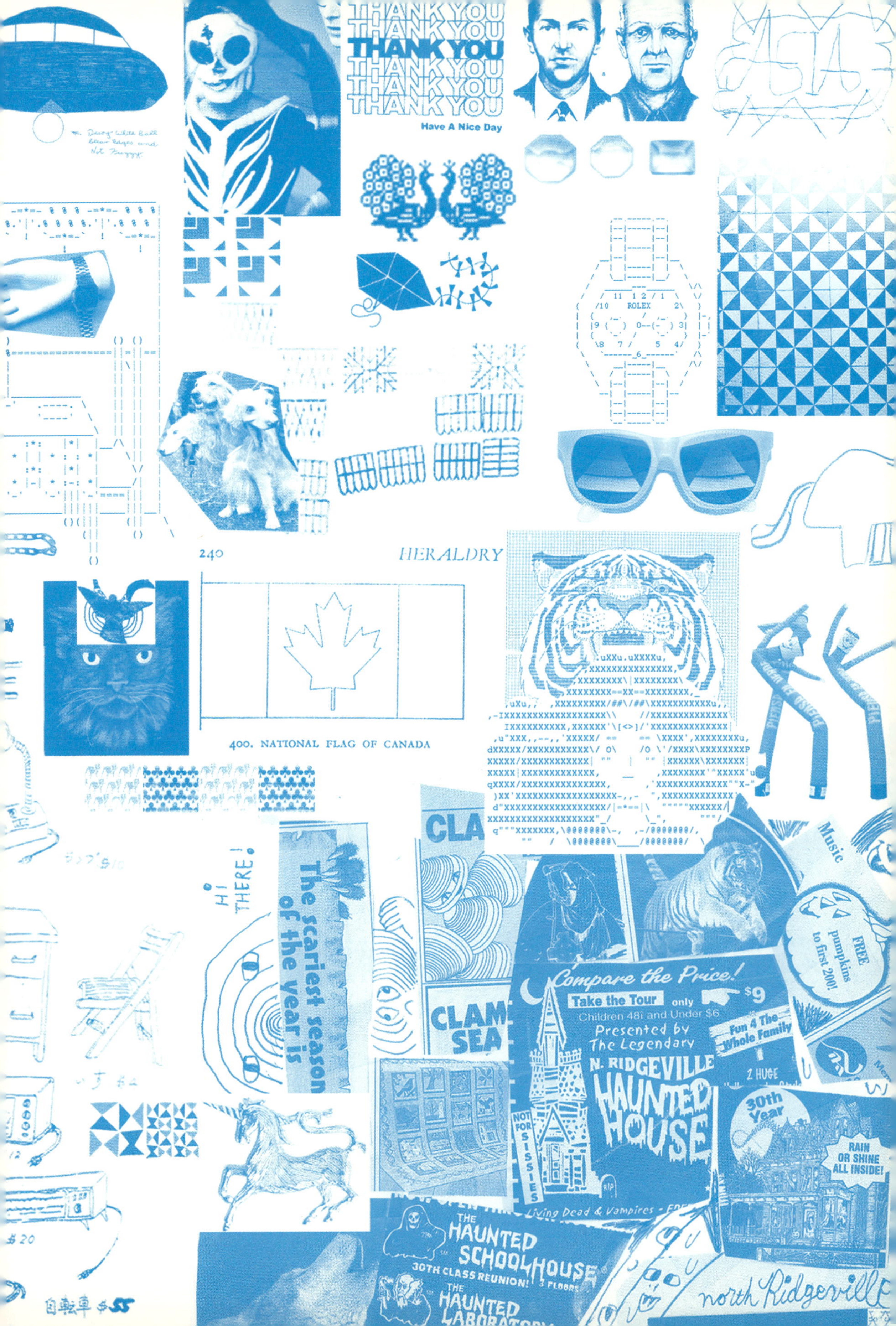
THANK YOU
THANK YOU
THANK YOU
THANK YOU
THANK YOU
Have A Nice Day
11 12 / 1
/10   ROLEX   2\
|9   0 -{-   3|
\8   7   5 4/
6
240
HERALDRY
400. NATIONAL FLAG OF CANADA
HI THERE!
The scariest season of the year is
CLA
CLAM SEA
Music
Compare the Price!
Take the Tour   only $9
Children 48i and Under $6
Presented by
The Legendary
N. RIDGEVILLE
HAUNTED HOUSE
NOT FOR SISSIES
Living Dead & Vampires
FREE pumpkins to first 200!
Fun 4 The Whole Family
2 HUGE
30th Year
RAIN OR SHINE ALL INSIDE!
THE HAUNTED SCHOOLHOUSE
30TH CLASS REUNION! 3 FLOORS
THE HAUNTED LABORATORY
north Ridgeville
自転車 $5

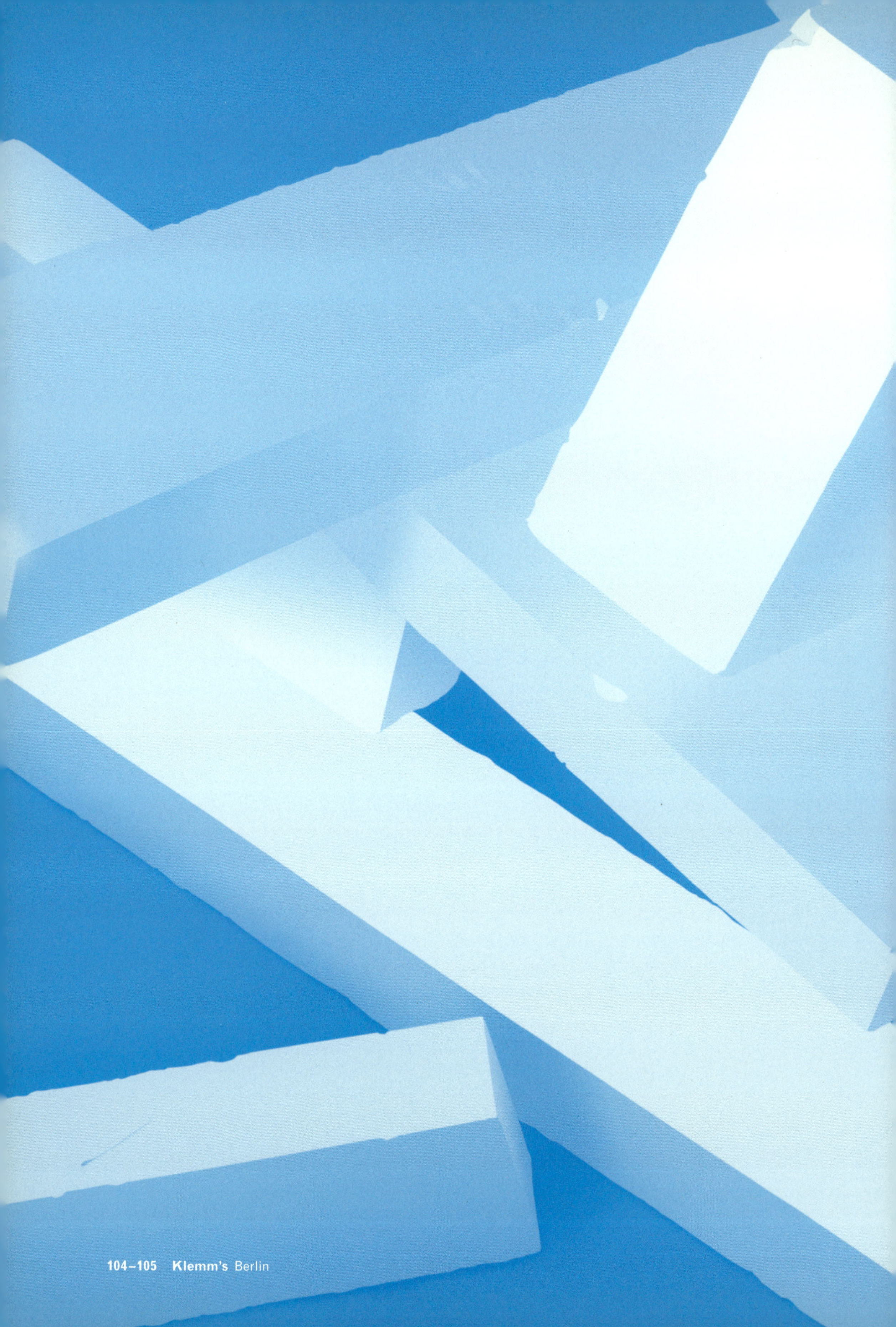

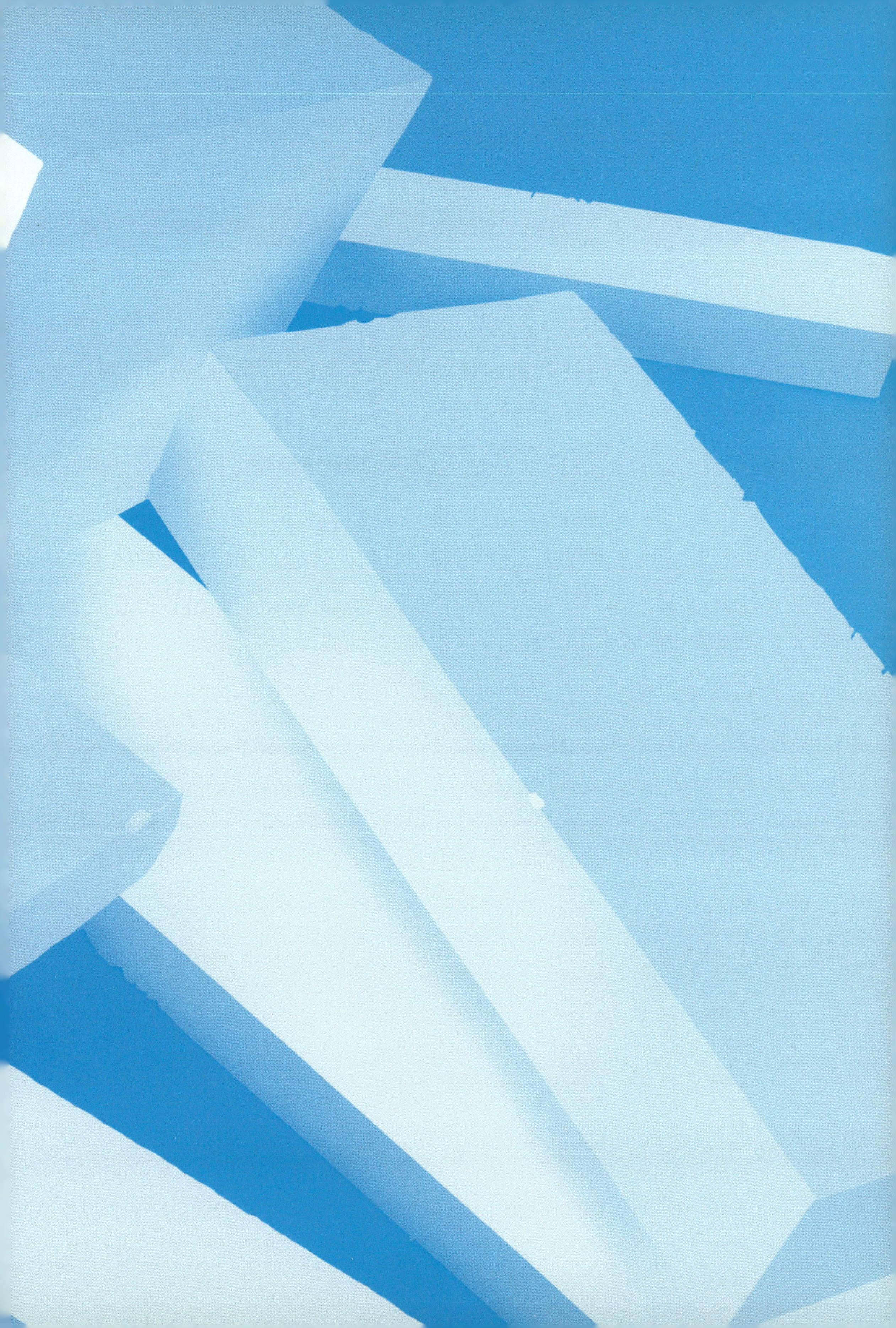

THE FIRST TIME
EVER I SAW
YOUR FACE
I THOUGHT THE
SUN ROSE IN
YOUR EYES

THE LAST TIME
EVER I SAW
YOUR FACE YOU
WERE TALKING
SHIT ABOUT A
PRETTY SUNSET

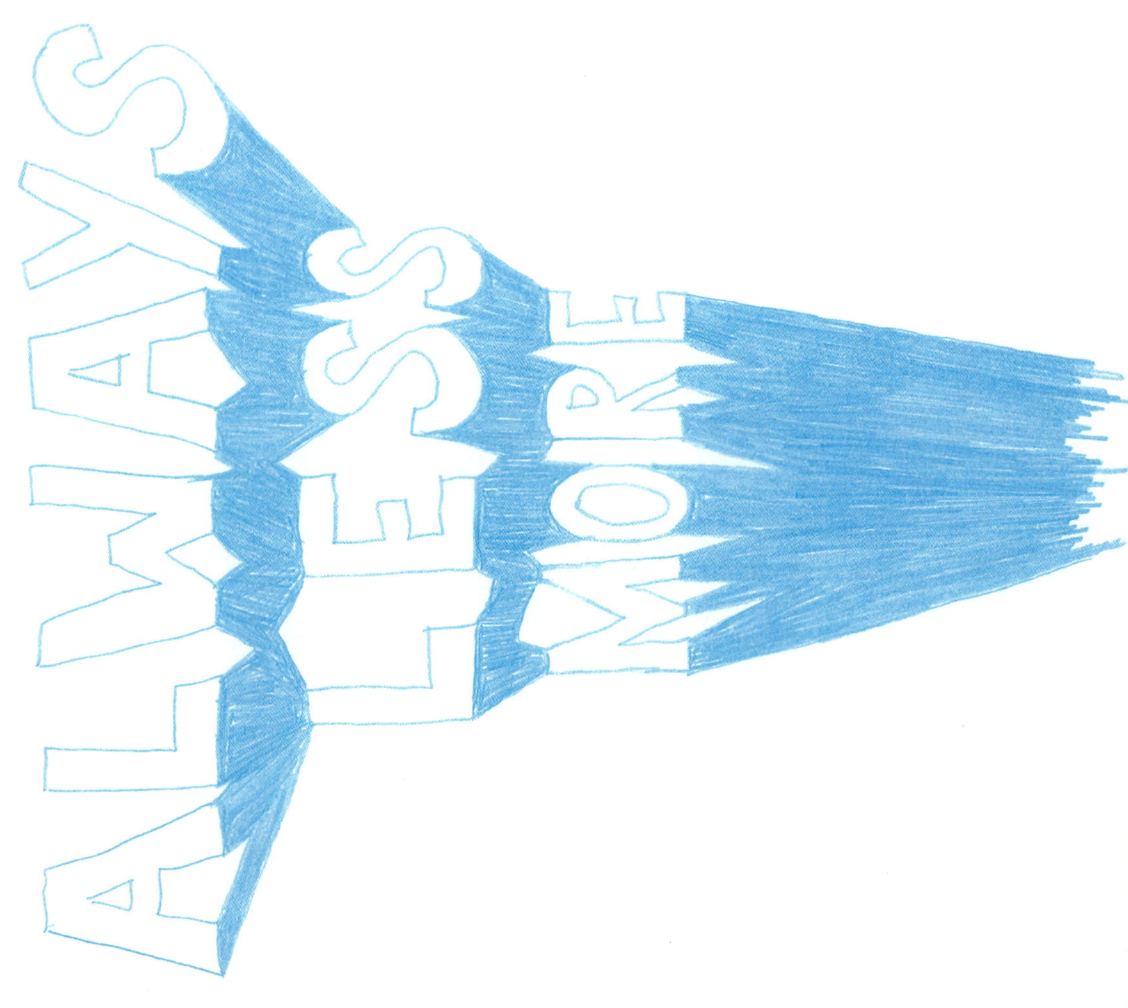

ALWAYS
LESS
MORE

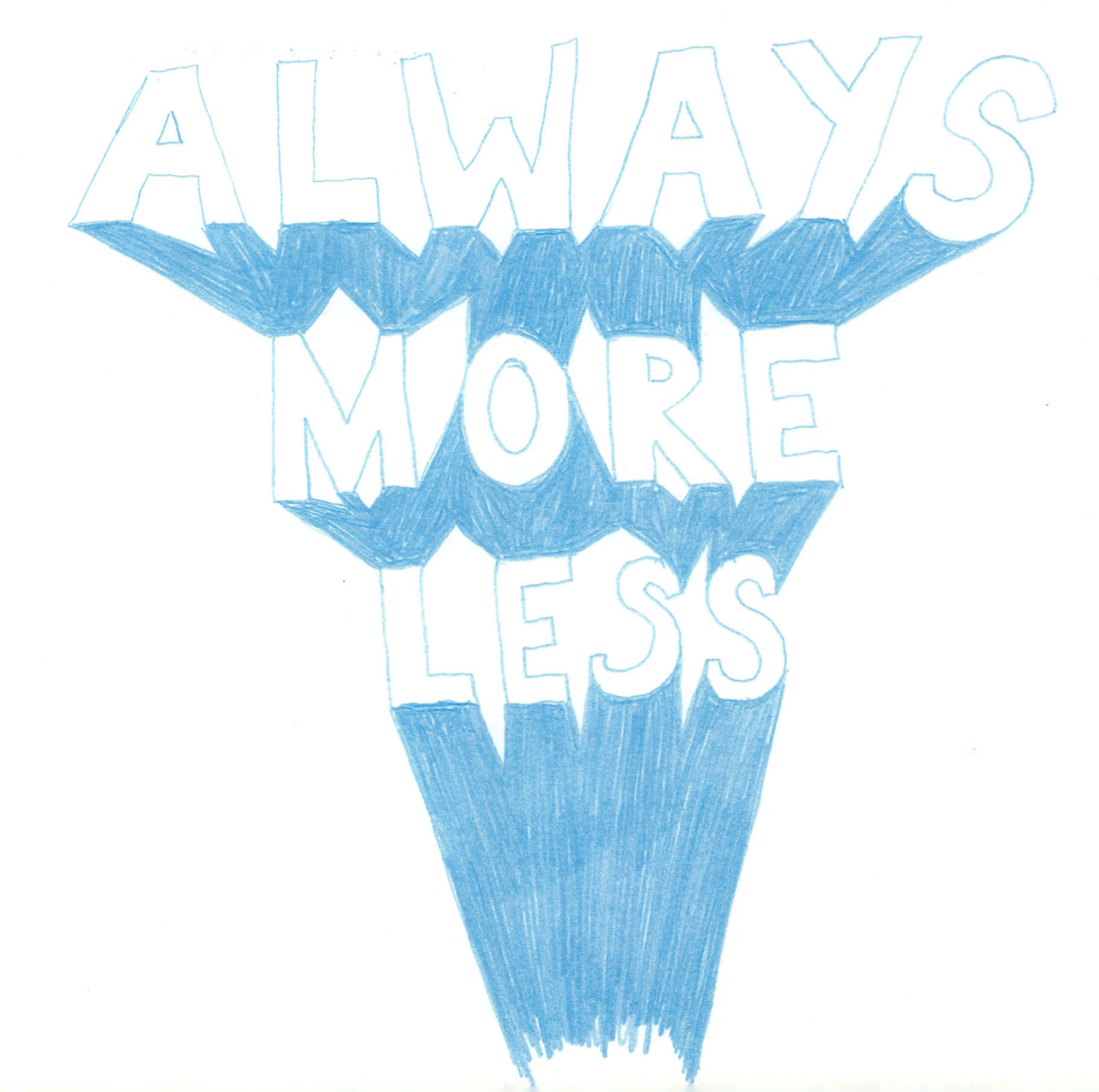

ALWAYS
MORE
LESS

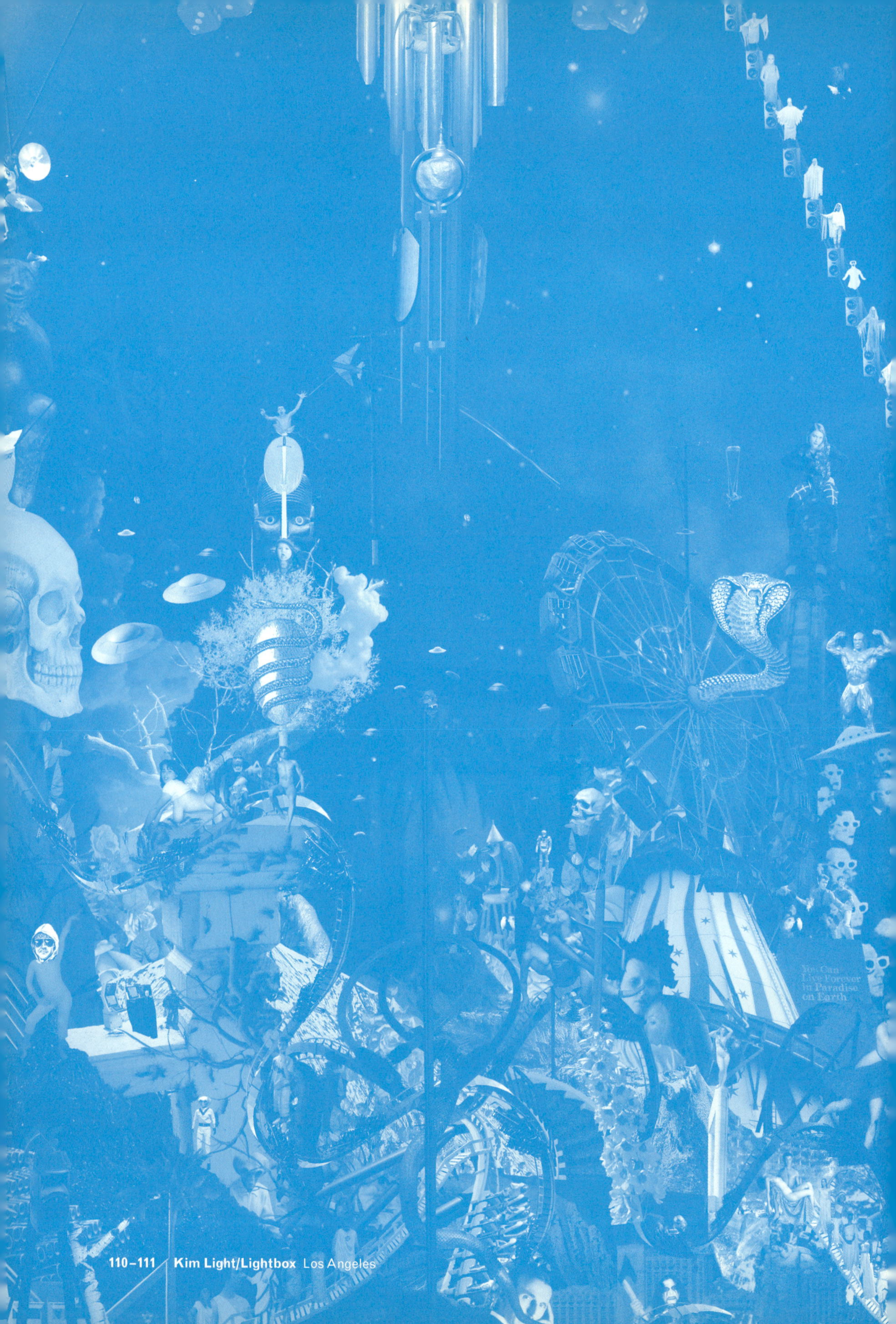
You Can
Live Forever
In Paradise
on Earth

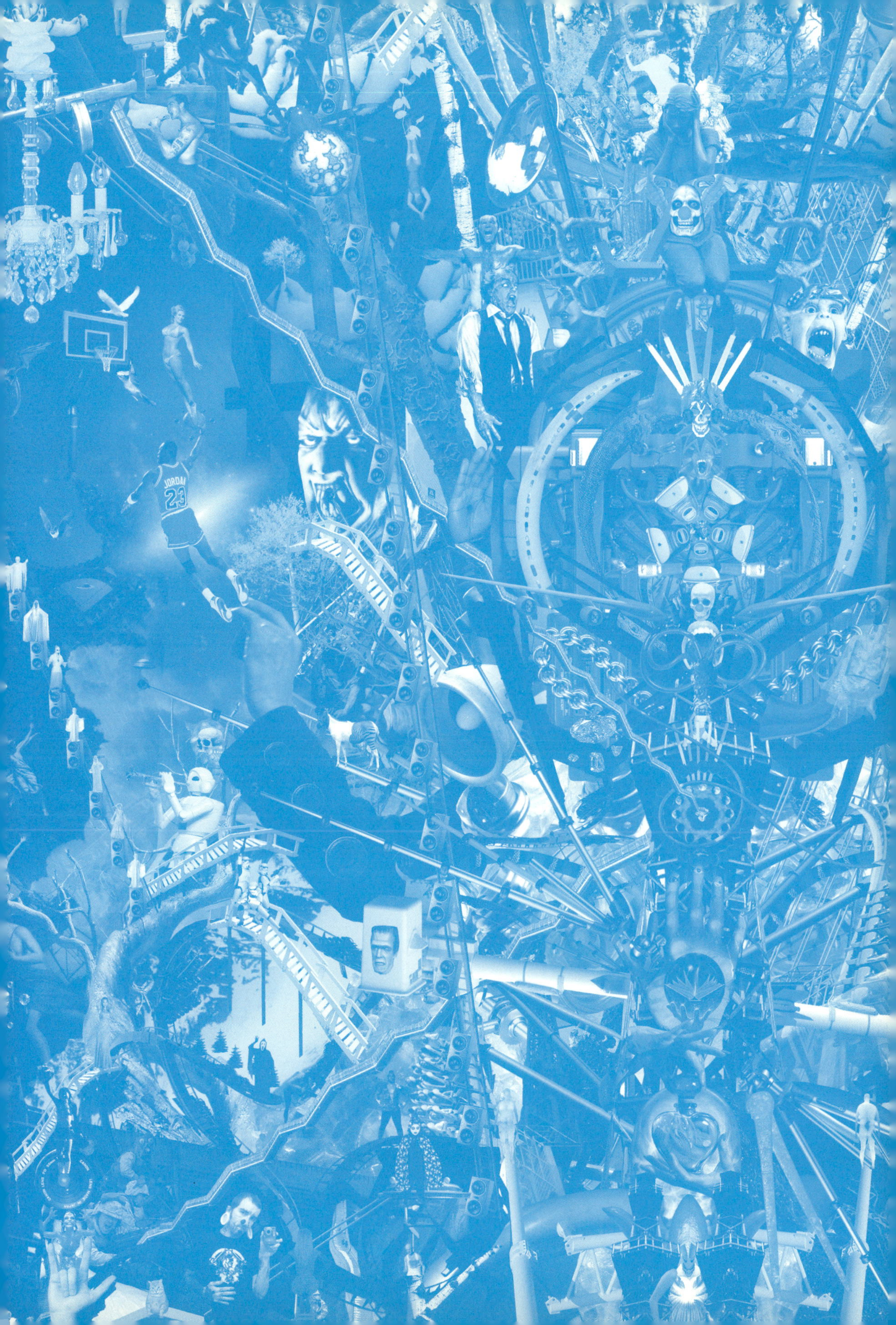

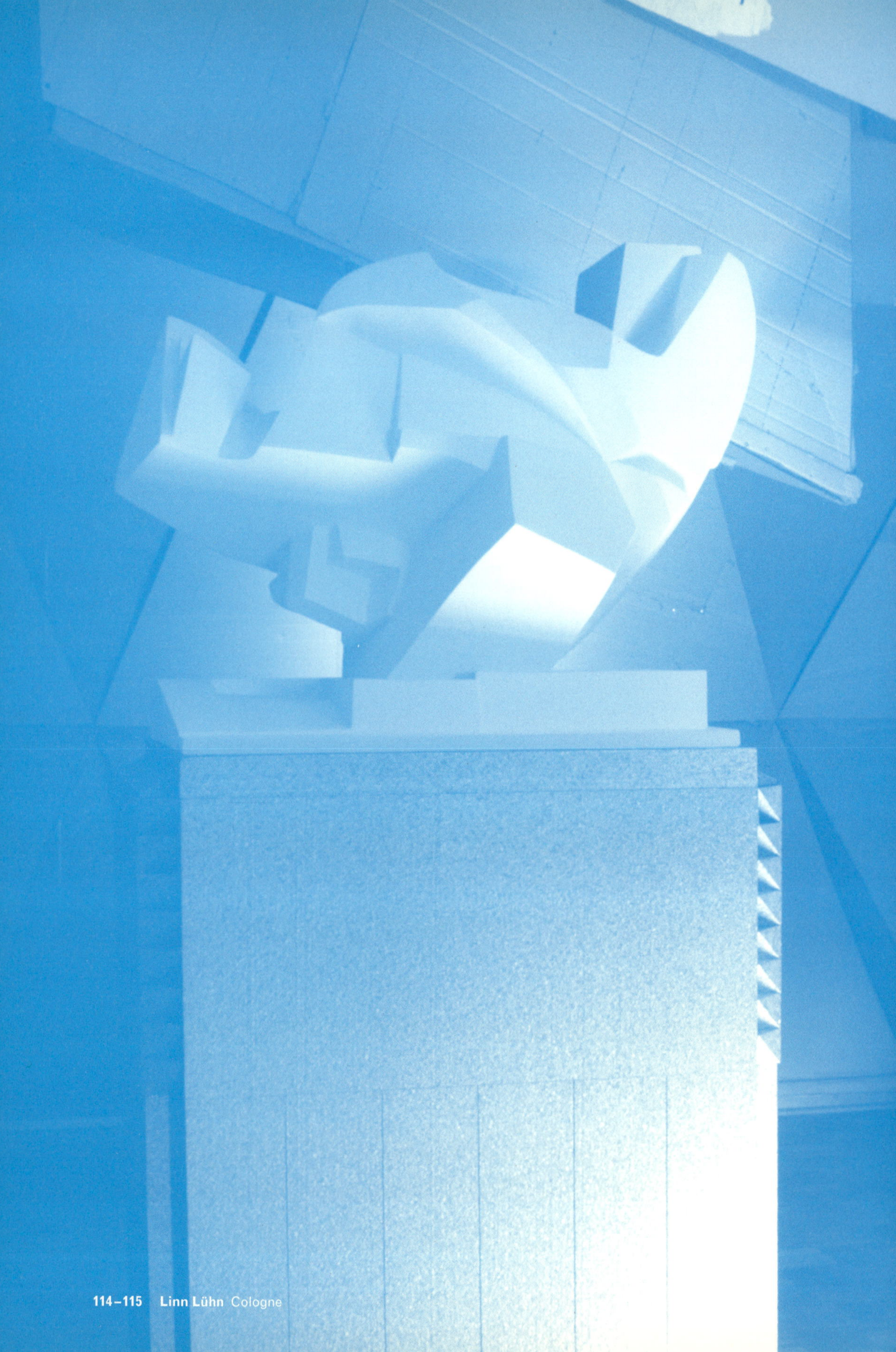

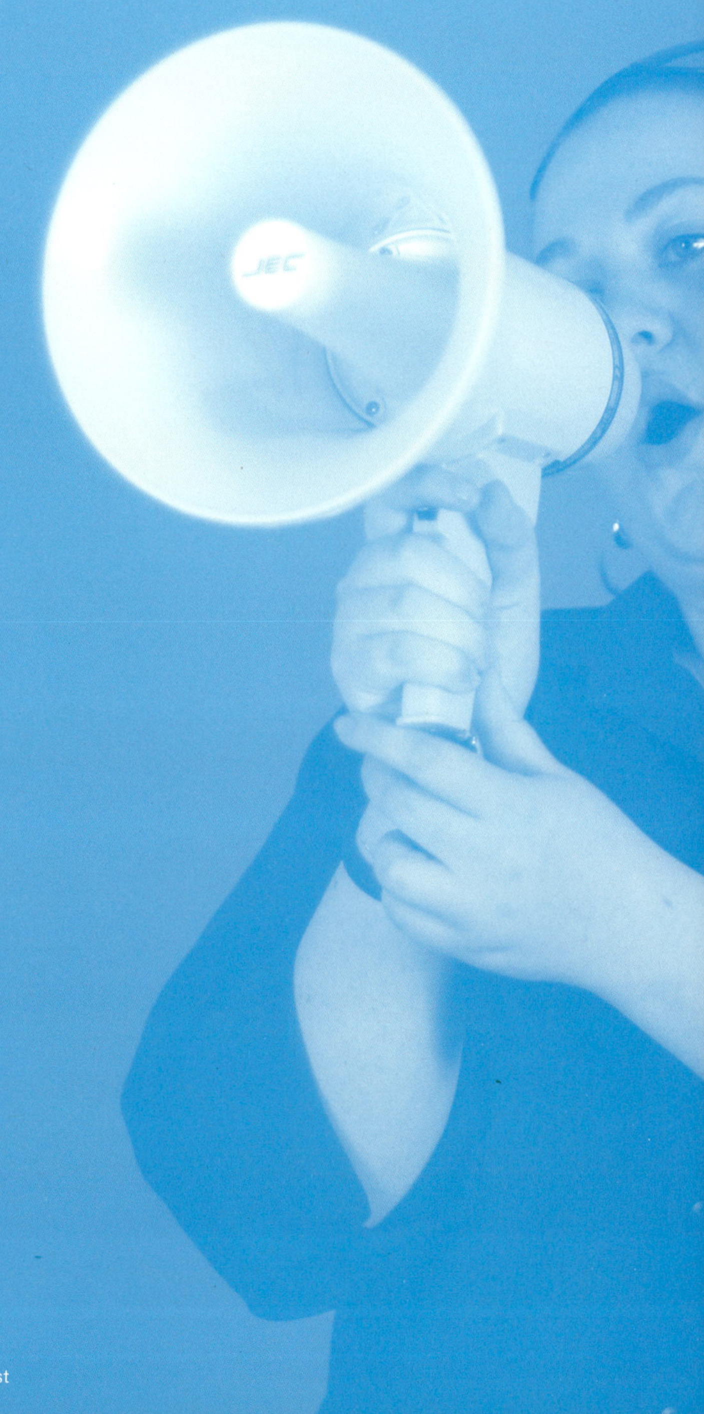

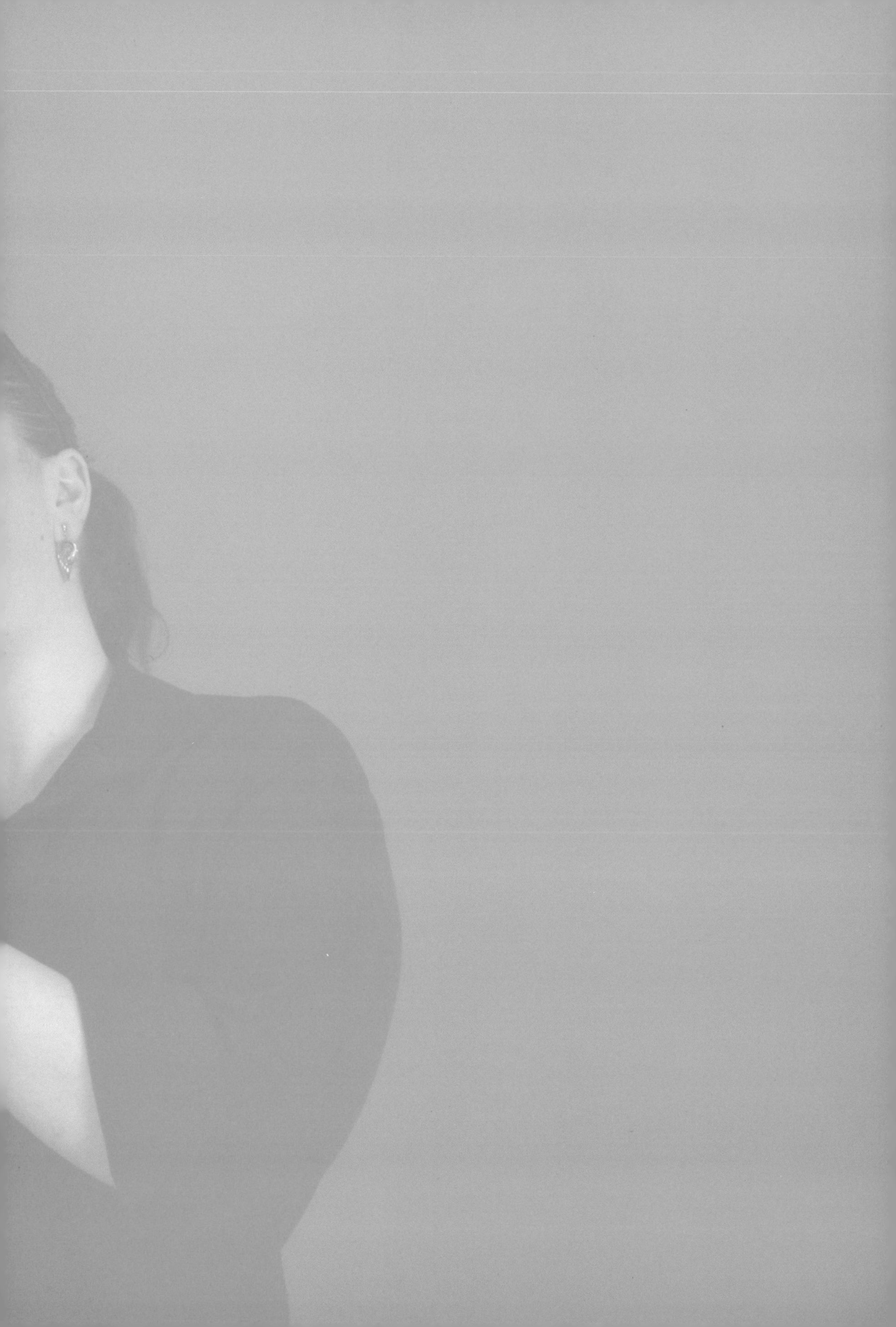

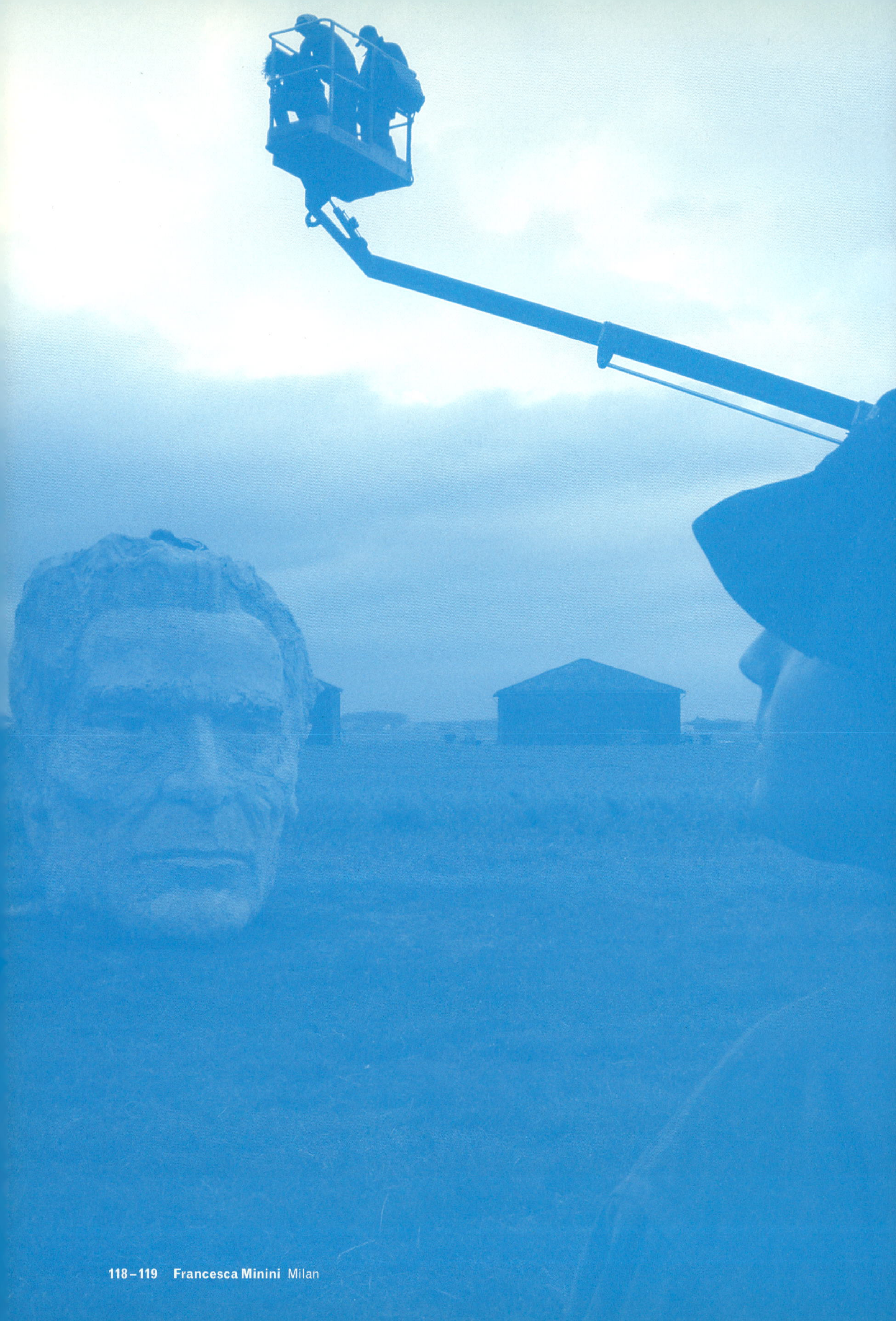

118–119 **Francesca Minini** Milan

Black Bikini

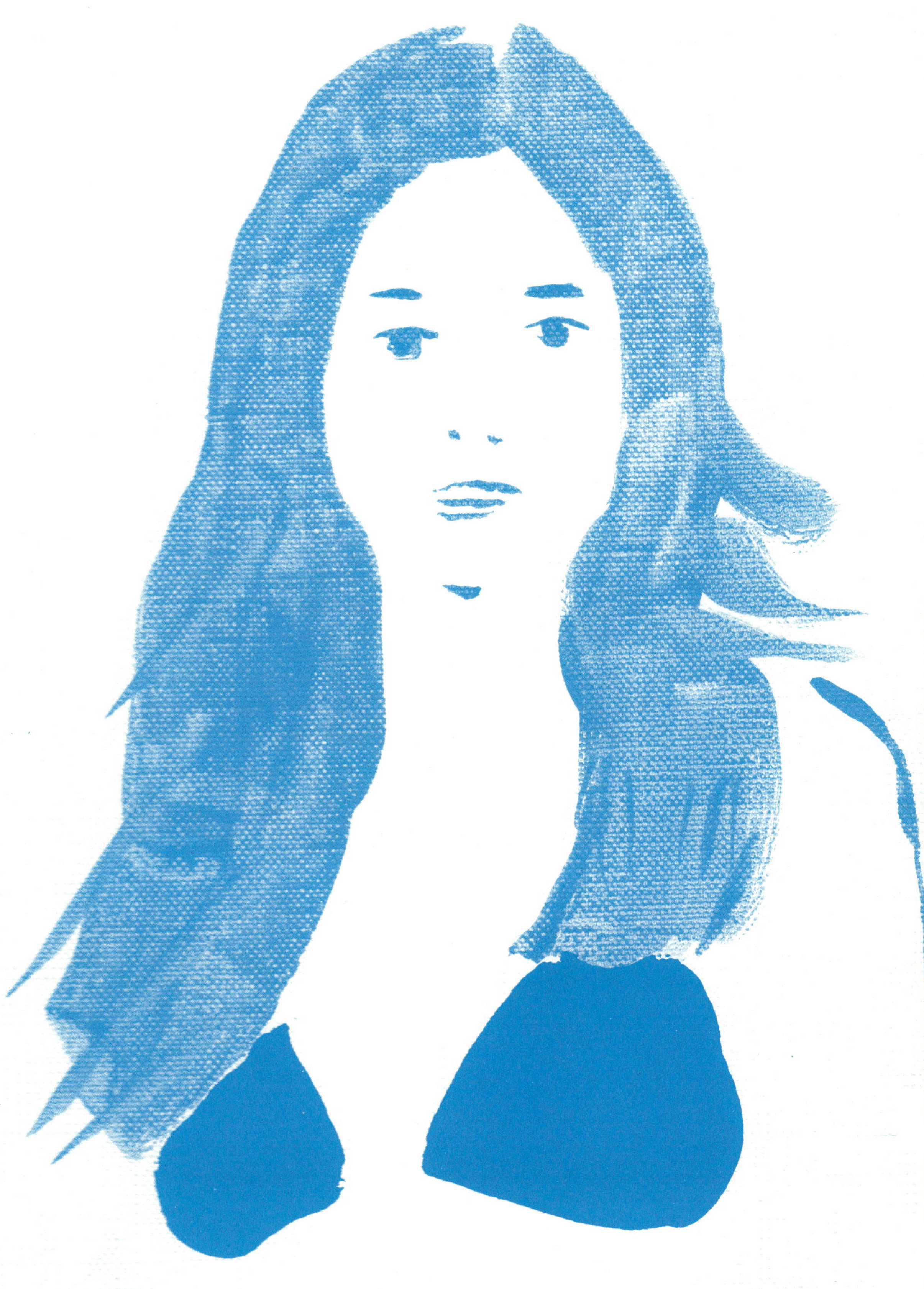

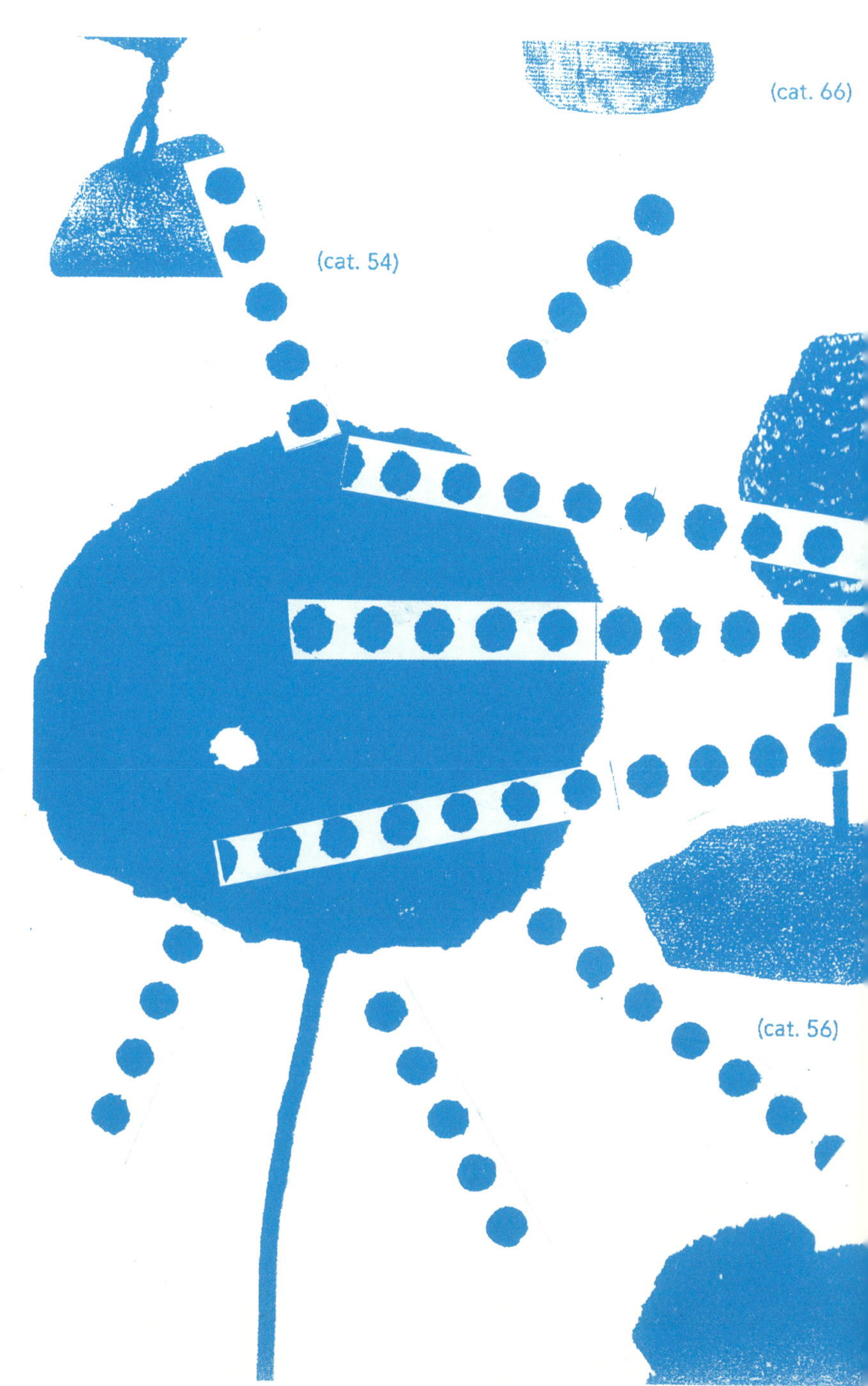

(cat. 66)
(cat. 54)
(cat. 56)

timately yielding gold and causing a
with this role of fire from his study of
provided further confirmation.

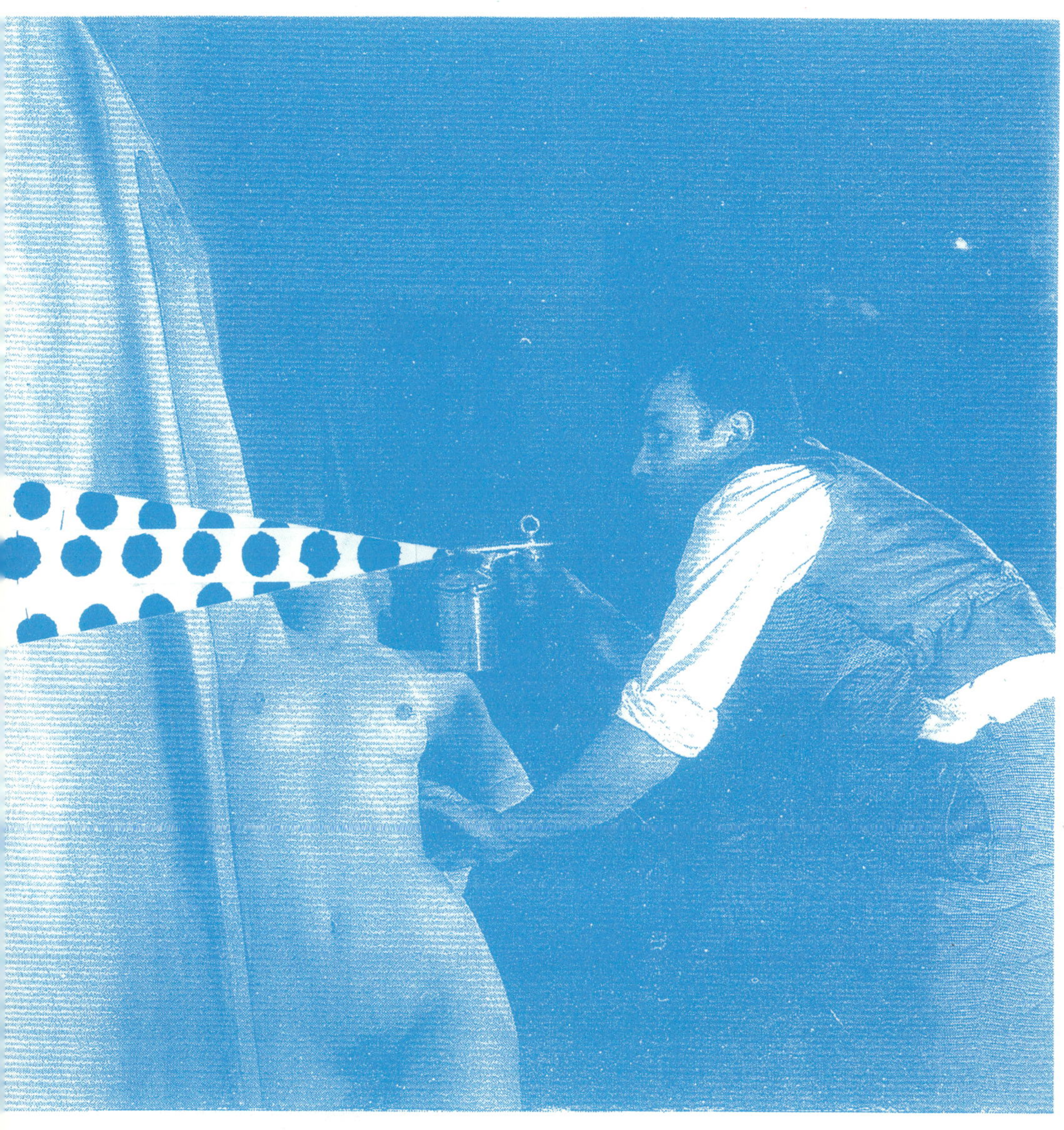

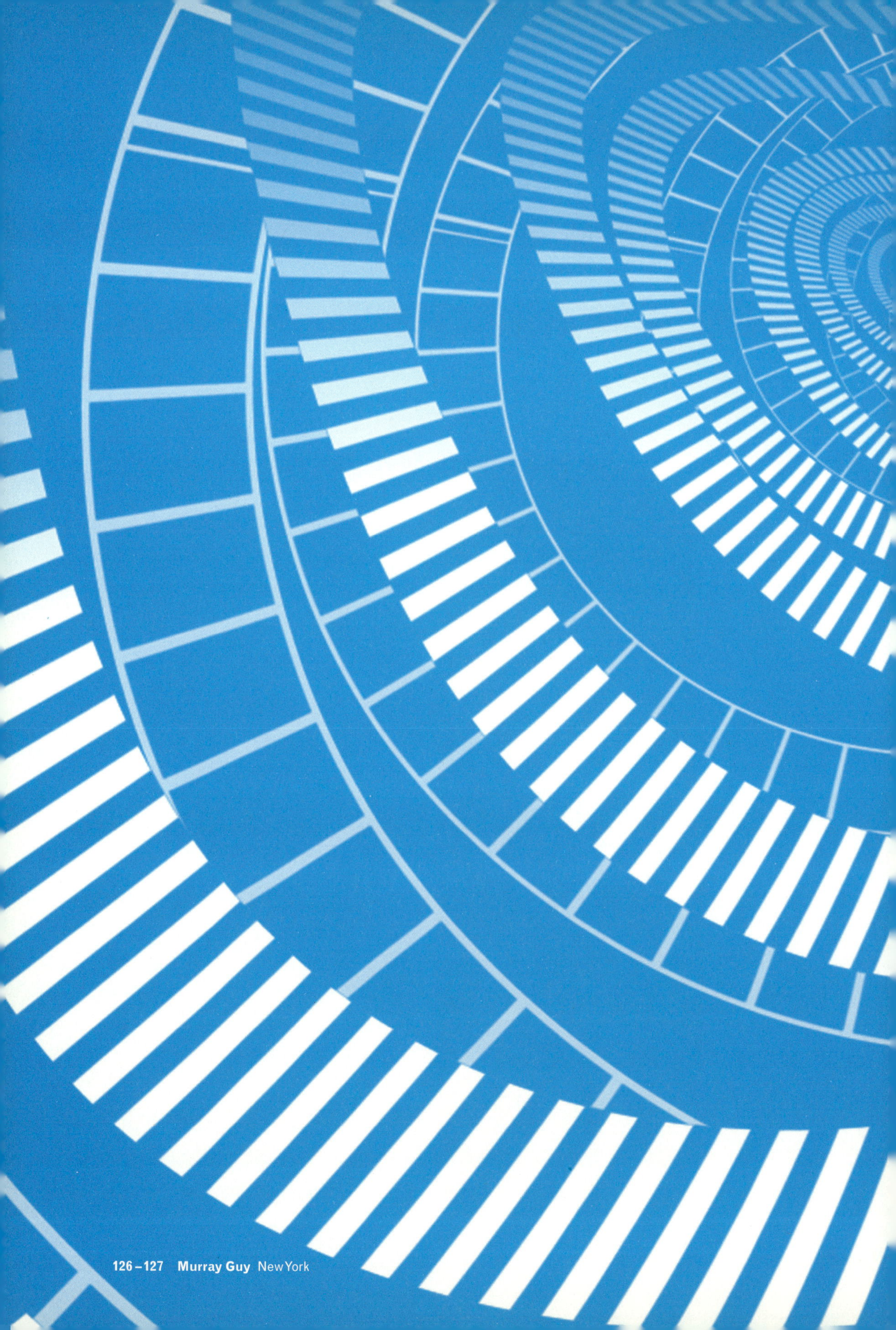

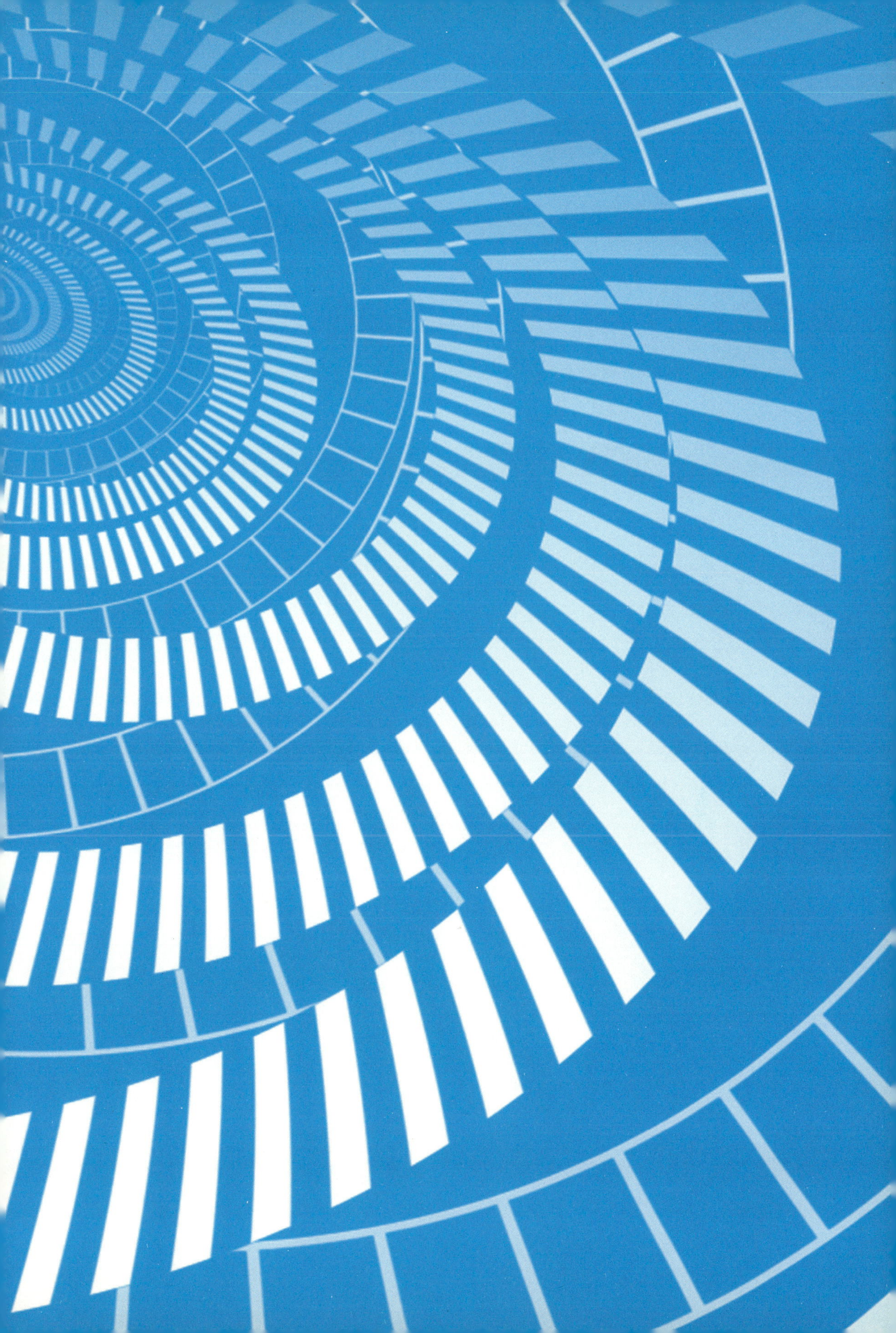

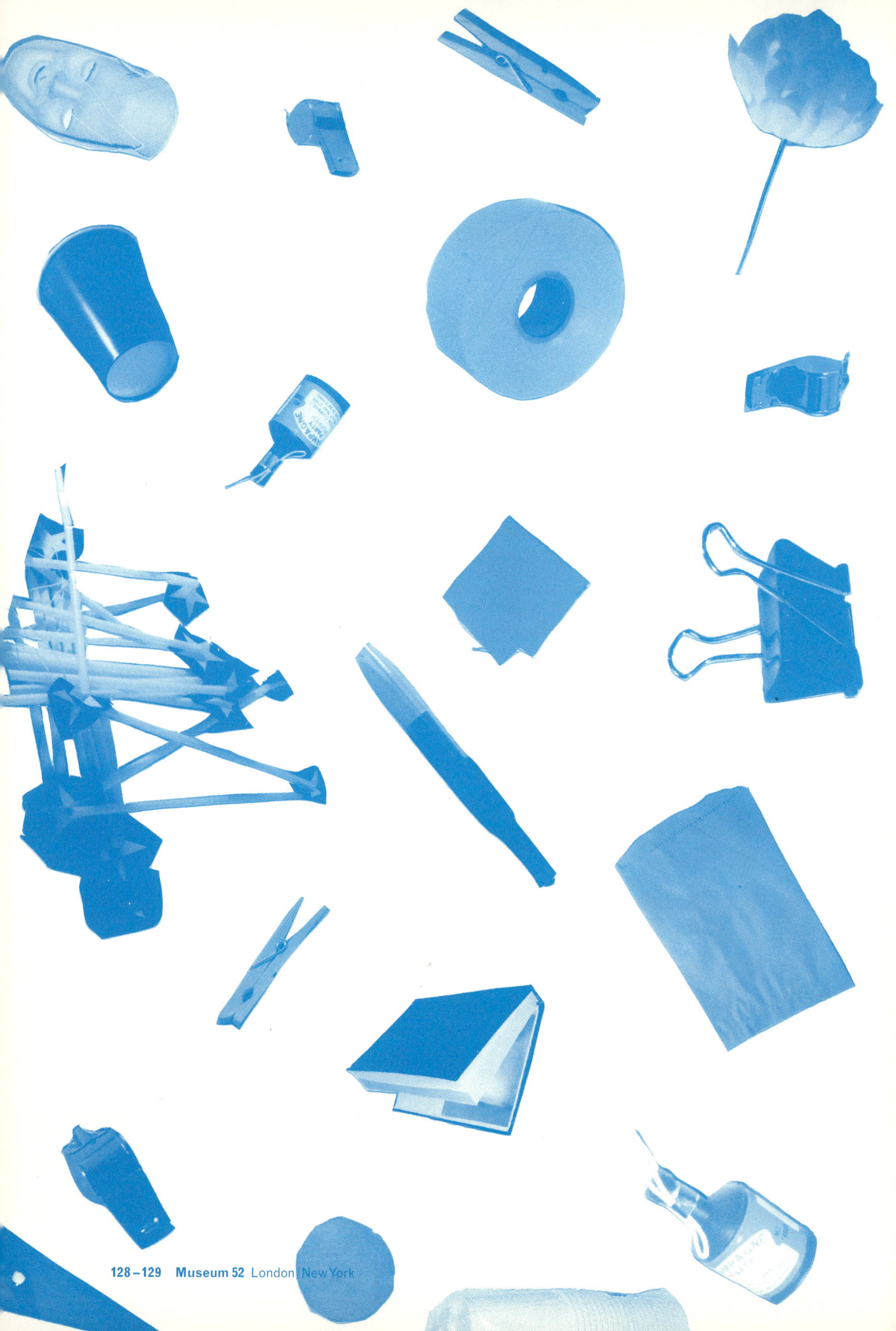

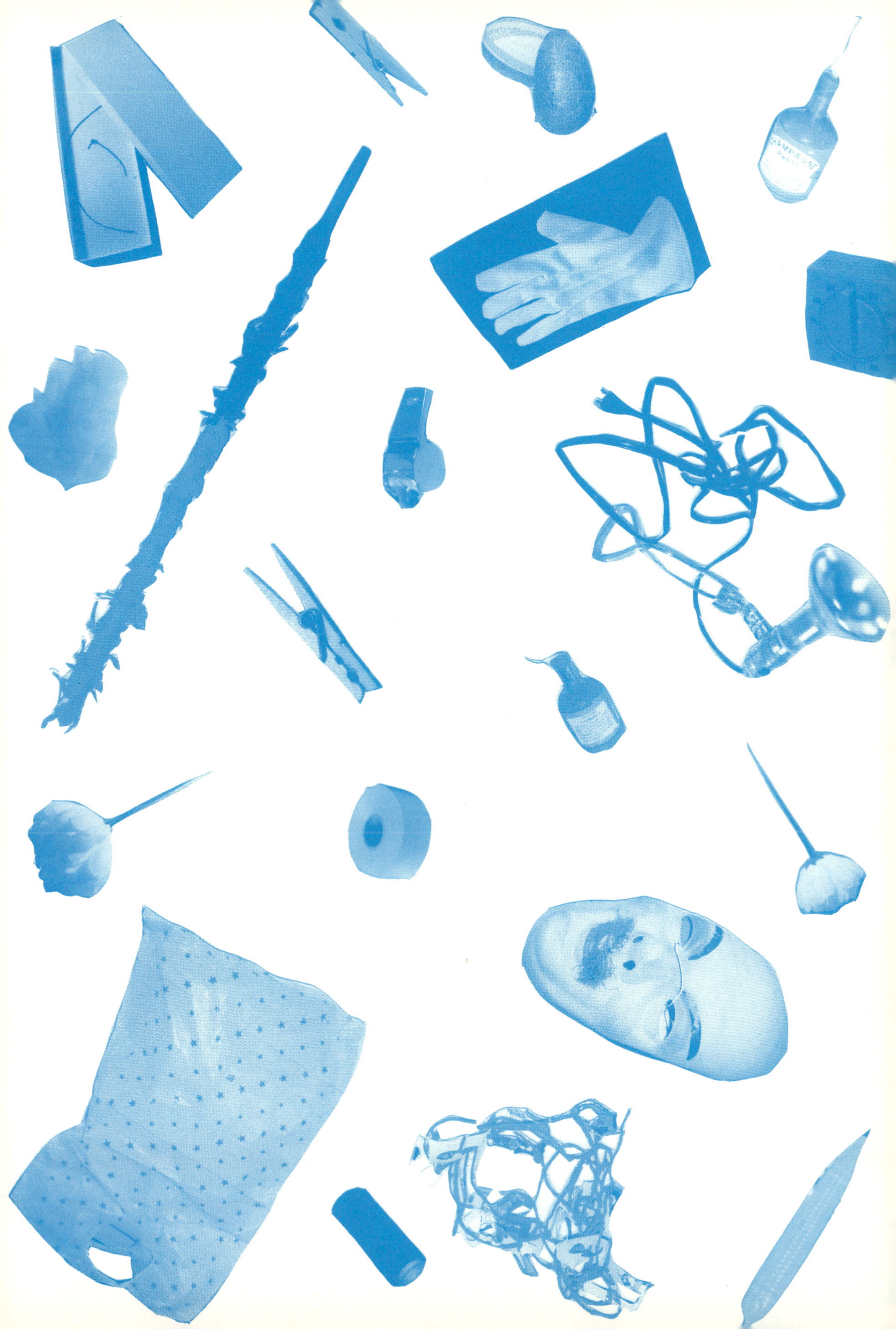

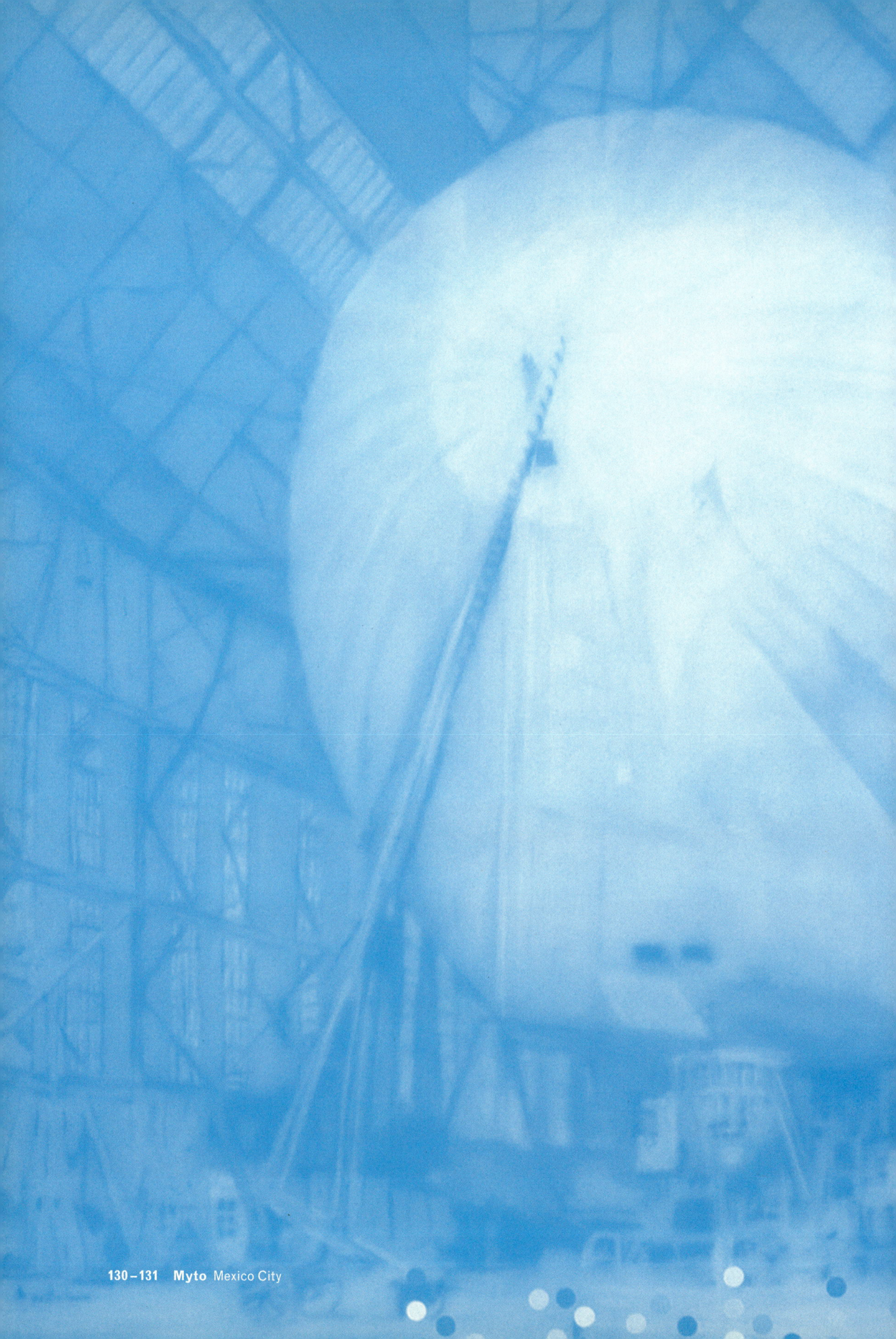

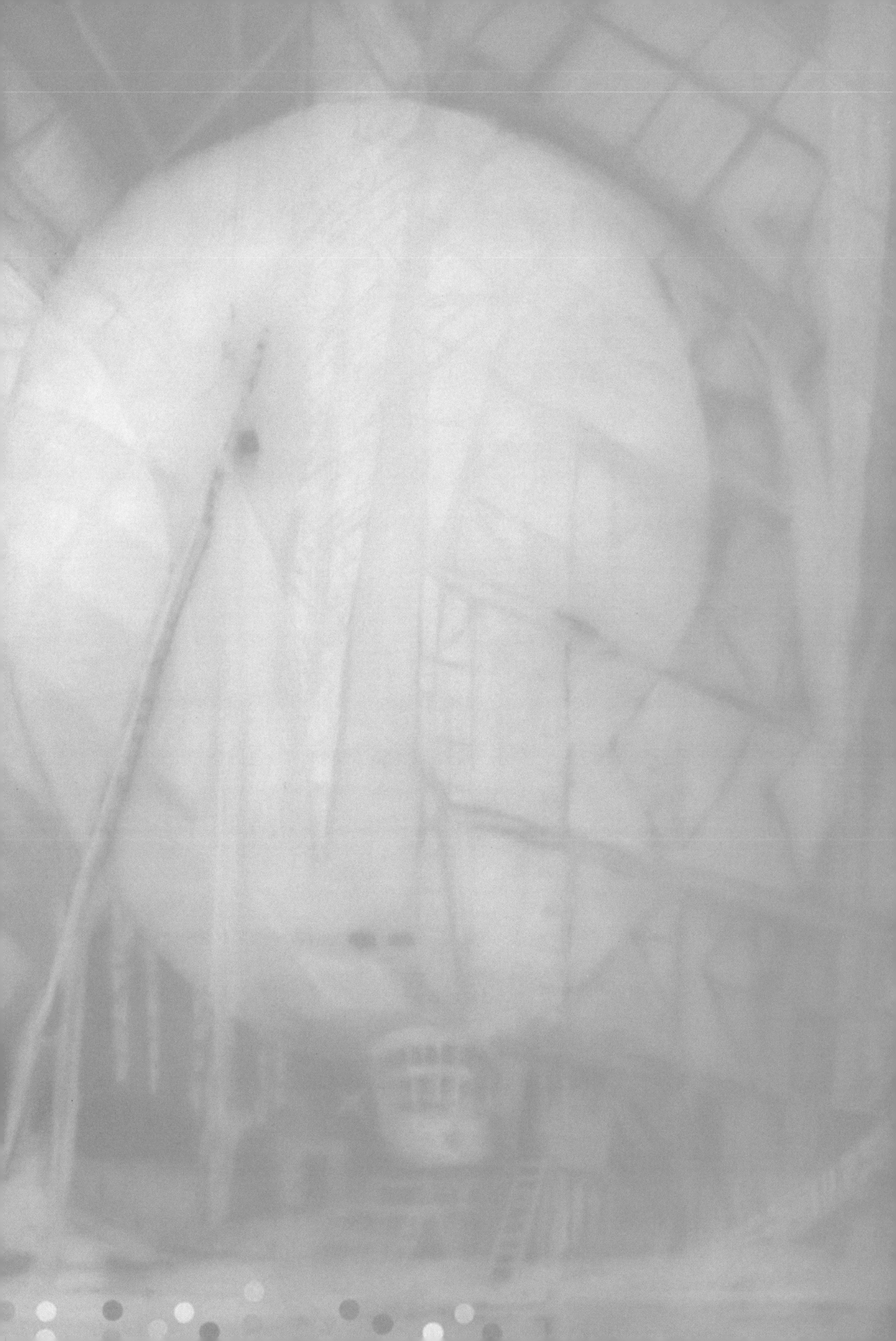

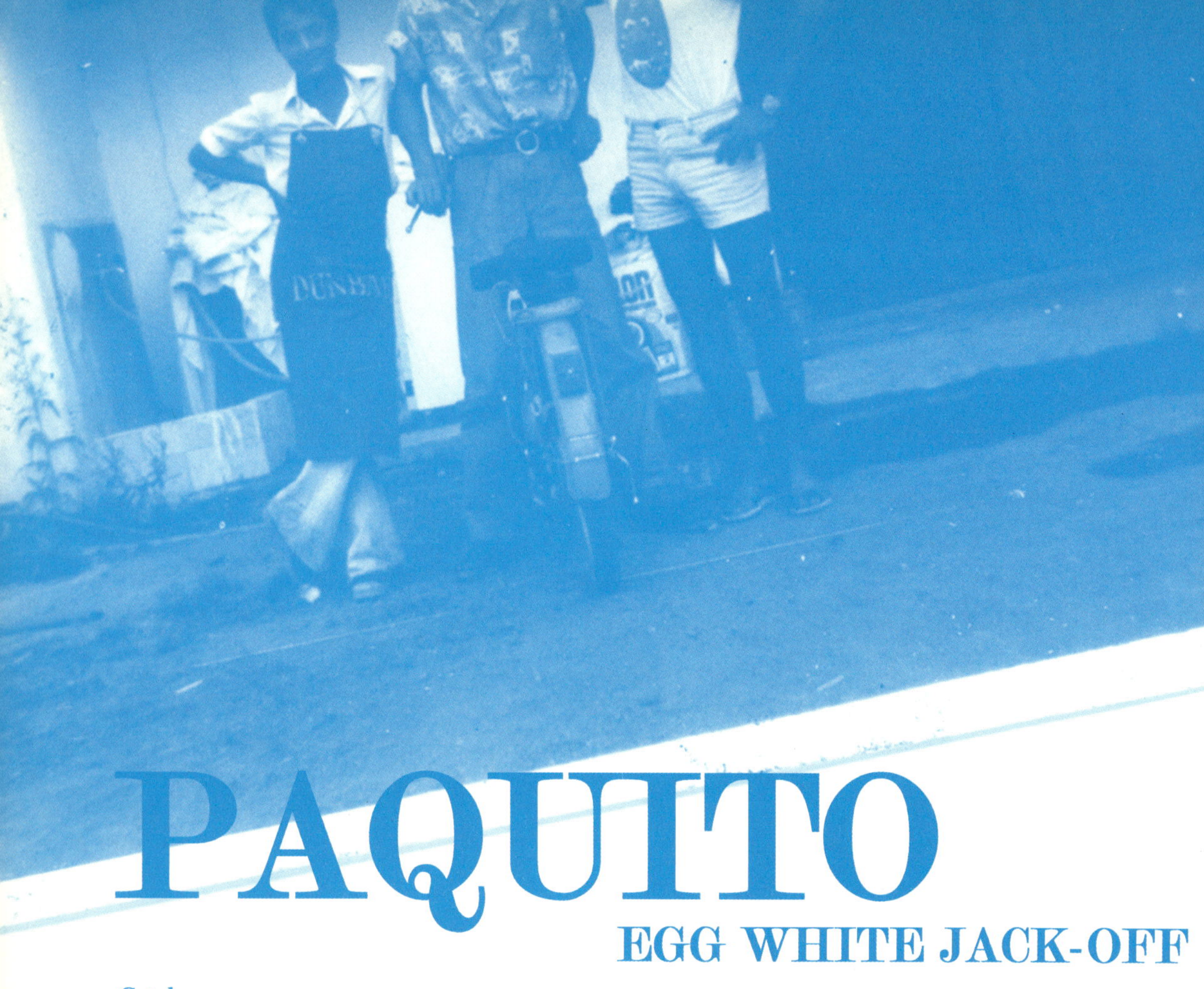

PAQUITO

EGG WHITE JACK-OFF

Catalunya, 1973.

Although Paquito was also a virgin, I gained little sympathy from this fact, as it was not an abnormal circumstance at the age of 16. Sharing this in common with him only served to emphasize the perversity of my own situation where, already at 26, I had surrendered hopes of ever having a sexual encounter. Increasingly I withdrew from the world of actions into an interior sexual world that grew so rich and consuming that by the summer that Paquito came to work at the Hotel Munber, it was near impossible to stop the two parts of my life from running haplessly into one another.

It was the hottest summer that I can remember and Franco's grip was like the oppressive sun that bore down on all the towns and peoples of the dry landscape. I had taken to masturbating only during the late evenings, rather than my favored time during the noonday siesta, so as to conserve my energies for serving the hoards of icy holidaymakers - the peroxide armies – and with them the teams of Franco guards that came to savor our notoriously rich Tortillas. Paquito had proved himself to be a versatile and quick-witted kitchen hand. However, the demand for our omelettes grew such that for a period of time we stopped serving anything else, and for some weeks Paquito's occupation was solely to buy and prepare stacks of fresh eggs.

As he was only a boy when he came to us, Paquito never played a part in my hidden sexual world. We had become so familiar that I did not notice that he had outgrown his boyhood frame and was becoming a man. Paquito had taken to removing his shirt from under his apron when he worked in the hot kitchens, twisting his torso in precise motions as he separated eggs and tossed shells onto the floor. Under the blaring kitchen lights I noticed firstly that his hands had grown large and strong, that his forearms bore light sun-kissed hairs that furred over his slender muscles and that his shoulders were now broad and commandeering over his monotonous task. Streams of sweat trickled down his neck, his chest, and then slowly over his firm stomach before disappearing under his gaping stained apron. When he finally noticed my gaze, I stood frozen. He continued his task automatically, now staring directly up at me with the large white porcelain bowl swimming full with gleaming egg yolks, sitting squarely between his legs. This was the first incident that led me to begin to use egg whites as a sexual aid to my masturbation, returning every night to my room with an egg delicately concealed in my apron before ritually cracking the shell and siphoning off the yolk.

Day and night the heat maintained its cruel grip, and we could not serve the impatient, relentless visitors quickly enough. Pepe, the head chef, grew cantankerous and unreasonable. Paquito and I kept up our industry, but inside we were frayed and unnerved. It came as no surprise, then, that this was when Paquito's accident should have happened. It was such that however well we armed ourselves with supplies against the mobs, there would be a point in the evening when eggs supplies would run close to dry and Paquito would jump onto his pop-pop bike and zip into town to collect more cartons. One night Paquito returned at an unusually early time than usual, ripping up the road towards the car park. As the sound of the moto approached and grew louder we began to hear the sound of brakes screeching followed by a loud crashing and scraping of metal and sand. I tailed Pepe as he burst out of the kitchen towards where Paquito lay, surrounded by a small group of bewildered tourists. The wheels of the moto turned angrily in the air and pressed Paquito's exposed body to the ground. Blood collected on his elbows and knees, and his head lay limp on the gravel dust. His torso was stretched out on a carpet of 100 broken eggshells and the slime of yolk and white began to run slowly over parts of his torso, arms and legs, mixing with blood and dirt. Whilst Pepe and the guests ran to his aid, the astonishing scene seized me with a terrific sexual thrust that ran through me as I had never before known and compelled me, in a contrary motion to the others, to make away from the scene so as to preserve the purity of the image. As voices called from the outer world, I lurched back through the kitchen doors towards the large porcelain bowl, frantically furrowing in my loins, and released my cock, dropping wads of hot cum into the folds of the glistening eggs. From then on I remember only the blue ambulance lights flashing through the open kitchen door, as I lay half-conscious, shivering on the tiled floor.

When Paquito returned to us the following year he had aged - he had developed a limp. Although Munber's notoriety of the tortilla days had subsided, we now served a prize winning Osso Bucco, which continued to draw in the tourists and kept the kitchen busy cutting and preparing the meat and bones. As I work I often wonder back to the evening of the accident and I debate at length who could have been the next to order an omelette that night,

whether it could have been a Franco soldier swallowing down the tortilla with my own special ingredient or an unassuming tourist - a family man - a honeymooning groom. I continue my nightly practices, and have expanded into new fields of perversion. However, to this day, I must say that the consistency of egg white is a hard one to beat.

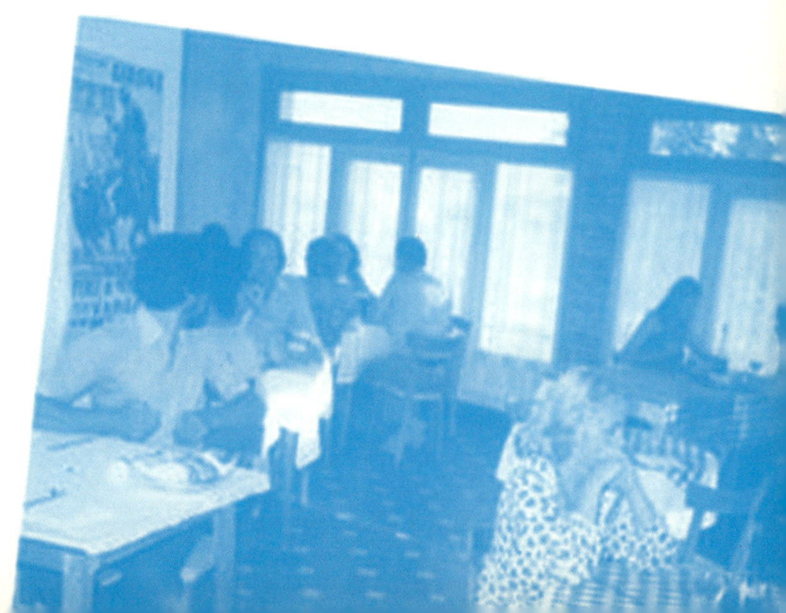

comm

nev

happ

unism

ver

ened

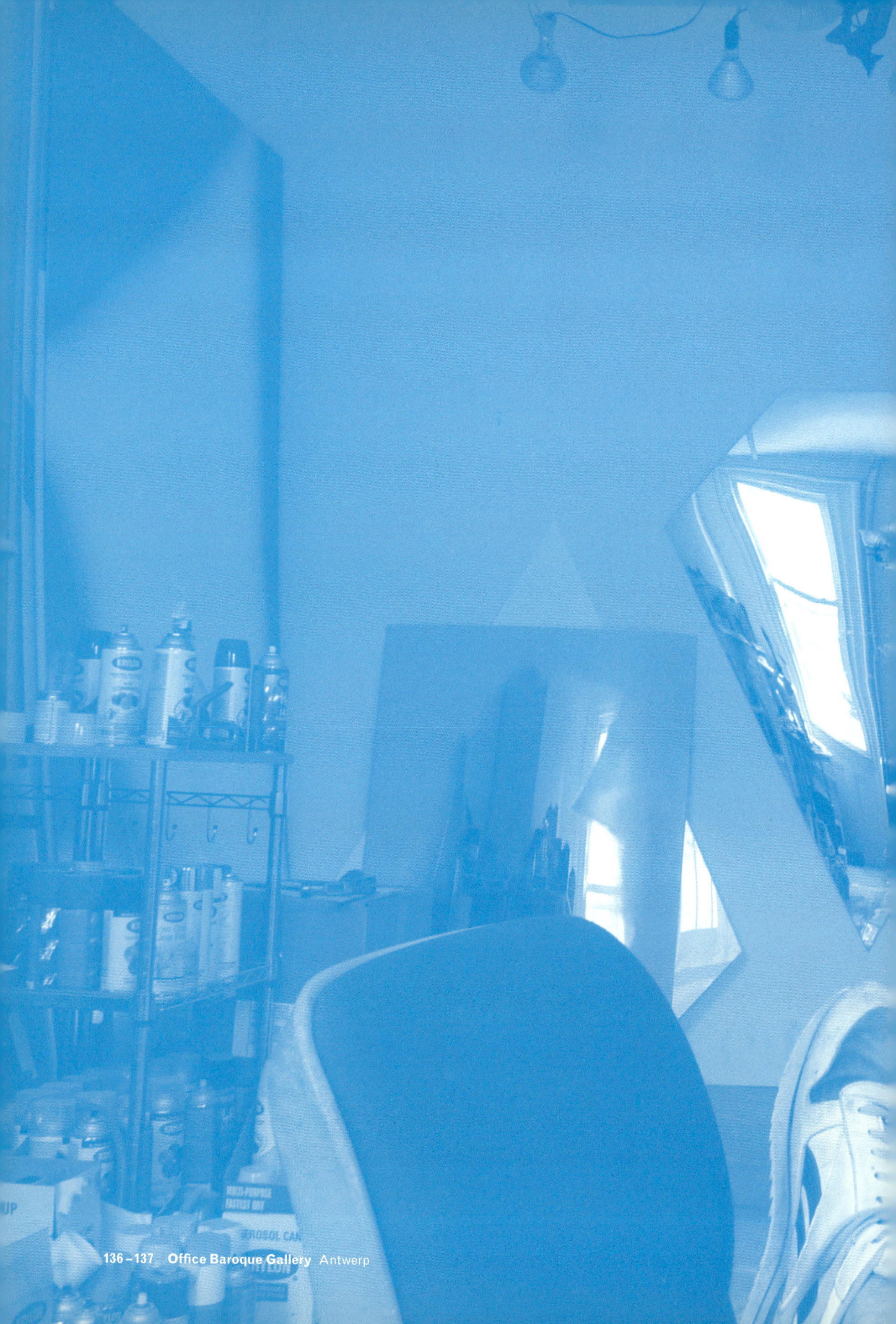

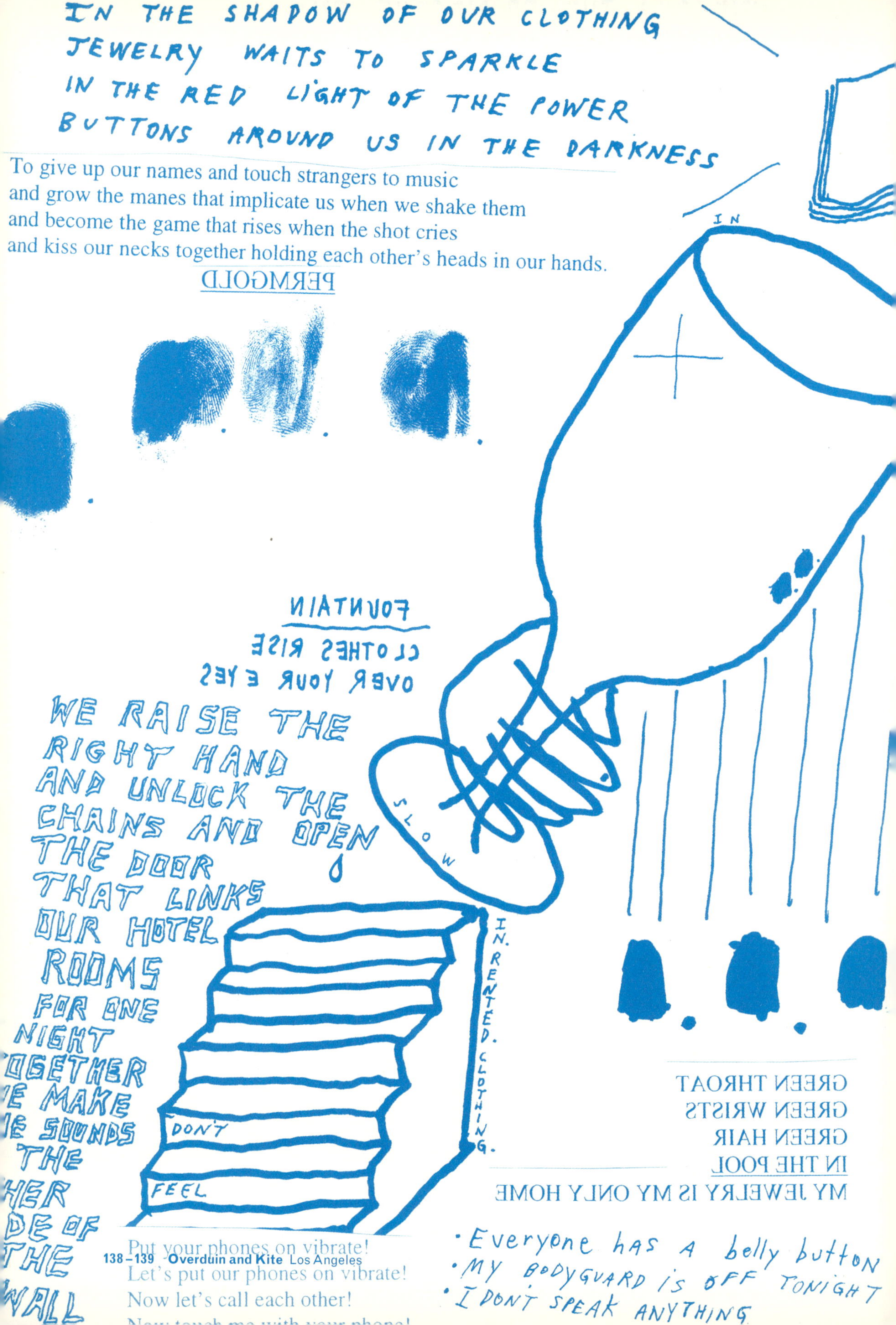

IN THE SHADOW OF OUR CLOTHING
JEWELRY WAITS TO SPARKLE
IN THE RED LIGHT OF THE POWER
BUTTONS AROUND US IN THE DARKNESS

To give up our names and touch strangers to music
and grow the manes that implicate us when we shake them
and become the game that rises when the shot cries
and kiss our necks together holding each other's heads in our hands.

PERMGOLD

FOUNTAIN
CLOTHES RISE
OVER YOUR EYES

WE RAISE THE
RIGHT HAND
AND UNLOCK THE
CHAINS AND OPEN
THE DOOR
THAT LINKS
OUR HOTEL
ROOMS
FOR ONE
NIGHT
TOGETHER
WE MAKE
THE SOUNDS
THE
OTHER
SIDE OF
THE
WALL

SLOW
DON'T
FEEL
IN
IN. RENTED. CLOTHING.

GREEN THROAT
GREEN WRISTS
GREEN HAIR
IN THE POOL
MY JEWELRY IS MY ONLY HOME

•Everyone has a belly button
•MY BODYGUARD IS OFF TONIGHT
•I DON'T SPEAK ANYTHING

Put your phones on vibrate!
Let's put our phones on vibrate!
Now let's call each other!

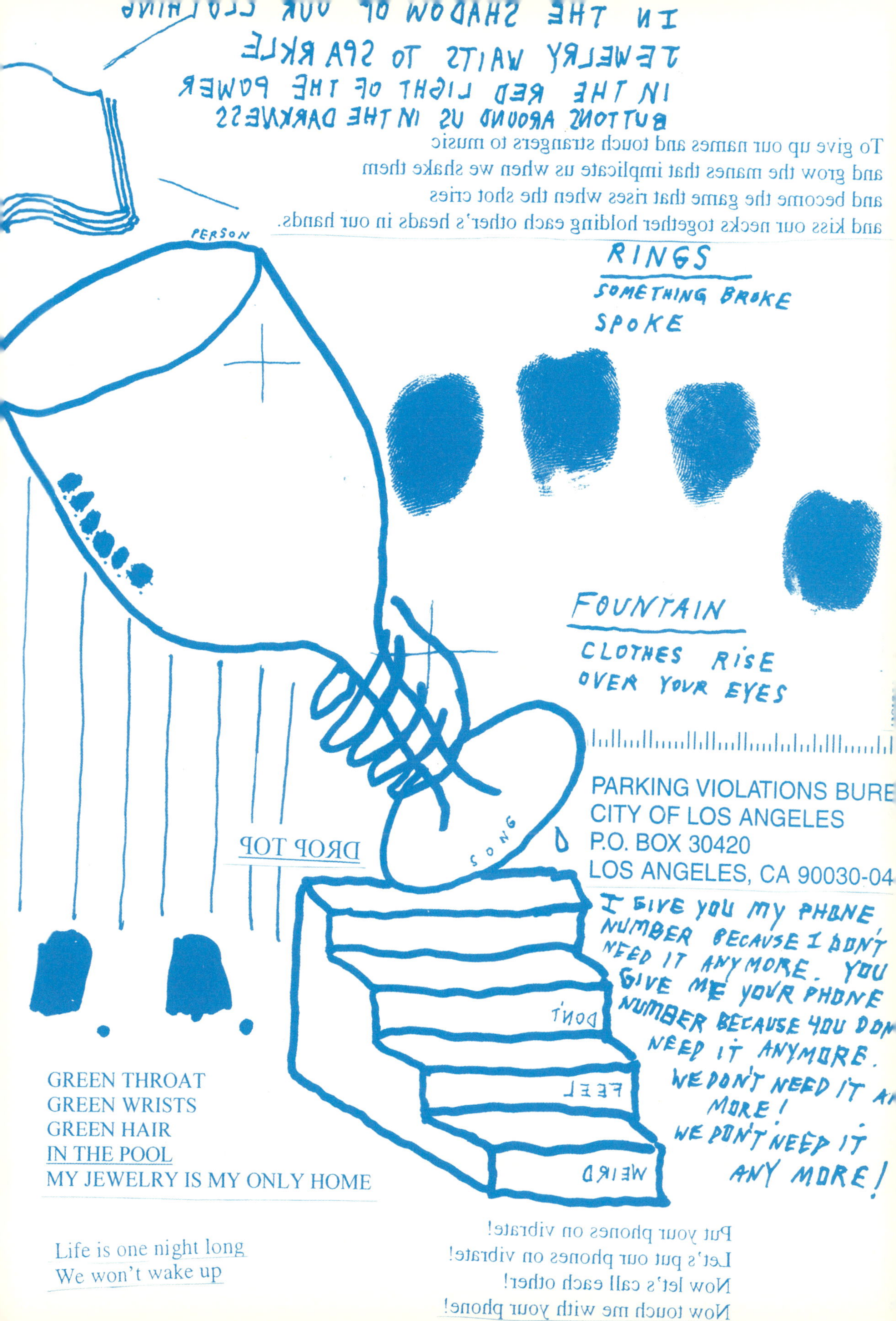

IN THE SHADOW OF OUR CLOTHING
JEWELRY WAITS TO SPARKLE
IN THE RED LIGHT OF THE POWER
BUTTONS AROUND US IN THE DARKNESS
To give up our names and touch strangers to music
and grow the names that implicate us when we shake them
and become the game that rises when the shot cries
and kiss our necks together holding each other's heads in our hands.
RINGS
SOMETHING BROKE
SPOKE
PERSON
FOUNTAIN
CLOTHES RISE
OVER YOUR EYES
PARKING VIOLATIONS BURE
CITY OF LOS ANGELES
P.O. BOX 30420
LOS ANGELES, CA 90030-04
DROP TOP
SONG
I GIVE YOU MY PHONE NUMBER BECAUSE I DON'T NEED IT ANYMORE. YOU GIVE ME YOUR PHONE NUMBER BECAUSE YOU DON'T NEED IT ANYMORE. WE DON'T NEED IT ANY MORE! WE DON'T NEED IT ANY MORE!
DON'T
FEEL
WEIRD
GREEN THROAT
GREEN WRISTS
GREEN HAIR
IN THE POOL
MY JEWELRY IS MY ONLY HOME
Life is one night long
We won't wake up
Put your phones on vibrate!
Let's put our phones on vibrate!
Now let's call each other!
Now touch me with your phone!

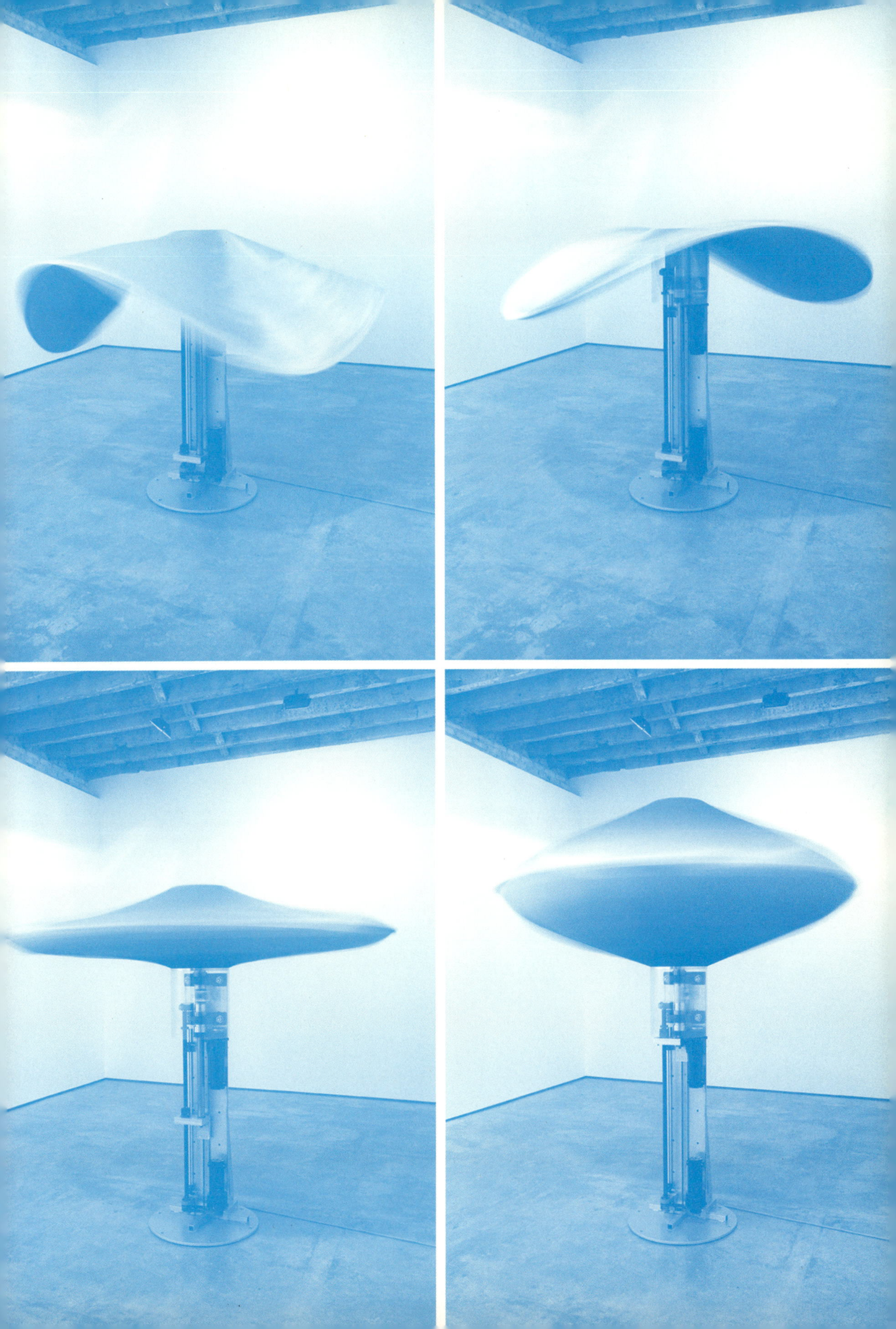

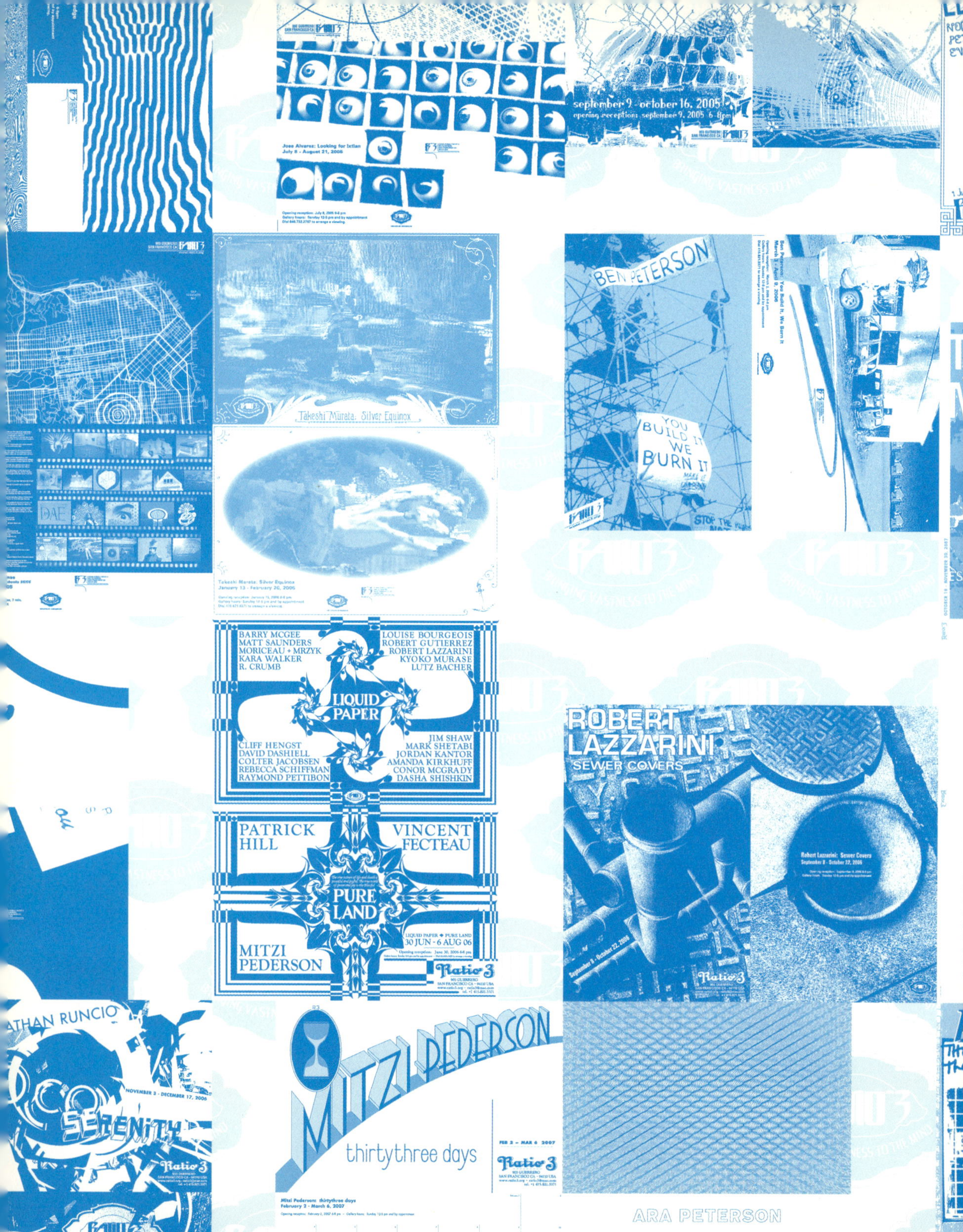

RATIO 3 903 GUERRERO SAN FRANCISCO CA 94110 USA

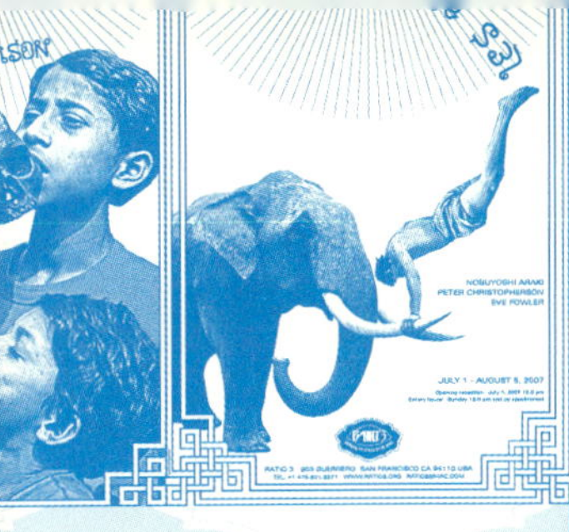
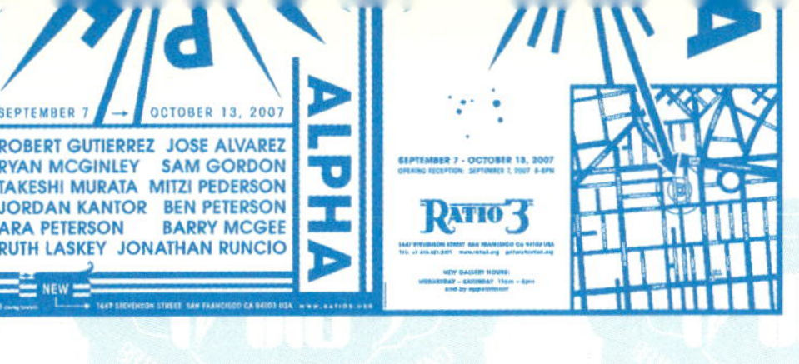
ALPHA
SEPTEMBER 7 — OCTOBER 13, 2007
ROBERT GUTIERREZ   JOSE ALVAREZ
RYAN MCGINLEY   SAM GORDON
TAKESHI MURATA   MITZI PEDERSON
JORDAN KANTOR   BEN PETERSON
ARA PETERSON   BARRY MCGEE
RUTH LASKEY   JONATHAN RUNCIO
NEW
RATIO 3
SEPTEMBER 7 - OCTOBER 13, 2007

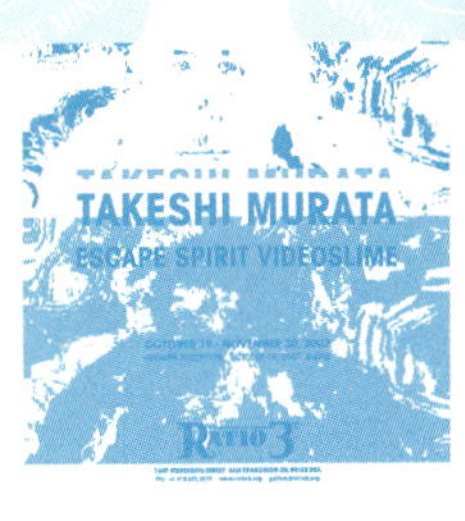
TAKESHI MURATA
ESCAPE SPIRIT VIDEOSLIME
RATIO 3

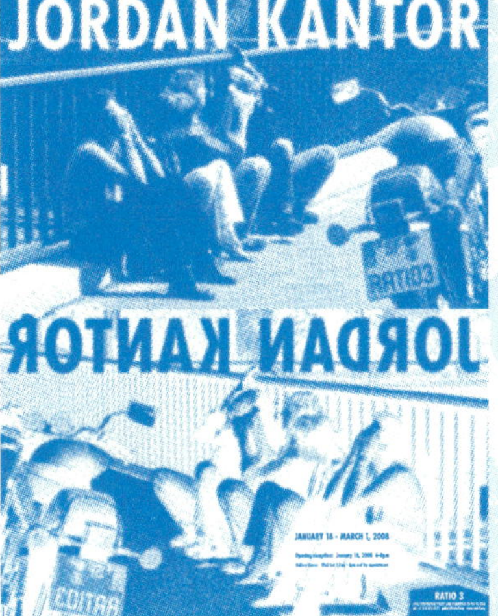
JORDAN KANTOR
JORDAN KANTOR
JANUARY 18 — MARCH 1, 2008
RATIO 3

Ruth Laskey
7 Weavings
March 14 - April 26, 2008
RATIO 3

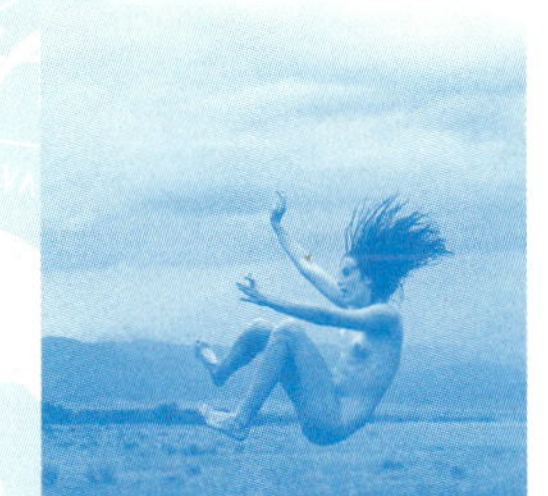
RYAN MCGINLEY
Spring and By Summer Fall
May 9 - June 21, 2008
Opening reception: May 9, 2008 6-8pm
RATIO 3

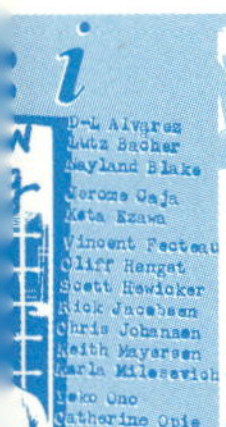
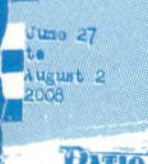
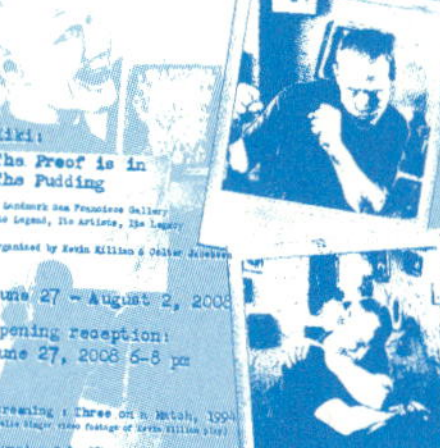
Kiki!
The Proof is in
The Pudding
June 27 - August 2, 2008
Opening reception:
June 27, 2008 5-8 pm
RATIO 3

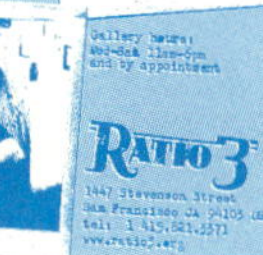

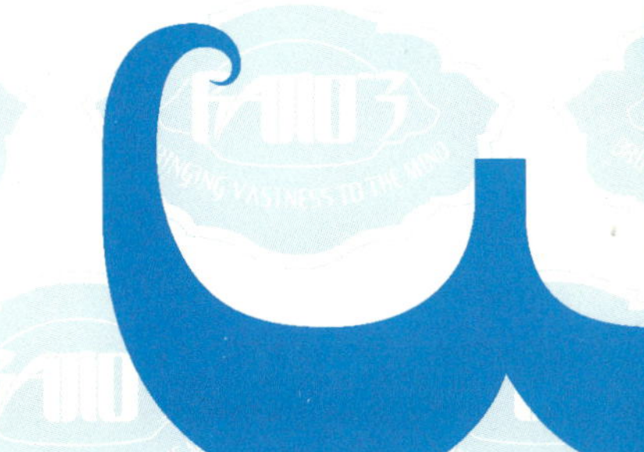
RATIO 3
SAN FRANCISCO
www.ratio3.org

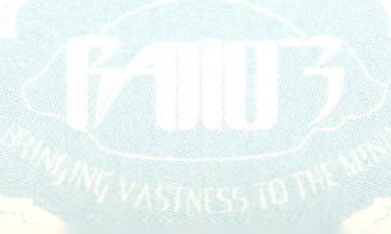
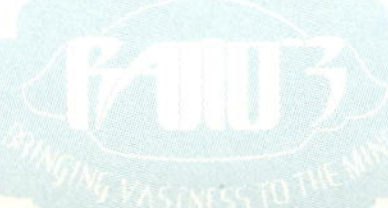

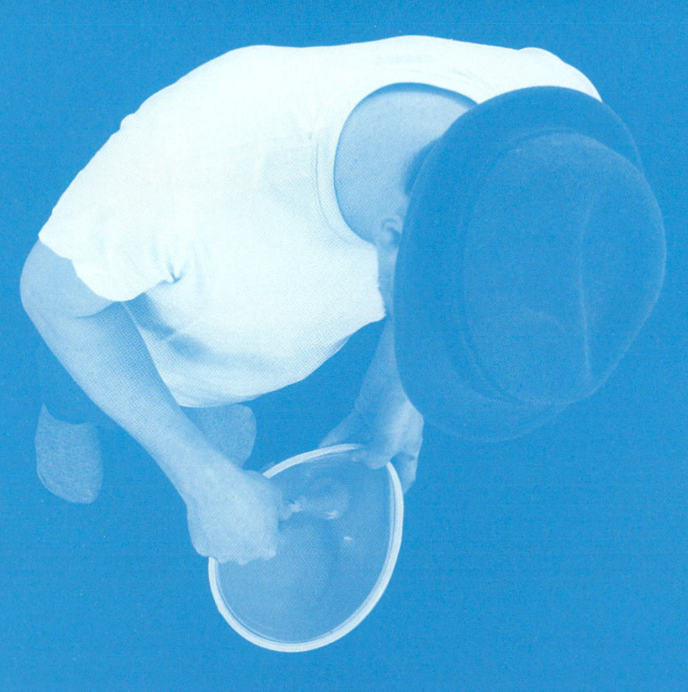

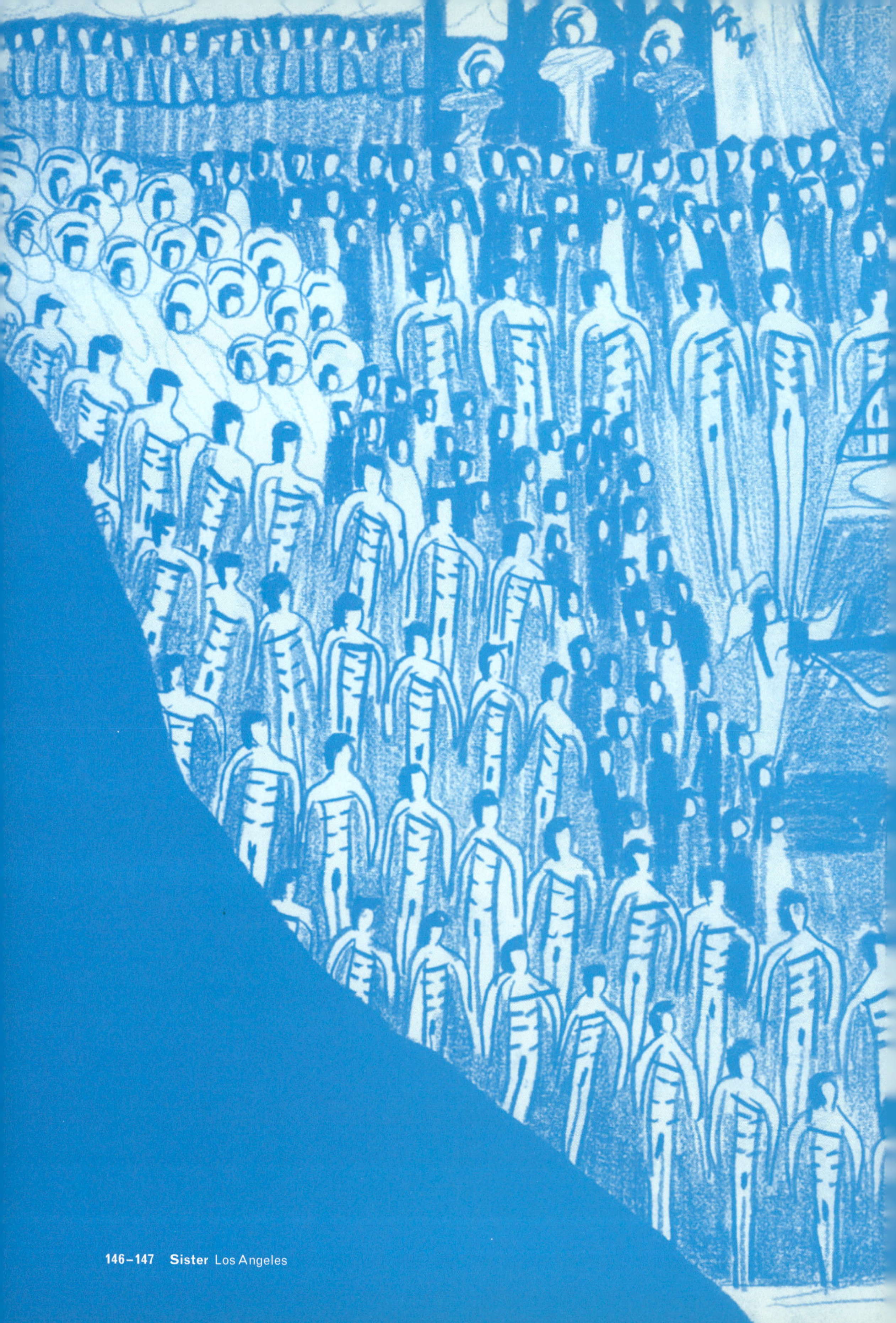

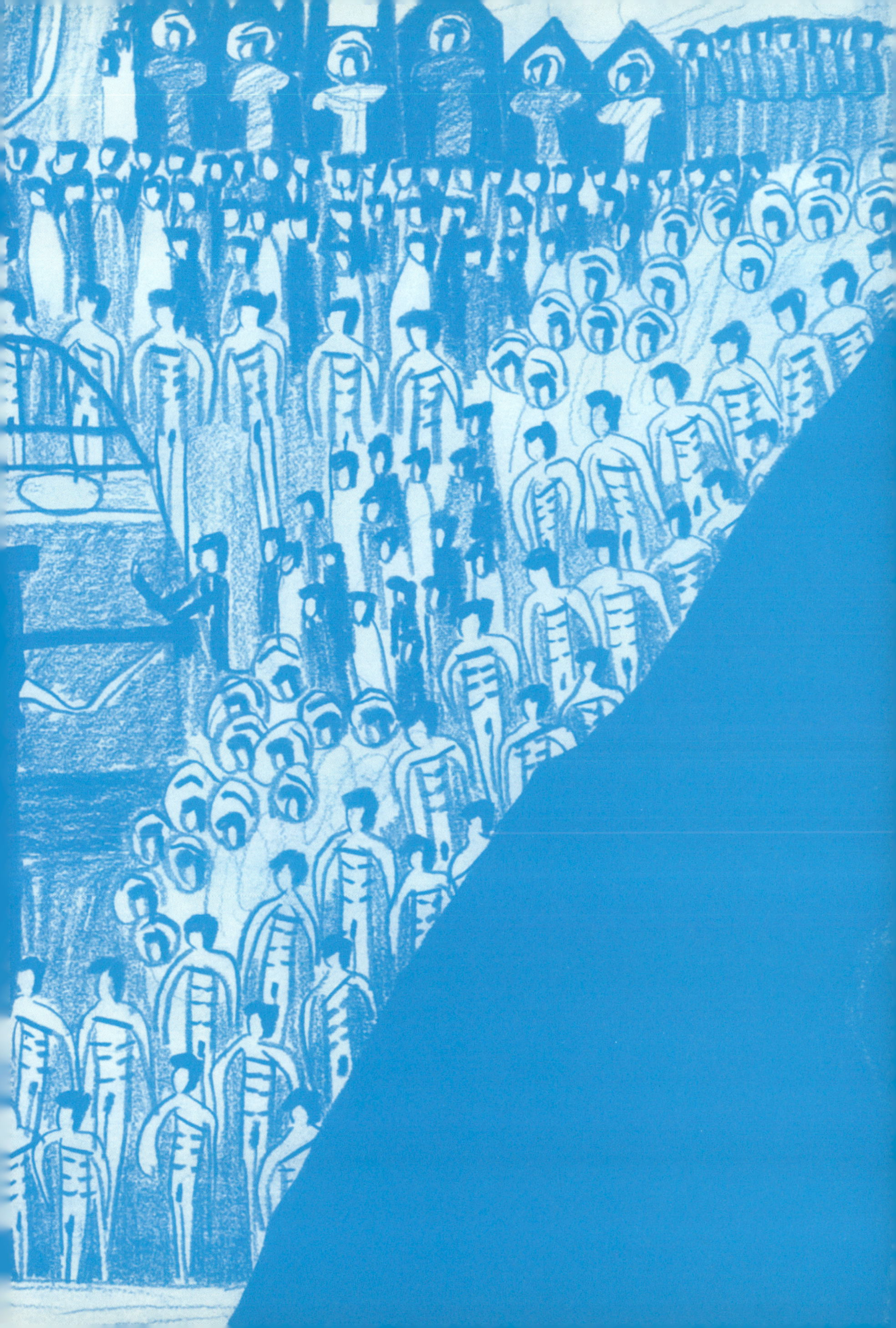

Awakened with a sense of urgency, I wrote these words and returned to bed.

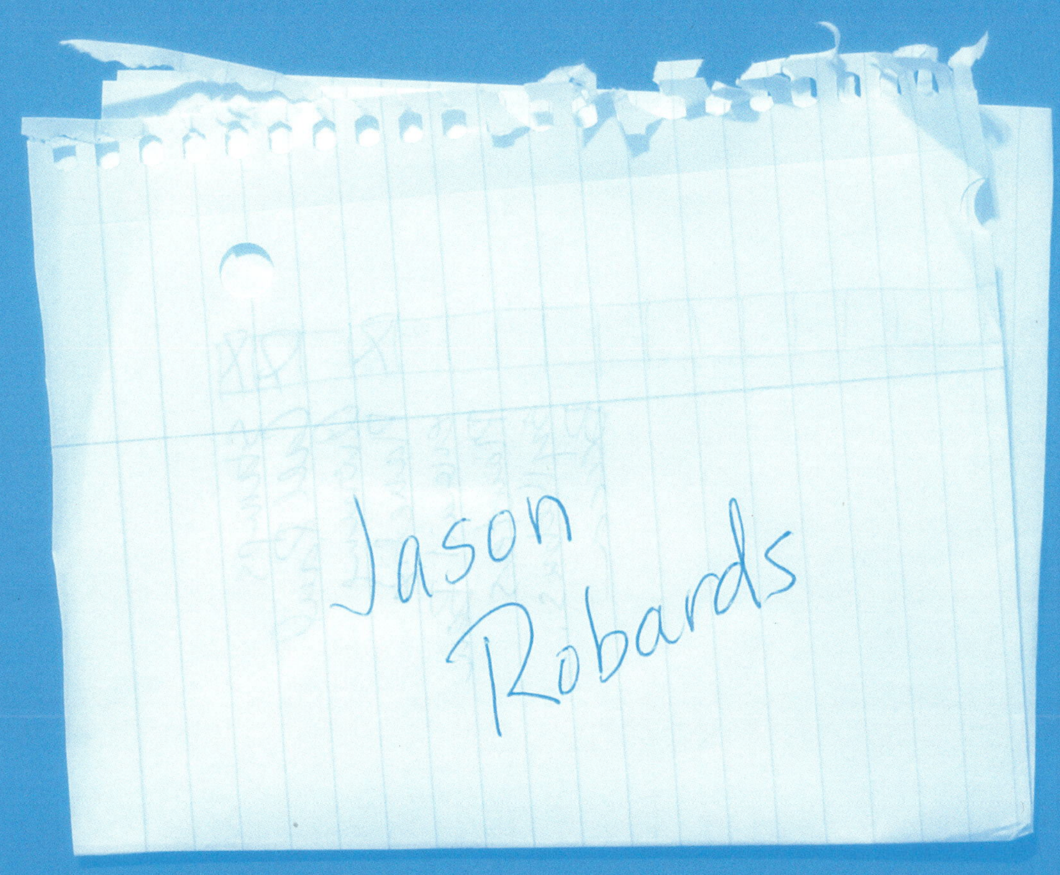

Jason
Robards

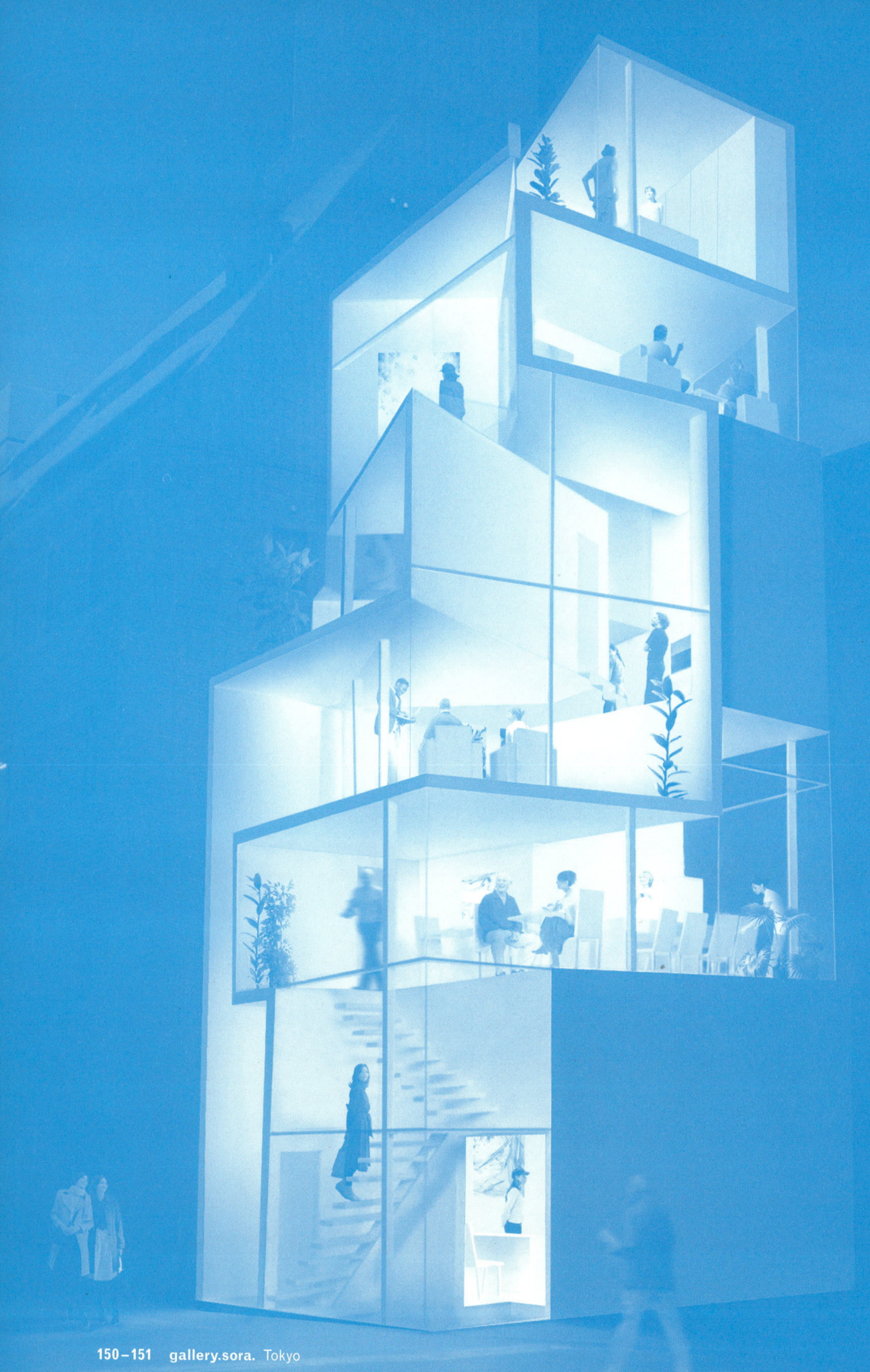

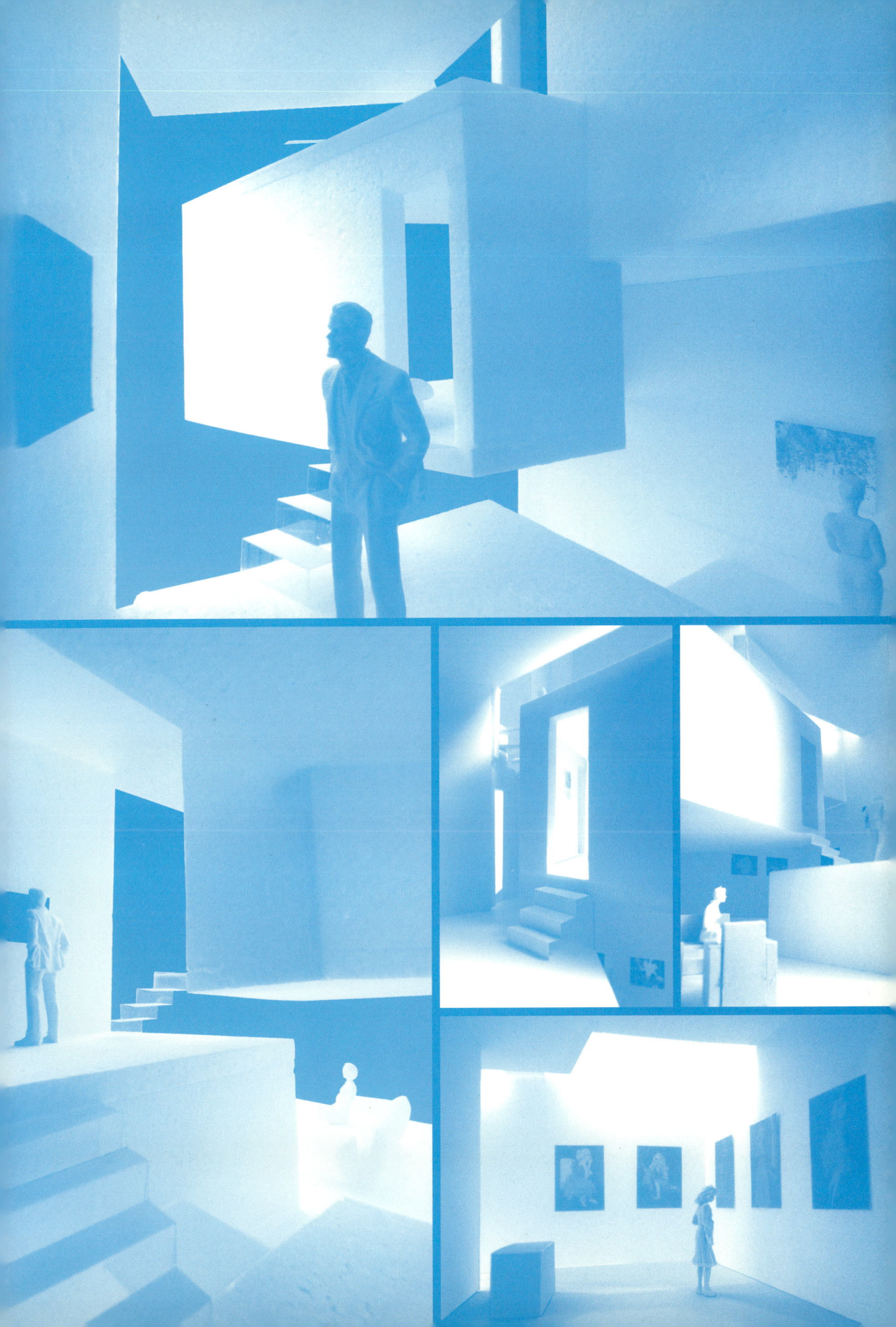

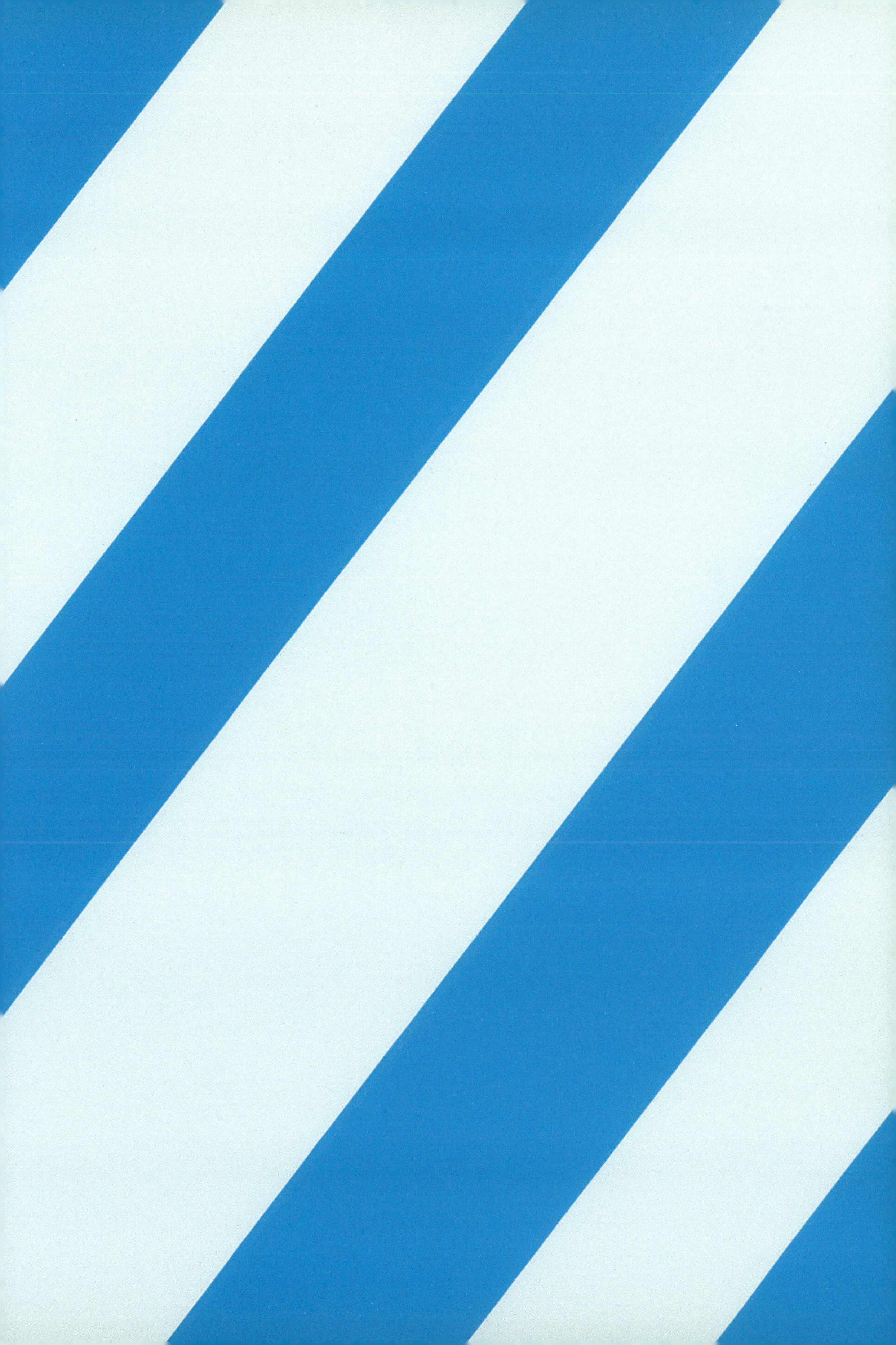

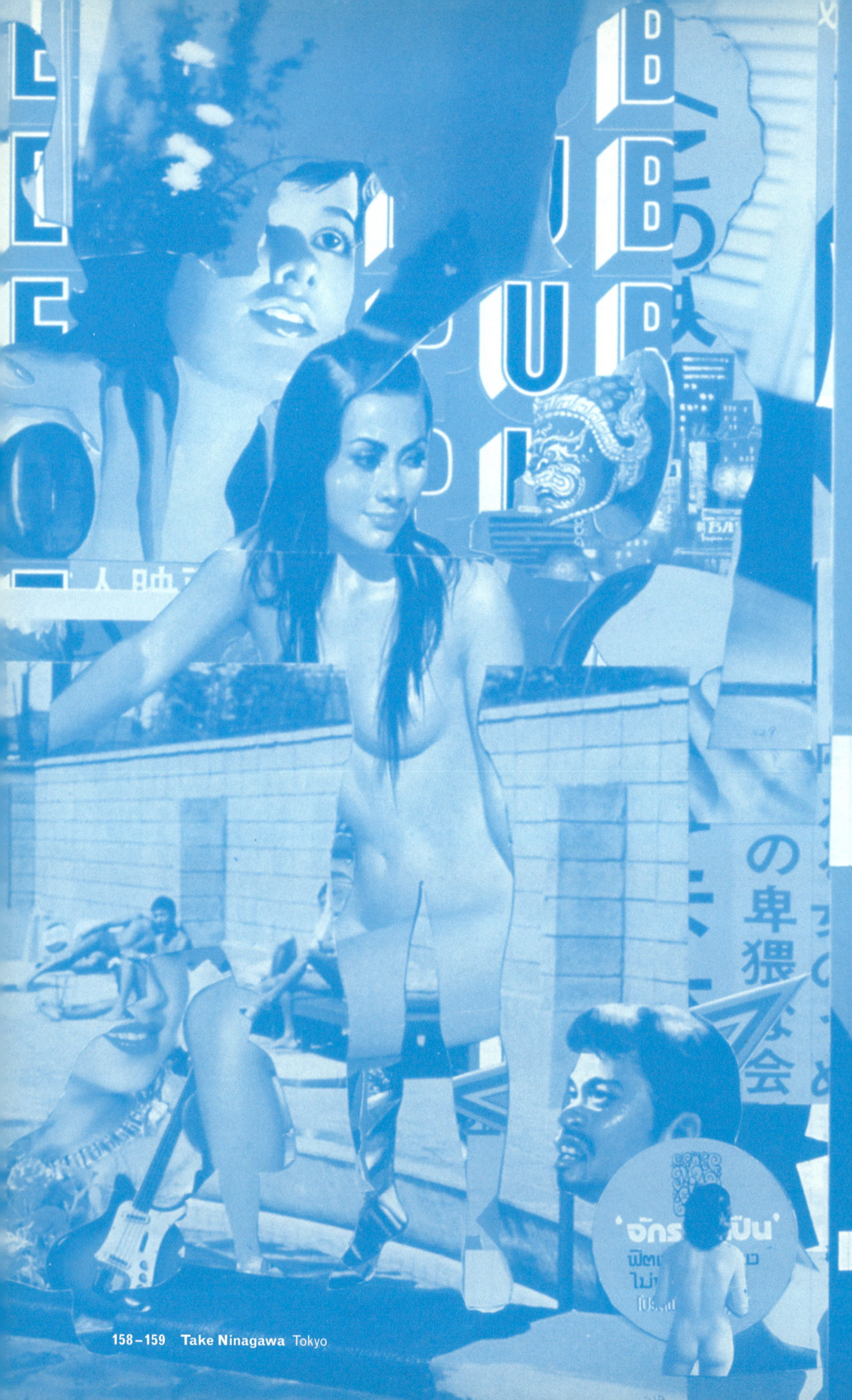

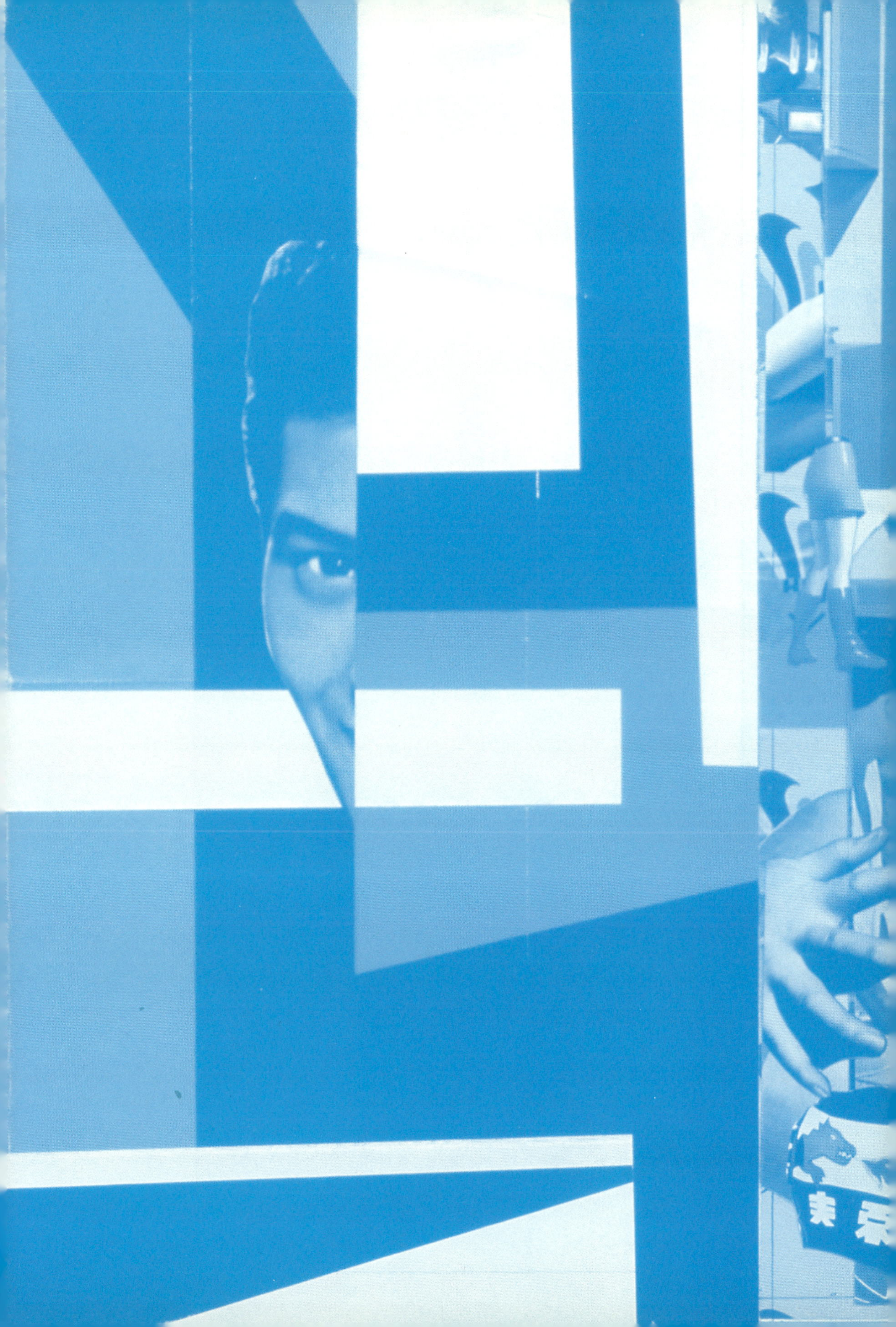

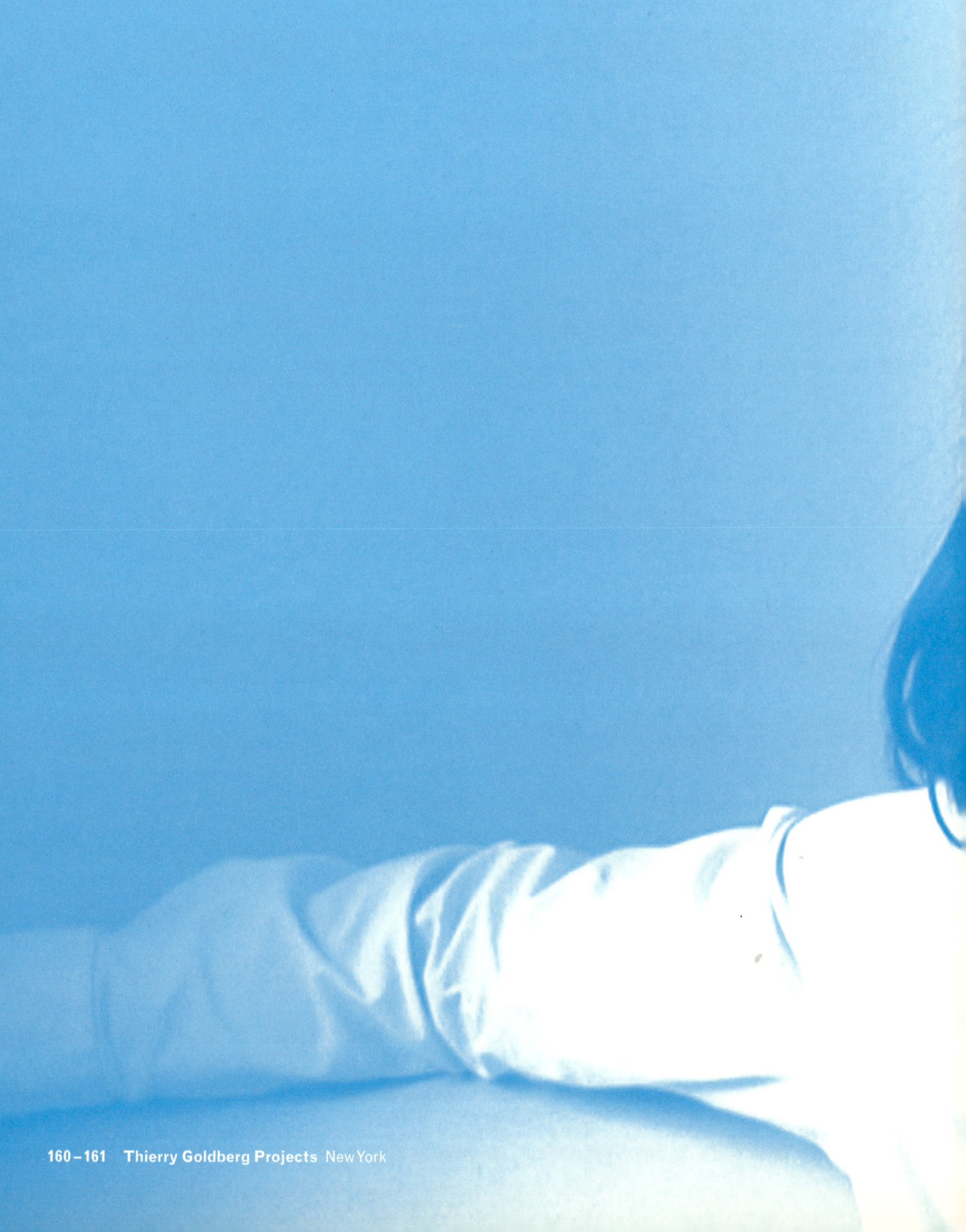

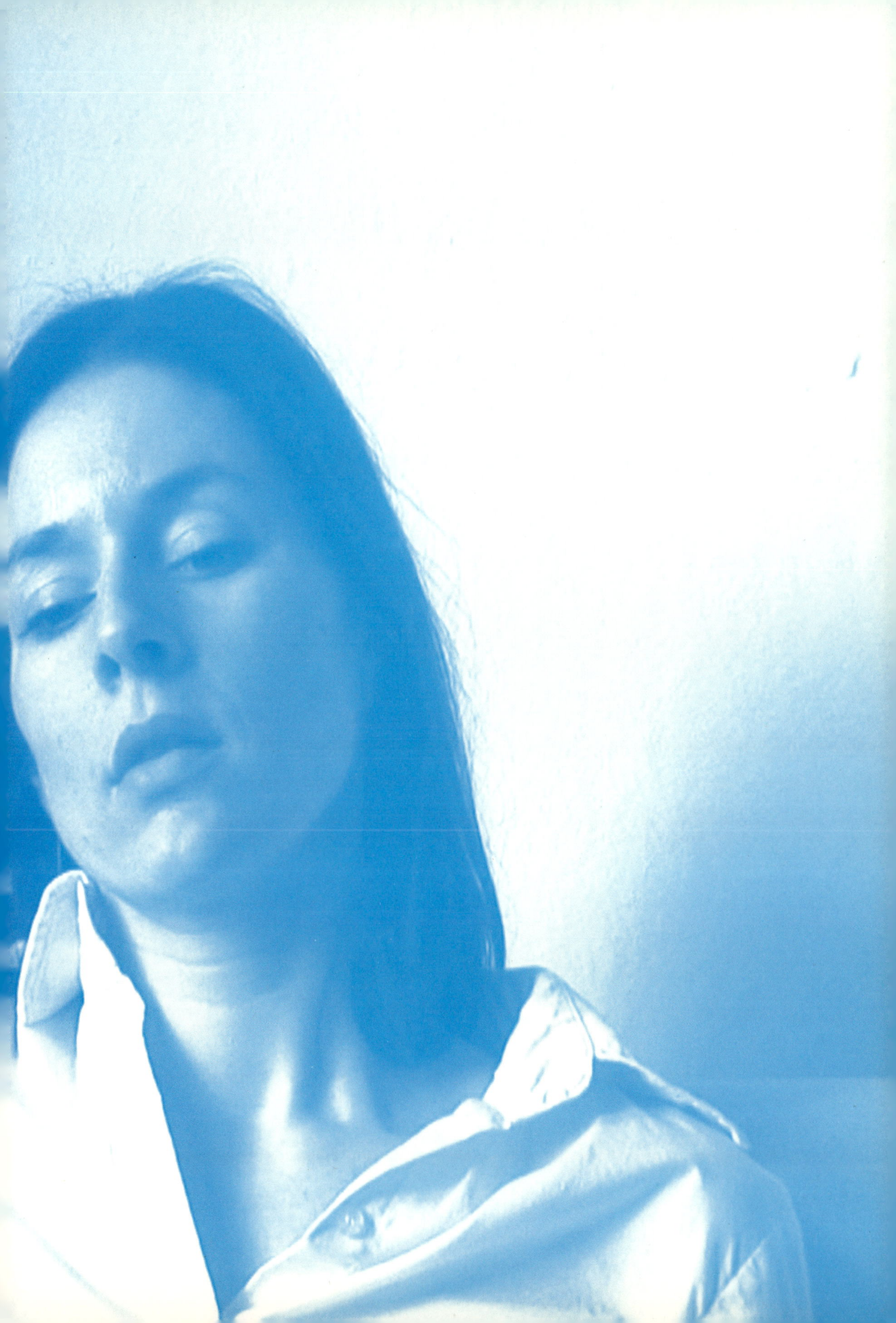

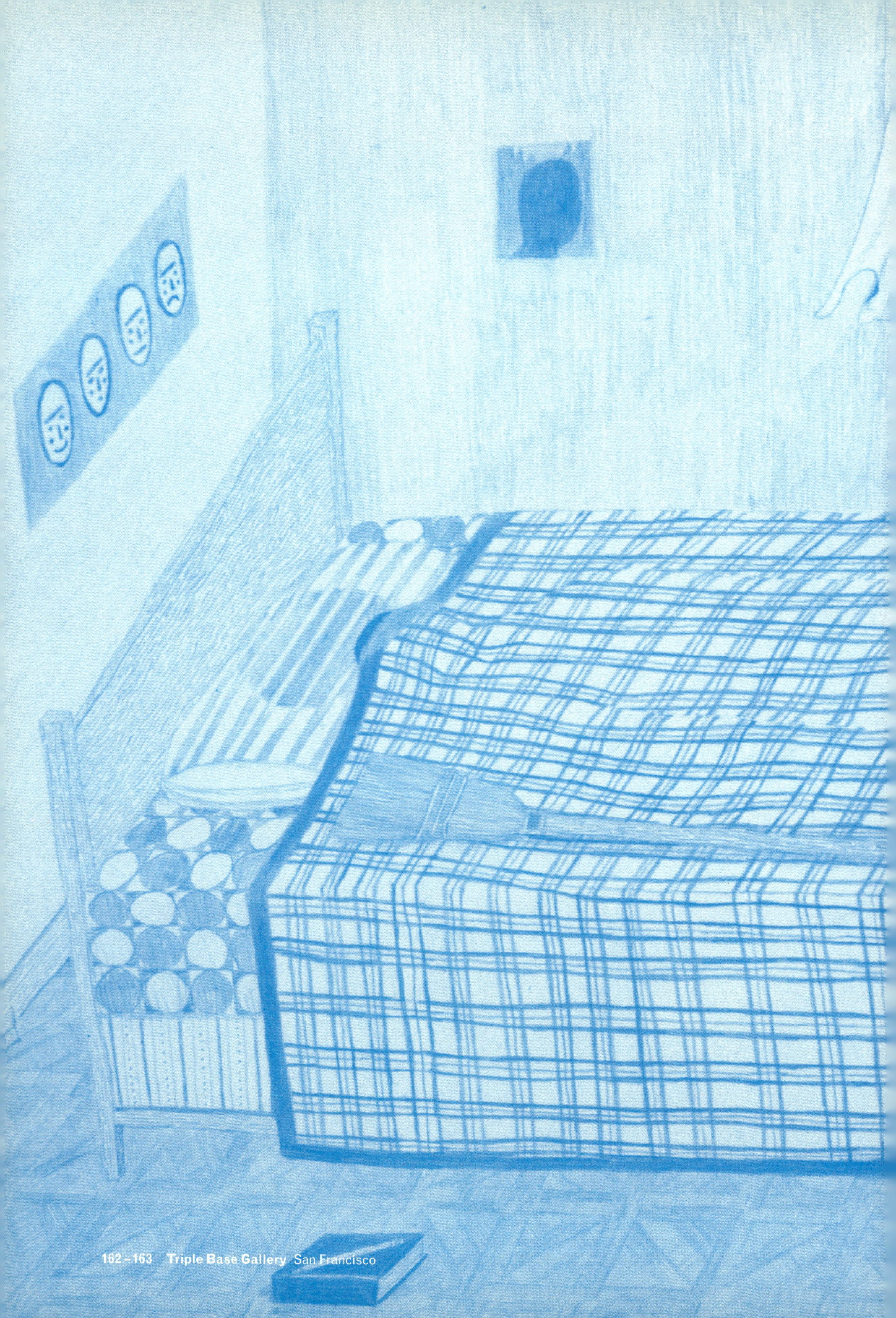

 Triple Base Gallery San Francisco

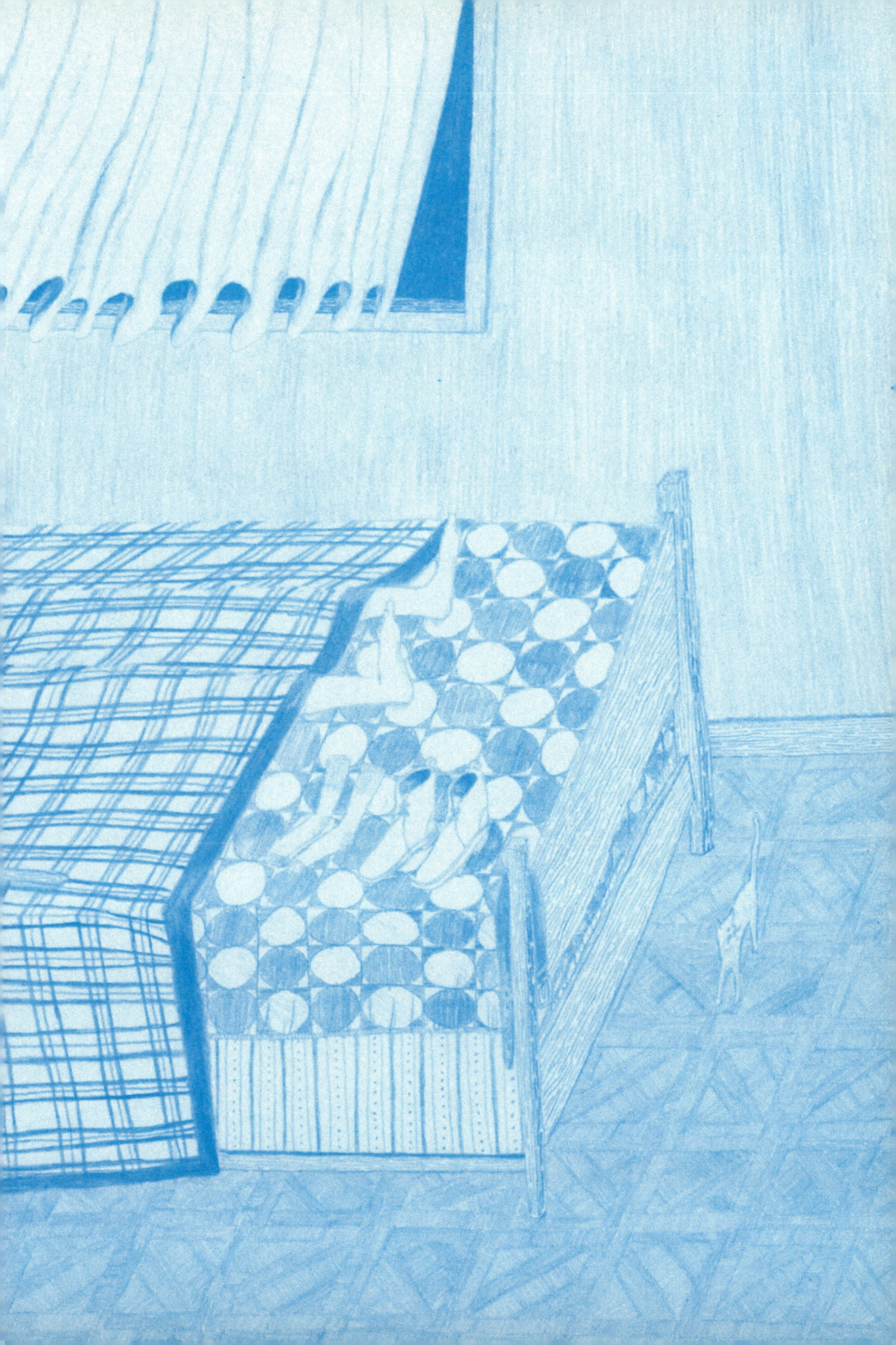

Such a
you are,
as I am y
Wealth, hon
are of n
the hour o

I was
and such
ou will be.
r and power
value at
your death.

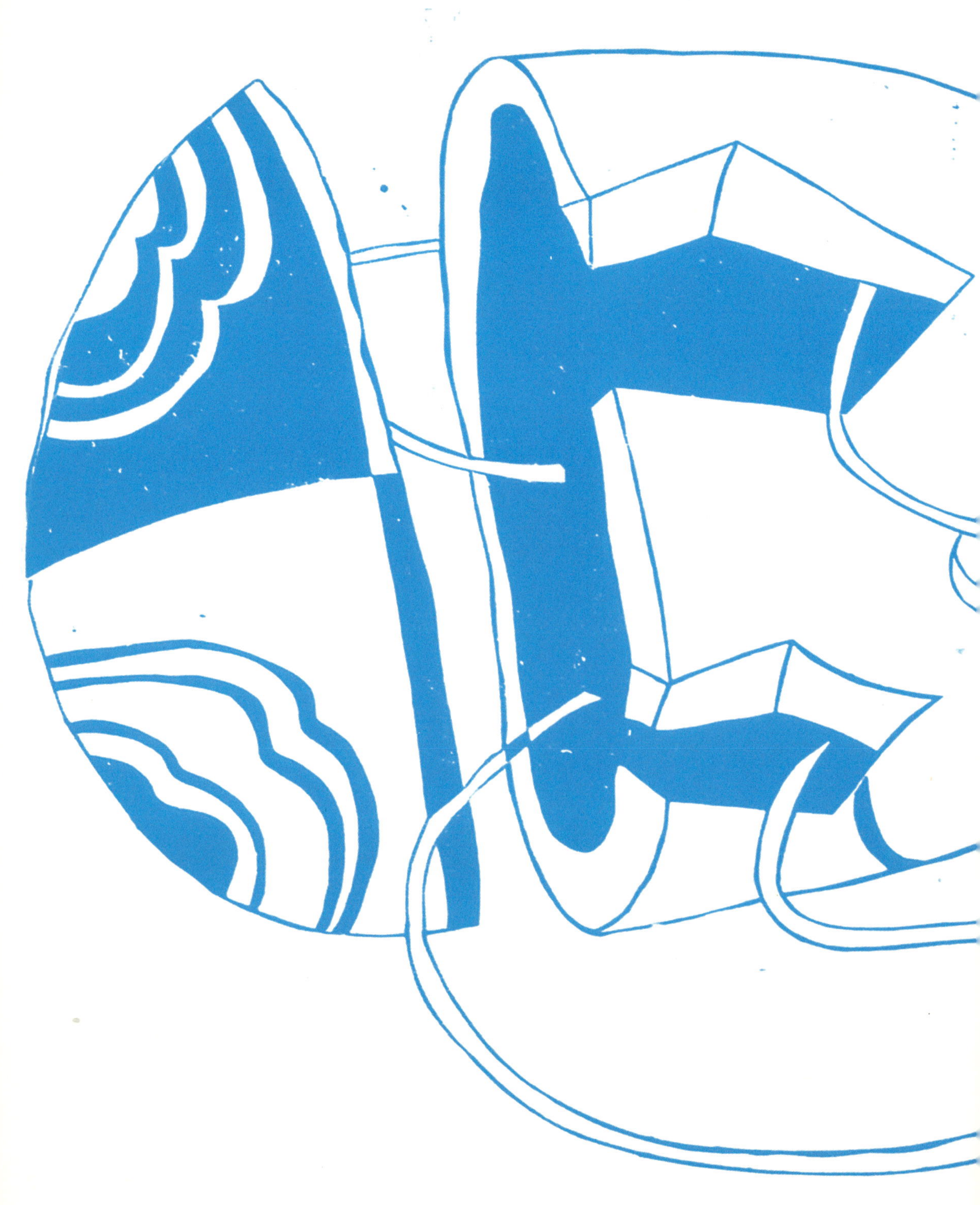

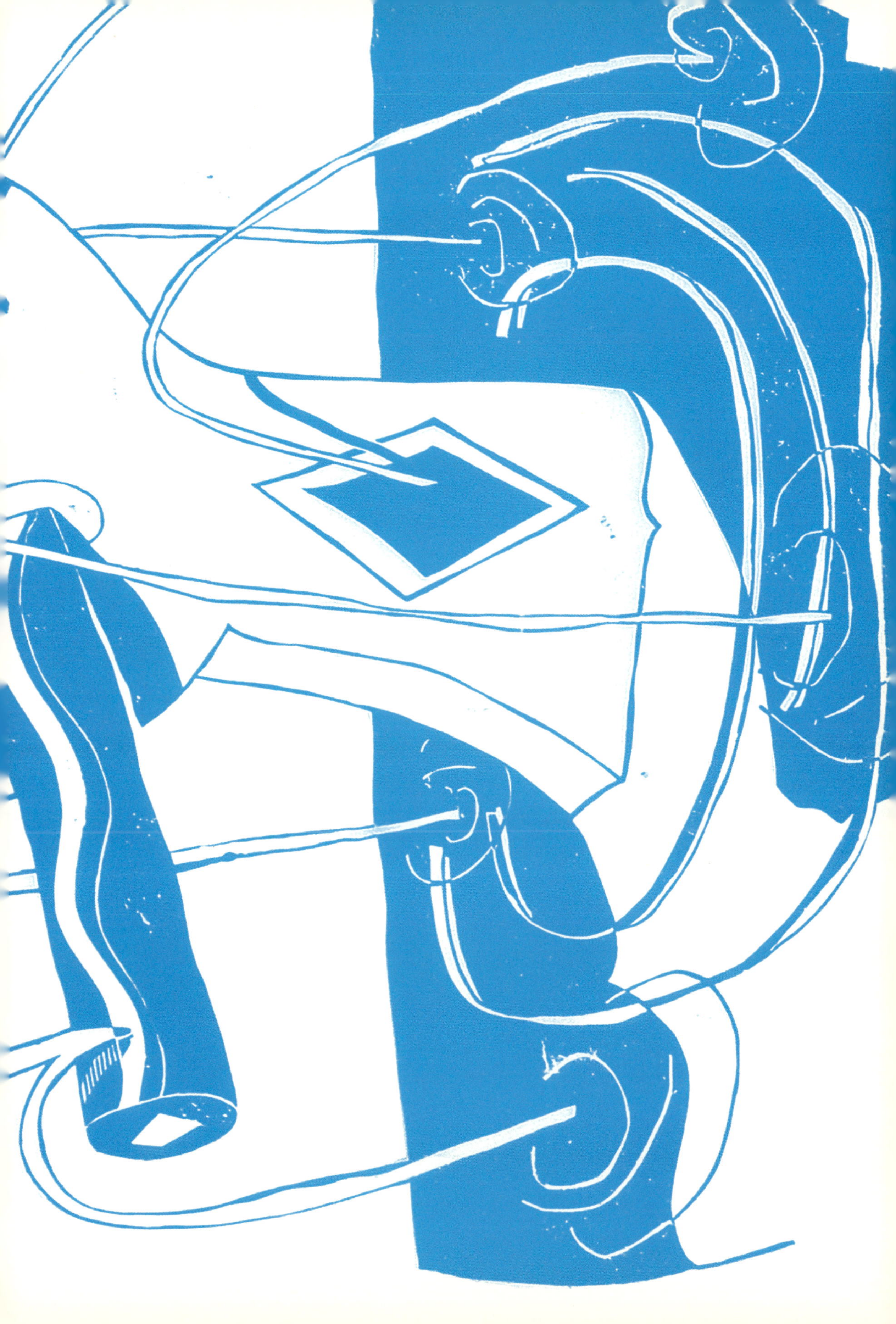

PLEASE
FREE ALSO
THIS
COLOUR
FROM
PANTONE
PRISON

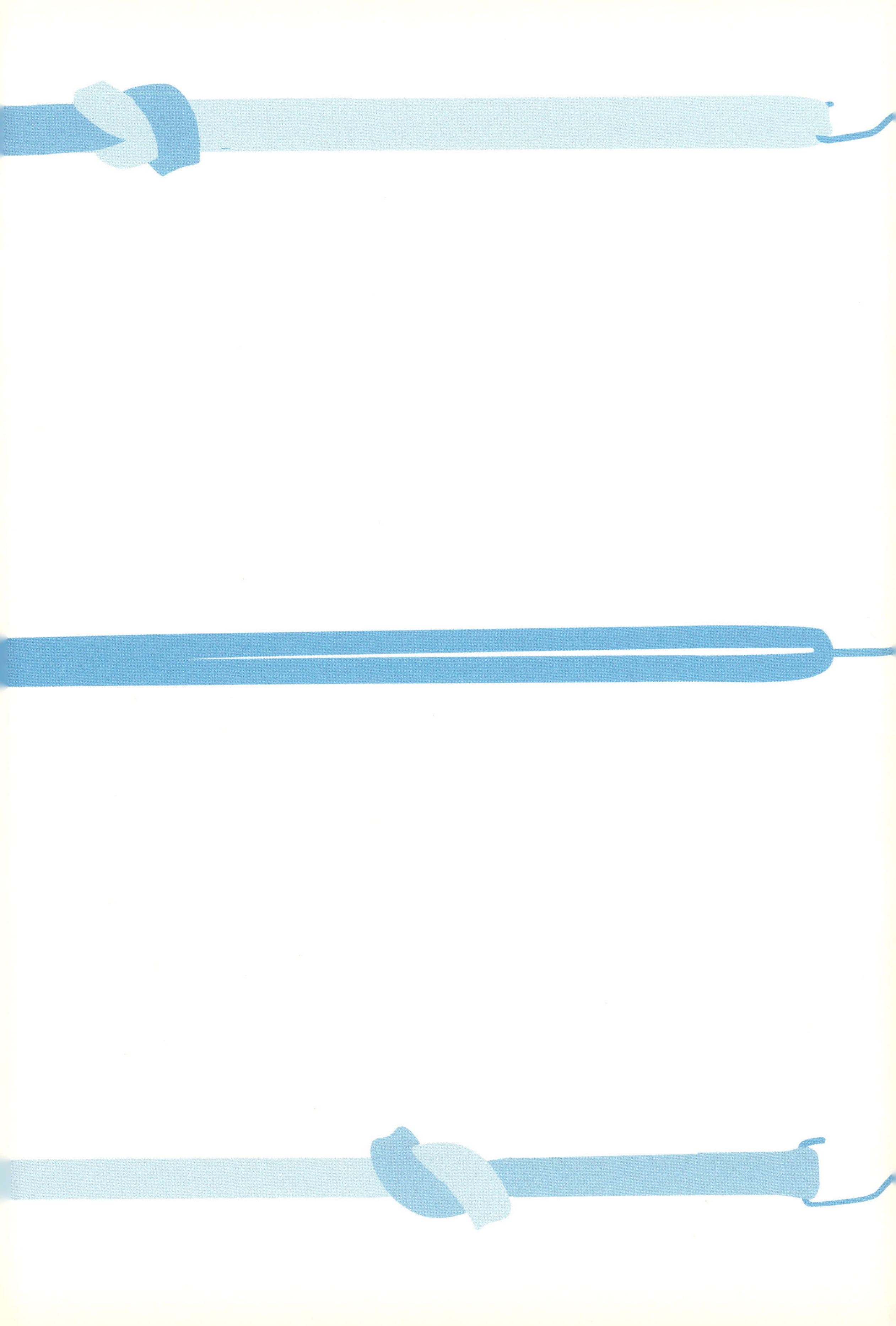

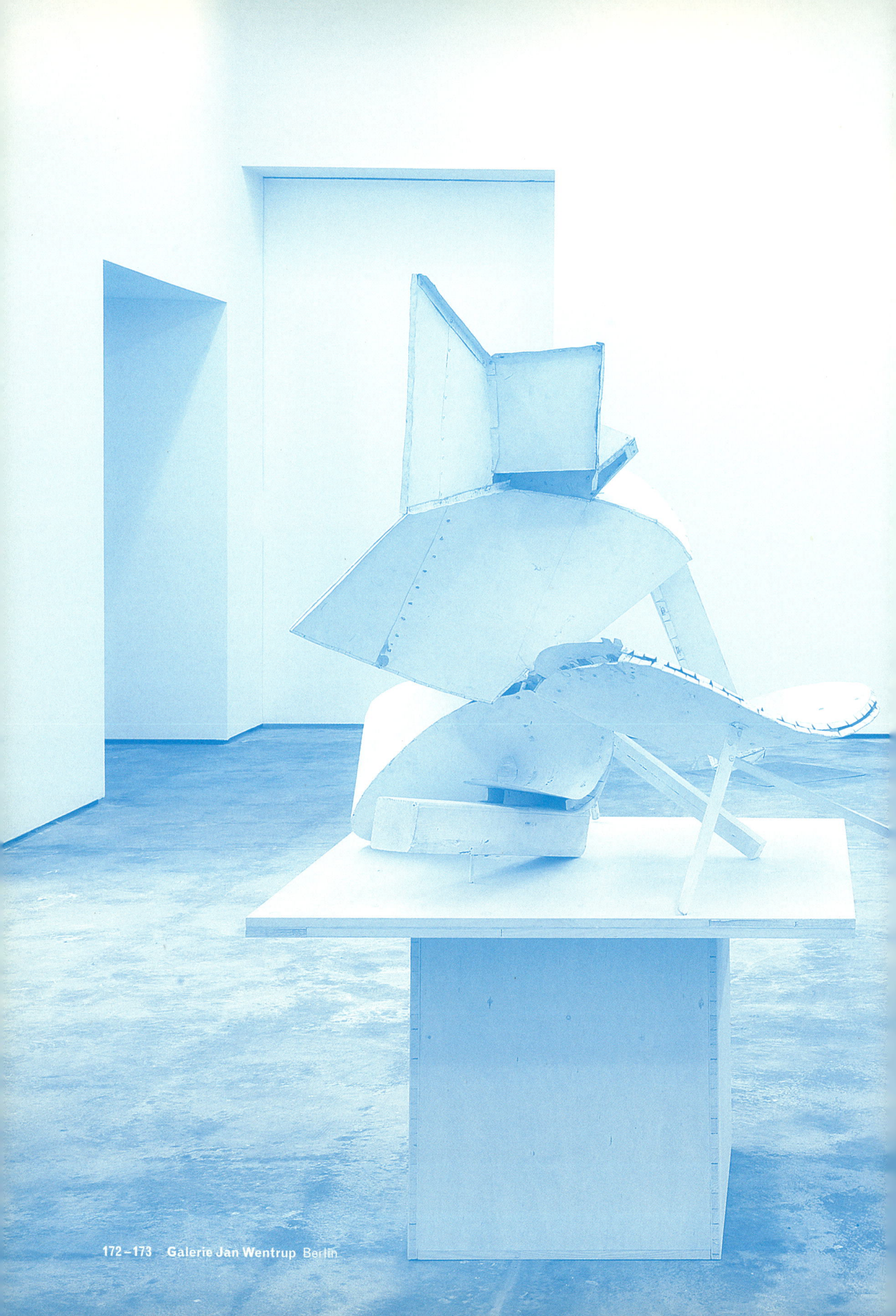

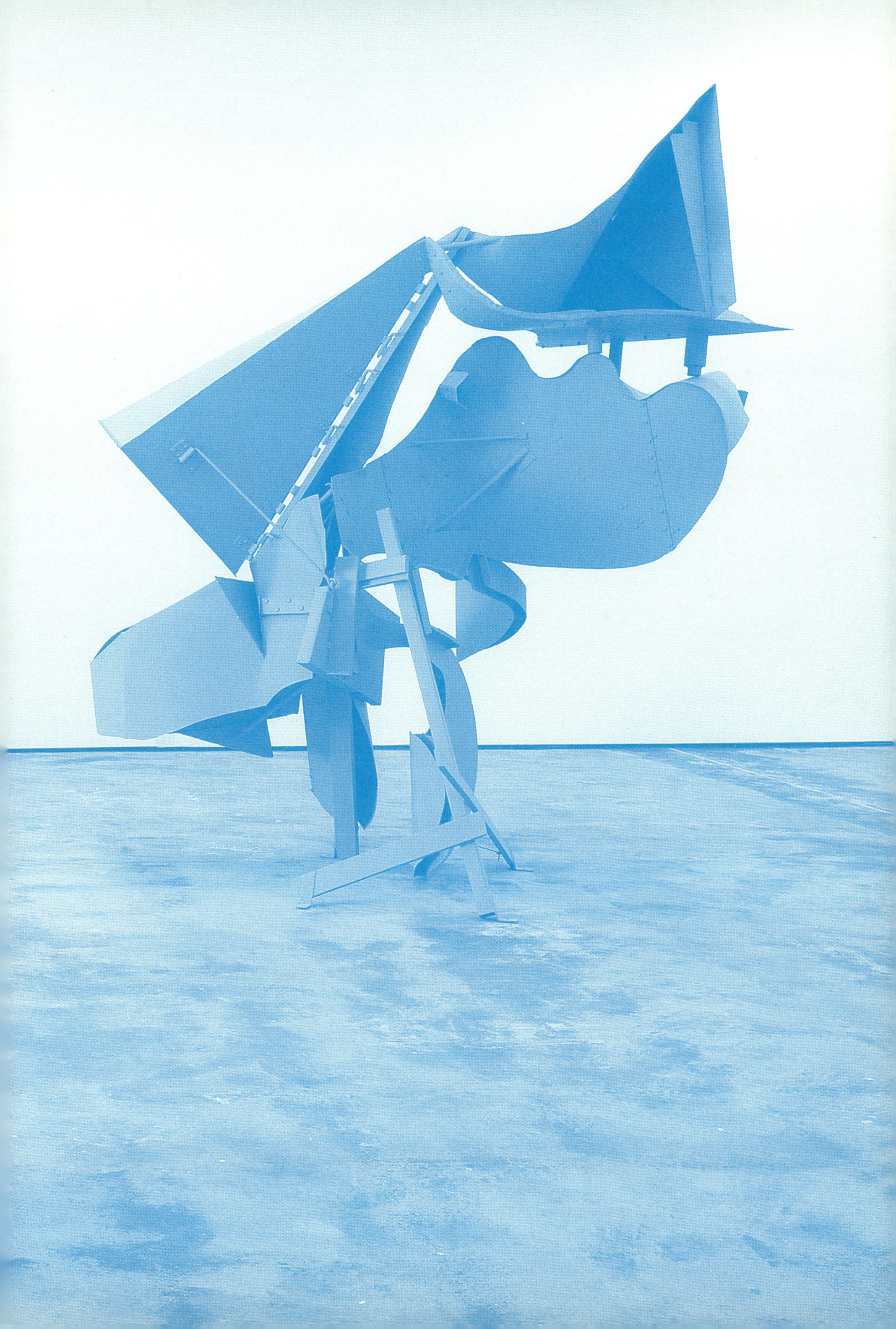

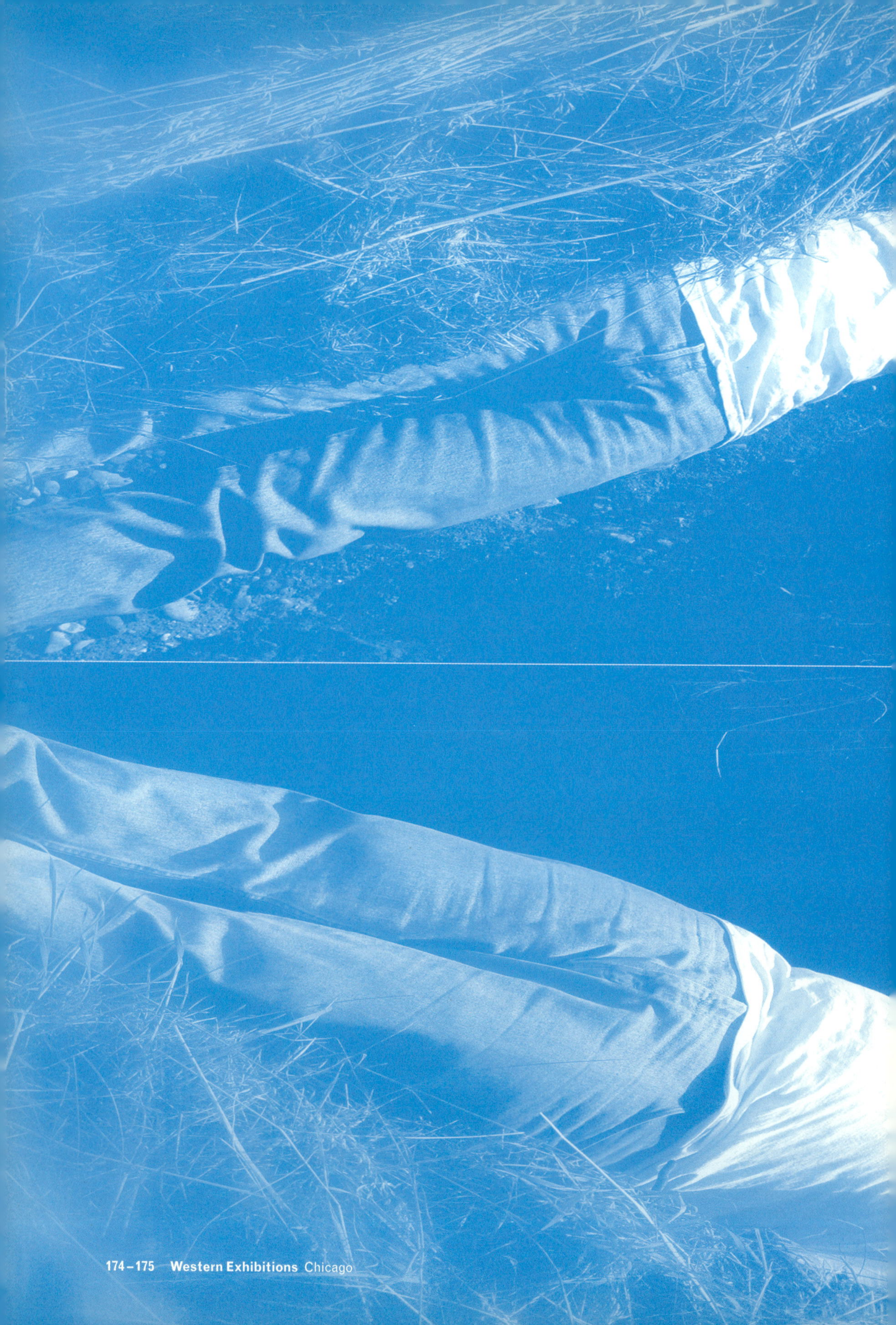

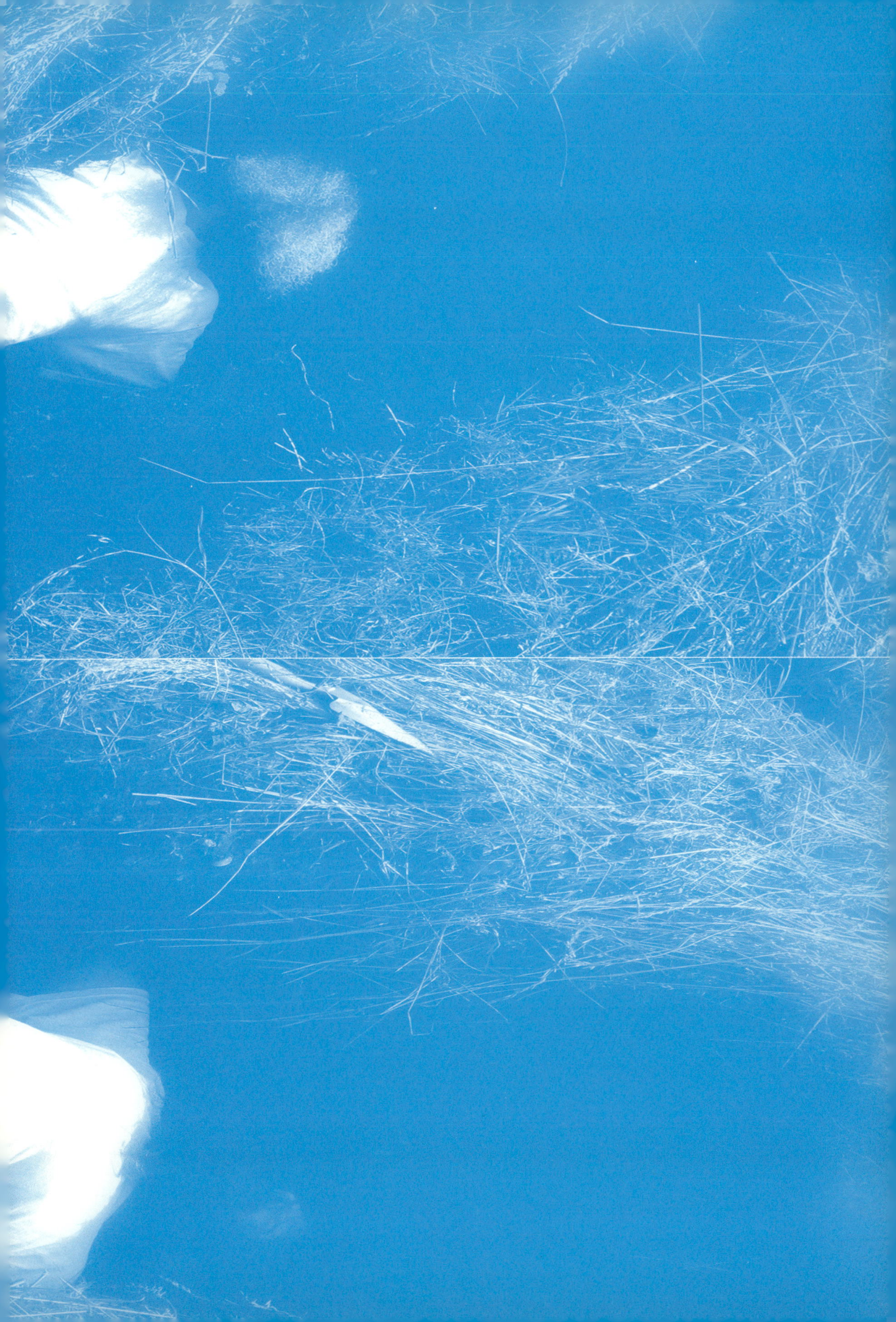

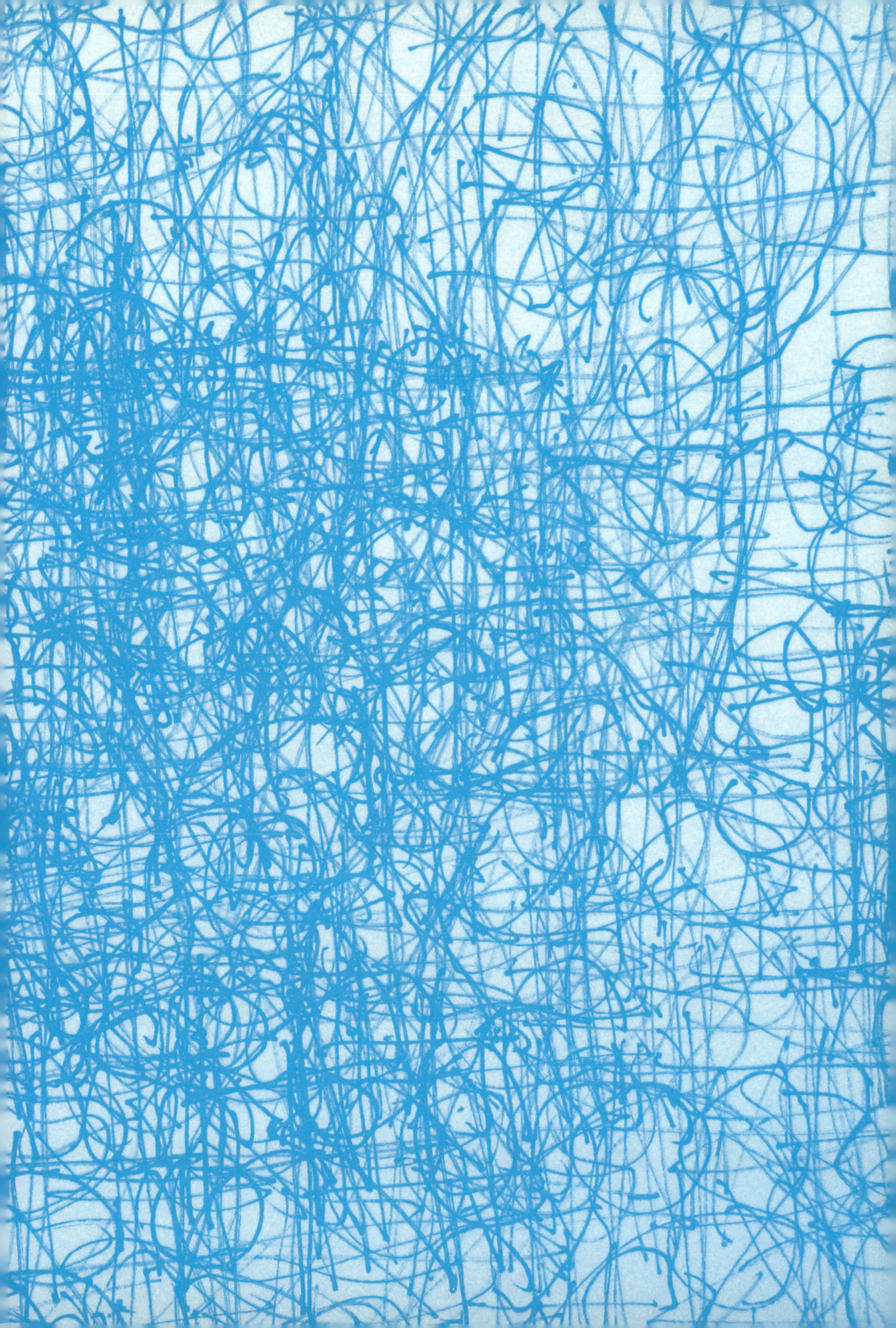

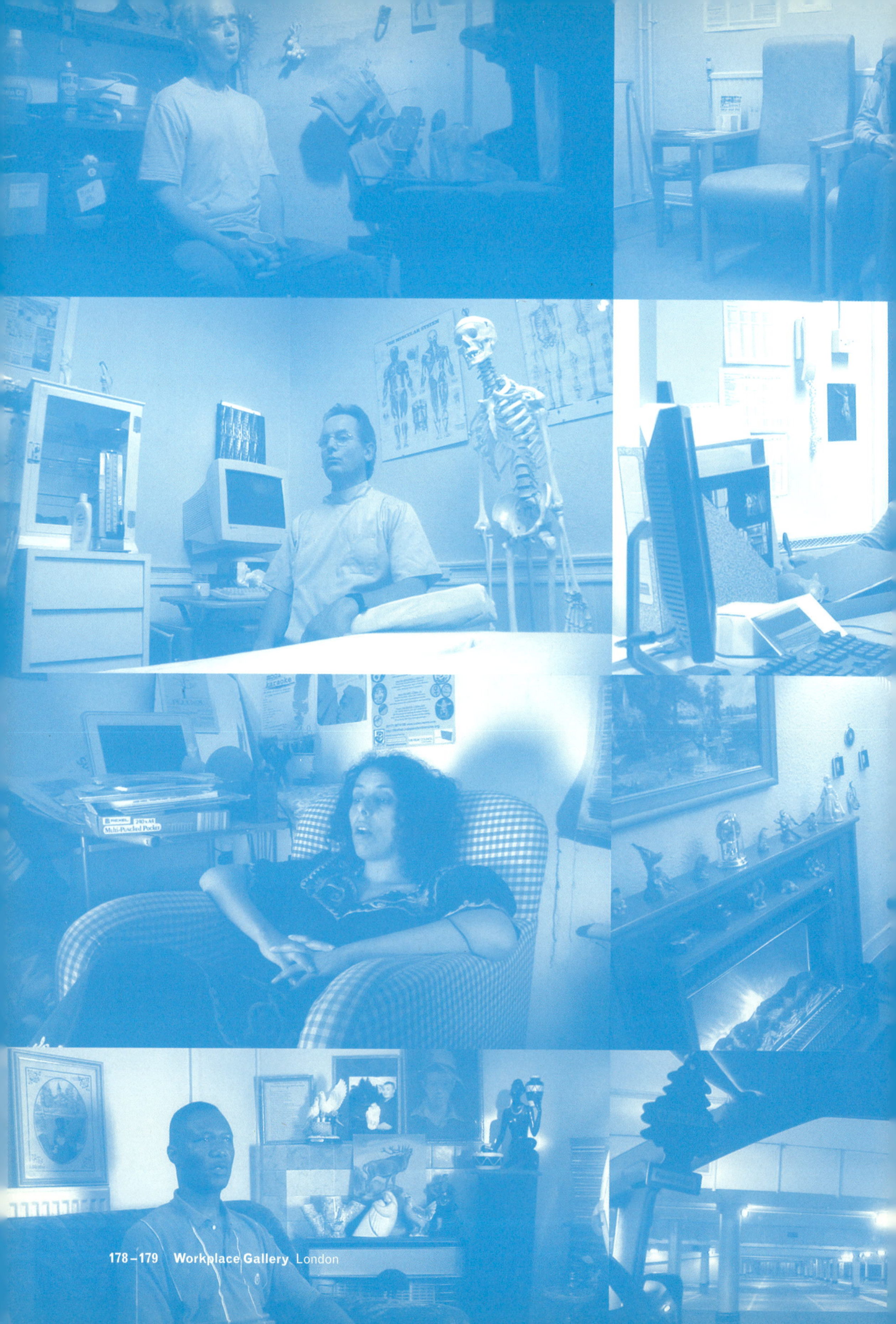

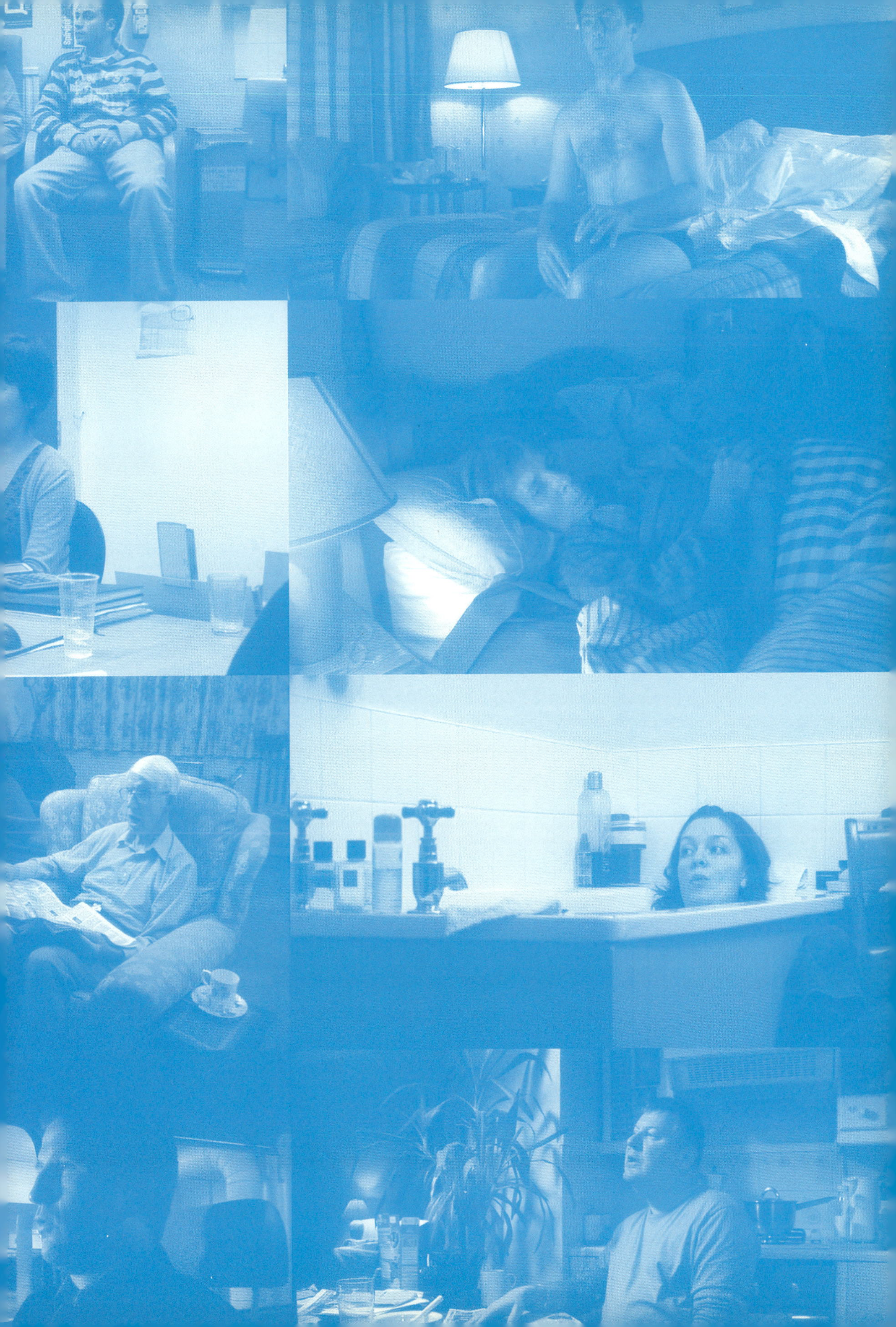

180–181 ZieherSmith New York

Gallery Index

Ancient & Modern
201 Whitecross Street
London EC1Y 8QP, UK
T +44 (0) 20 7253 4550
F +44 (0) 20 7253 4550

mail@ancientandmodern.org
www.ancientandmodern.org

STAFF
Bruce Haines, Rob Tufnell

ARTISTS
Eva Bernedes
Peter Linde Busk
Ruth Ewan
Melissa Gordon
Des Hughes
Alan Kane

Arquebuse
14 Rue de l'Arquebuse
1204 Geneva, Switzerland
T +41 (0) 22 807 0440
F +41 (0) 22 807 0441

info@arquebusegalerie.com
www.arquebusegalerie.com

STAFF
Faye Fleming

ARTISTS
Athanasios Argianas
Charles Avery
Pauline Boudry
Tim Braden
Ruth Claxton
Tami Ichino
Nick Laessing
Dietmar Lutz
Dave Miko
Brendan Monroe
André Niebur
Karen Russo
DJ Simpson
Barry Thompson
Marie Velardi
Lynette Yiadom-Boakye

ATM Gallery
621 West 27th Street
New York, NY 10001, USA
T (212) 375 0349
F (212) 260 2627
M (917) 417 7559

william@atmgallery.com
www.atmgallery.com

STAFF
Bill Brady

ARTISTS
Huma Bhabha
Yayoi Deki
Anne Eastman
Alison Fox
Tomoo Gokita
Yoko Kawamoto
Min Kim
Tamami Kobuta
Mike Pare
Miguel Angelo Rocha
Noam Rappaport
Eric Sall
Saeko Takagi
Gordon Terry

Page 6–7
Ruth Ewan, *Re-mould it nearer
to the heart's desire*, 2008
Adapted drawing by Lauren McKay
(aged 13) copied from the cover
of the Fabian Society Tract, 428 (1975)
14.25 × 10 inches

Page 8–9
Ruth Claxton, *Nest (Crested Parrots)*, 2008
Wall-mounted sculpture in two parts:
welded steel, paint, mirror, glass,
vinyl, found porcelain figurines, Fimo
One: 39.4 × 72.8 × 39.4 inches
Two: 27.6 × 35.4 × 17.7 inches

Page 10–11
Mikiya Matsuda, *ATM*, 2008

Laura Bartlett
10 Northington Street
London WC1N 2JG, UK
T +44 (0) 20 7404 9251
F +44 (0) 20 7430 1731
M +44 (0) 7771 803 606

mail@laurabartlettgallery.org
www.laurabartlettgallery.org

STAFF
Laura Bartlett

ARTISTS
Becky Beasley
Nina Beier & Marie Lund
Harrell Fletcher
Cyprien Gaillard
Elizabeth McAlpine
Andrei Roiter
Martin Skauen

Bellwether Gallery
134 10th Avenue
New York, NY 10011, USA
T (212) 929 5959
F (212) 929 5912

info@bellwethergallery.com
www.bellwethergallery.com

STAFF
Becky Smith, Allison Kave,
Elisabeth Schnieder, Greg Hopkins

ARTISTS
Ellen Altfest
Zoe Beloff
Tanyth Berkeley
Sarah Conaway
Adam Cvijanovic
Daphne Fitzpatrick
Dana Frankfort
Brent Green
Jonah Groeneboer
Everest Hall
Anne Hardy
Jocelyn Hobbie
Trevor Paglen
Chihcheng Peng
Alyssa Pheobus
Jansson Stegner
Marc Swanson
Abbey Williams
Paula Wilson

Josée Bienvenu Gallery
529 West 20th Street, 2nd Floor
New York, NY 10011, USA
T (212) 206 7990
F (212) 206 8494

info@joseebienvenu.com
www.joseebienvenu.com

STAFF
Josée Bienvenu, Alita Giacone,
Samuel Roeck

ARTISTS
Noriko Ambe
Marti Cormand
Annabel Daou
Juan Manuel Echavarria
Dario Escobar
Robert Jack
Ricardo Lanzarini
Marco Maggi
Stefana McClure
Adam Ogilvie
Mathias Schmied
Ken Solomon
Julianne Swartz
Yuken Teruya
Aaron Wexler

Page 12–13
Nina Beier and Marie Lund, *Two Women*,
1969–2008
Photographs of fathers' previous wives
hand printed by the artists
Courtesy of the artists and Laura
Bartlett Gallery

Page 14–15
Dana Frankfort, *MEATBALLS*, 2008
Gouache on paper, 14.25 × 10 inches

Page 16–17
Ken Solomon, *Class of '69*, 2008
Ink on paper, 14.25 × 10 inches

Blanket Contemporary Art Inc.
6-758 Alexander Street
Vancouver, British Columbia
V6A 1E3, Canada
T (604) 709 6100
F (604) 649 8159

info@blanketgallery.com
www.blanketgallery.com

STAFF
Sarah Macaulay, Natalia Tkachev

ARTISTS
Eli Bornowsky
Lutz Brown
Neil Campbell
Matthew A. Chambers
Matthias Dornfeld
Jeremy Hof
Brett Lund
Elizabeth McIntosh
Charlie Roberts
Peter Schuyff
Jeremy Shaw
Corin Sworn

BolteLang
Limmatstr. 214
8005 Zurich, Switzerland
T +41 (0)44 273 00 10
F +41 (0)44 273 00 12

info@boltelang.com
www.boltelang.com

STAFF
Anna Bolte, Chaja Lang

ARTISTS
Vanessa Billy
Paul Cherwick
Daniel Gustav Cramer
Haris Epaminonda
Christina Forrer
Florian Germann
Swantje Hielscher
Pamela Rosenkranz
Tif Sigfrids
Lukas Wassmann

Brown
42 Hoxton Square
Lower Ground Floor
London N1 6PB, UK
T +44 (0) 20 7729 1290
F +44 (0) 20 7729 1290

info@browngallery.co.uk
www.browngallery.co.uk

STAFF
Kimberly Brown, Robert Simons,
Kristin Lim

ARTISTS
Kristoffer Akselbo
Tamy Ben-Tor
Philomene Pirecki
Sam Porritt
Ry Rocklen
Shaan Syed

Galerie Sandra Bürgel
Hedemannstr. 25
D-10969 Berlin, Germany
T +49 (0) 30 258 006 30
M +49 (0) 173 54 37 247

info@galerie-buergel.de
www.galerie-buergel.de

STAFF
Sandra Bürgel, Celia Solf

ARTISTS
Franziska Cordes
Raphael Danke
Aleana Egan
James Evans
Alex Frost
Martina Heinz
Nina Rhode
Thomas Schroeren
Paul Snowden
Jean-Michel Wicker
Klaus Winichner

Shane Campbell Gallery
1431 West Chicago Avenue
Chicago, IL 60622, USA
T (312) 226 2223

info@shanecampbellgallery.com
www.shanecampbellgallery.com

STAFF
John Schmid, Heather Guertin,
Shira Ballon, Kevin Gallagher

ARTISTS
Jesse Chapman
Ann Craven
Kim Fisher
Michelle Grabner
Joanne Greenbaum
Mark Grotjahn
Jay Heikes
Patrick Hill
Suzanne McClelland
Jason Meadows
Rebecca Morris
Aliza Nisenbaum
William J. O'Brien
Anthony Pearson
Zak Prekop
Elizabeth Saveri
Mary Weatherford
Jonas Wood

Canada
55 Chrystie Street
New York, NY 10002, USA
T (212) 925 4631
M (413) 687 9888

gallery@canadanewyork.com
www.canadanewyork.com

STAFF
Sarah Braman, Suzanne Butler,
Philip Grauer, Wallace Whitney,
Sadie Laska

ARTISTS
David Askevold
Devendra Banhart
Brian Belott
Katherine Bernhardt
Joe Bradley
Sarah Braman
Matt Connors
Phil Grauer
Xylor Jane
Tom Johnson
Lily Ludlow
Michael Mahalchick
Frankie Martin
Carrie Moyer
Luke Murphy
Elena Pankova
Robin Peck
Jocelyn Shipley
Anke Weyer
Wallace Whitney
Michael Williams

Page 24–25
Klaus Winichner

Page 26–27
Jonas Wood, *Two Pots*, 2008
Graphite on paper, 8.5 × 11 inches

Page 28–29
Lily Ludlow & Allen Cordell,
Sowing Circle, 2008

Cardenas Bellanger
43, rue Quincampoix
75004 Paris, France
T +331 4887 4765
F +331 4887 4765

info@cardenasbellanger.com
www.cardenasbellanger.com

STAFF
Carlos Cardenas,
Amélie Bellanger Mathieu

ARTISTS
Devendra Banhart
Sophie Bueno-Boutellier
Kyle Field
Amy Granat
Andrew Hahn
Clément Rodzielski
Jérôme Saint Loubert-Bié
Amy Sarkisian
Olivier Soulerin

Cerealart
149 North 3rd Street
Philadelphia, PA 19106, USA
T (215) 627 5060
F (215) 627 5061

info@cerealart.com
www.cerealart.com

STAFF
Larry Mangel, Debbie Mangel,
Shiya Mangel

ARTISTS
Olaf Breuning
Chris Caccamise
Maurizio Cattelan
Marcel Dzama
Elmgreen & Dragset
Kirsten Hassenfeld
Yayoi Kusama
Nathan Mabry
Walter Martin & Paloma Munoz
Allan McCollum
Adam McEwen
Keegan McHargue
Taylor McKimens
Yoshitomo Nara
Yoshua Okon
Elizabeth Peyton
Kenny Scharf
Shirana Shahbazi
David Shrigley
Laurie Simmons
Andreas Slominski
Shinique Smith
Mickalene Thomas
Momoyo Torimitsu
Lawrence Weiner
Tommy White
Kehinde Wiley

**Portfolio to Benefit Youth
AIDS and the Cambodian
Children's Fund**
Works by: **Michael Bevilacqua,
Jeremy Deller, Kenny Scharf,
Laurie Simmons, Shinique Smith,
Mickalene Thomas, Kelley Walker**

Page 30–31
Clément Rodzielski, *Untitled*, 2008
Folded offset print, unique, 8.5 × 11 inches

Page 32–33
Chris Caccamise, *Birdhouse*, 2008
Edition of 40, painted resin,
13.25 × 8.5 × 9 inches

Galerie Chez Valentin

9, rue Saint Gilles
75003 Paris, France
T +33 (0) 1 48 87 42 55

galerie@galeriechezvalentin.com
www.galeriechezvalentin.com

STAFF
Philippe Valentin,
Frederique Valentin, Joe Tang,
Mathilde Landivier

ARTISTS
Pierre Ardouvin
Eric Baudart
Etienne Bossut
Véronique Boudier
Franck David
Olivier Dollinger
Sophie Dubosc
Babak Ghazi
Laurent Grasso
Yves Grenet
Carlos Kusnir
Mathieu Mercier
Nicolas Moulin
Anne Neukamp
François Nouguiès
David Renggli
Joe Scanlan
Gitte Schäfer
Veit Stratmann
Donelle Woolford

Cohan and Leslie

138 10th Avenue
New York, NY 10011, USA
T (212) 206 8710
F (212) 206 8711

info@cohanandleslie.com
www.cohanandleslie.com

STAFF
Andrew Leslie, Leslie Cohan,
Sarah Mattes, Joshua Kolbo

ARTISTS
Simon Aldridge
Marco Brambilla
Judith Eisler
Rob Fischer
Joseph Grigely
Rinko Kawauchi
Tim Lee
Euan Macdonald
Frank Magnotta
Todd Norsten
Melanie Schiff
Mark Soo
Tam Van Tran
Ned Vena
Uwe Wittwer
Shizuka Yokomizo

**COMA Centre for Opinions in
Music and Art**

Leipziger Str. 36
D-10117 Berlin, Germany
T +49 (0) 30 20648886
F +49 (0) 30 20649496

info@ancientandmodern.org
www.ancientandmodern.org

STAFF
Kolja Gläser, Thomas Hug,
Josephine Chetko, Saskia Draxler

ARTISTS
Lutz Dammbeck
Brock Enright
Nicolas Guagnini
Fabrice Gygi
Jan Hammer
Swetlana Heger
Christian Jendreiko
Michael Kunze
Gerhard Merz
Agnieszka Kurant
Michael Müller
Anna Parkina
Reynold Reynolds
Mika Tajima
Geerten Verheus
Sinta Werner

Page 34–35
Eric Baudart

Page 36–37
Mark Soo, *That's That's Alright Alright
Mama Mama*, 2008
Two C-prints, 3D glasses, angled wall
Each print 71 × 93 inches, wall dimensions
variable, Courtesy of the artist and
Cohan and Leslie, New York

Page 38–39
Brock Enright *Crystal Lines Basketball*, 2007
Swarovski crystals on Wilson basketball,
12 × 6 inches

Lisa Cooley
34 Orchard Street
New York, NY 10002, USA
T (212) 680 0564
F (212) 680 0565
M (347) 351 8075

frontdesk@lisa-cooley.com
www.lisa-cooley.com

STAFF
Lisa Cooley, Jeffrey Tranchell,
Scott Calhoun

ARTISTS
Andy Coolquitt
Alex Flemming
Frank Haines
Alan Reid
J. Parker Valentine

Country Club
424 Findlay Street
Cincinatti, OH 45214, USA
T (513) 792 9744
F (513) 792 9755

info@countryclubgallery.com
www.countryclubgallery.com

STAFF
Christian Strike, Matt Distel

ARTISTS
Kamrooz Aram
Jimmy Baker
Henry Chalfant
Jacob Dyrenforth
Cheryl Dunn
David Ellis
Justin Green
Estate of Charley Harper
Barry McGee
Ryan McGinness
Ohad Meromi
Aaron Morse
Shana Moulton
Kambui Olujimi
Todd Pavlisko
SIMPARCH
Chris Vorhees

Czarna Galeria
Marszalkowska Street 4 door 3
Warsaw, Mazowieckie 00 590, Poland
T +48 (0) 601 46 19 90

czarnagaleria@gmail.com
www.czarnagaleria.art.pl

STAFF
Aga Czarnecka

ARTISTS
Olaf Brzeski
Dorota Buczkowska
Anna Okrasko
Joanna Pawlik
Slawek Pawszak
Jadwiga Sawicka
Monika Wiechowska

Page 40–41
Frank Haines, *Untitled*, 2008

Page 42–43
SIMPARCH, Study for *Silvas Capitalis*, 2008
Pencil on paper, 11.625 × 17 inches

Page 44–45
Slawek Pawszak, *Untitled*, 2008
Oil on canvas, 59 × 43.3 inches

Elizabeth Dee Gallery
545 West 20th Street
New York, NY 10011, USA
T (212) 924 7545
F (212) 924 7671

info@elizabethdeegallery.com
www.elizabethdeegallery.com

STAFF
Elizabeth Dee, Jenny Moore
Jayne Drost, Tim Saltarelli

ARTISTS
Alex Bag
Eric Baudelaire
Harry Dodge and Stanya Kahn
Renée Green
Gareth James
Kevin Landers
Miranda Lichtenstein
Virgil Marti
Josephine Meckseper
Carl Ostendarp
Adrian Piper
Erik Schmidt
Meredyth Sparks
Mika Tajima / New Humans
Ryan Trecartin
Ryan Trecartin and Lizzie Fitch
Susan Turcot

doggerfisher
11 Gayfield Square
Edinburgh EH1 3NT, UK
T +44 (0)131 558 7110
F +44 (0)131 558 7179
M +44 (0) 779 056 9090

mail@doggerfisher.com
www.doggerfisher.com

STAFF
Susanna Beaumont, Charlotte
Jones, Becky Milling, Jenny Richards

ARTISTS
Charles Avery
Claire Barclay
Neil Clements
Nathan Coley
Graham Fagen
Moyna Flannigan
Franziska Furter
Ilana Halperin
Alexander Heim
Louise Hopkins
Tania Kovats
Janice McNab
Rosalind Nashashibi
Nashashibi / Skaer
Sally Osborn
Jonathan Owen
Lucy Skaer
Hanneline Visnes

ELASTIC
Ystadvägen 22 / Bragegatan 15
Malmö, SE-21430, Sweden
T +46 (0) 40 611 4319
F +46 (0) 40 611 4319
M +46 (0) 70 656 4319

info@elasticgallery.com
www.elasticgallery.com

STAFF
Ola Gustafsson

ARTISTS
Dave Allen
Luca Frei
Franziska Furter
Maria Hedlund
Knut Henrik Henriksen
Jone Kvie
Runo Lagomarsino
Anna Ling
Camilla Løw
Per Mårtensson
Anna Nordquist Andersson
Magnus Thierfelder
Anders Sletvold Moe

WORKS AVAILABLE BY
Catrin Andersson
Christian Andersson
Alexander Gutke
Kristina Matousch
Nilsmagnus Sköld
Astrid Svangren

Page 46–47
Mika Tajima, Still from *Untitled
(slow video)*, 2008
35mm slide film, dimensions variable

Page 48–49
Installation view, *Group*, 2008

Page 50–51
Luca Frei, *Untitled (Heads)*, 2007
Acrylic paint on wall, dimensions variable

Galerie Frank Elbaz

7, rue Saint-Claude

75003 Paris, France

T +33 1 48 87 50 04

F +33 1 48 87 52 93

M +33 6 03 33 85 85

info@galeriefrankelbaz.com

www.galeriefrankelbaz.com

STAFF

Frank Elbaz, Johana Carrier

ARTISTS

Olivier Babin

Davide Balula

Lilian Bourgeat

Wallace Berman

Swetlana Heger

Rainier Lericolais

Audrey Nervi

Kaz Oshiro

Gyan Panchal

Meredyth Sparks

Blair Thurman

Eleven Rivington

11 Rivington Street

New York, NY 10002, USA

T (212) 982 1930

F (212) 982 1936

office@elevenrivington.com

www.elevenrivington.com

STAFF

Augusto Arbizo, Kristen Lorello,

Elizabeth Raizes

ARTISTS

Hilary Berseth

Chris Caccamise

Caetano de Almeida

Matt Ducklo

Jacob Kassay

Cameron Martin

Florian Morlat

Jackie Saccoccio

Valeska Soares

Ishmael Randall Weeks

Michael Zahn

Kevin Zucker

Derek Eller Gallery

615 West 27th Street

New York, NY 10001, USA

T (212) 206 6411

F (212) 206 6977

info@derekeller.com

www.derekeller.com

STAFF

Derek Eller, Christine McLane

ARTISTS

D-L Alvarez

Jesse Bercowetz

Matt Bua

Carl D'Alvia

Lorenzo De Los Angeles

David Dupuis

André Ethier

Dan Fischer

Chris Hammerlein

Jessica Jackson Hutchins

Seth Kelly

Keith Mayerson

Dominic McGill

Christian Schwarzwald

Michelle Segre

Bettina Sellmann

Alyson Shotz

Whiting Tennis

Dan Torop

Ivan Witenstein

Page 52–53

Gyan Panchal, *standen*, 2008

Expanded polystyrene,

93.7 × 47.2 × 23.6 inches

Page 54–55

Caetano de Almeida, *Cruz*, 2007

Pollution on canvas, 19.68 × 15.75 inches

Page 56–57

Keith Mayerson, *The Nature of
Alexander (Alexander the Great)*, 2008

Oil on linen, 42 × 70 inches

Evergeene
7, rue de Vieux-Billard
1205 Geneva, Switzerland
T +41 22 321 37 40
F +41 22 321 37 43
M + 41 76 327 02 12

gallery@evergreene.ch
www.evergreene.ch

STAFF
Nicole Timonier, Samuel Gross

ARTISTS
Delphine Coindet
Andreas Dobler
Richard Dupont
Neil Farber
Jeremie Gindre
David **Hominal**
Laurence Huber
Renee Levi
Damien Navarro
Frederic Post
Didier Rittener
Christian Robert-Tissot
Alessandro Twombly
Pierre Vadi

Figge von Rosen Galerie
Aachener Str. 65
50674 Cologne, Germany
T +49 221 27 05 68 40
F +49 221-27 05 68 49
M +49 163 6383394
  +49 172 2093701

info@figgevonrosen.com
www.figgevonrosen.com

STAFF
Philipp Figge, Philipp von Rosen

ARTISTS
Shoja Azari
Koen van den Broek
Haïdée Henry
Nic Hess
Christian Hoischen
Anna Malagrida
Liza Nguyen
Sarah Ortmeyer
Ulrich Rückriem
Javier Téllez
Bas de Wit

Fruit & Flower Deli
53A Stanton Street
New York, NY 10002, USA

keeper@fruitandflowerdeli.com
www.fruitandflowerdeli.com

STAFF
Keeper

ARTISTS
David Adamo
Julieta Aranda
Fia Backström
Judith Braun
Jota Castro
Rainer Ganahl
Nicolás Guagnini
Tracy Nakayama
Trong Nguyen
Ylva Ogland

Page 58–59
Andreas Dobler, *Autumn Shelves*, 2007
Acrylic and oil on canvas, 63.8 × 82.7 inches
Photo by Annik Wetter

Page 60–61
Bas de Wit

Page 62–63
Arte et Veritas

James Fuentes
35 St. James Place
New York, NY 10038, USA
T (212) 577 1201
F (212) 577 1202

info@jamesfuentes.com
www.jamesfuentes.com

STAFF
Becky James, James Fuentes

ARTISTS
Lizzi Bougatsos
Brian DeGraw
Alejandro Cardenas
John McAllister
Agathe Snow

Galerie Laurent Godin
5, rue de grenier Saint Lazare
75003 Paris, France
T +33 (0)1 42 71 10 66
F +33 (0)1 42 71 10 77

info@laurentgodin.com
www.lauretgodin.com

STAFF
Laurent Godin, Agathe Lacroix,
Virginie Jacquet, Isabelle Chen,
Xavier Fontaine

ARTISTS
Scoli Acosta
Hsia-Fei Chang
Claude Closky
Liz Cohen
Delphine Coindet
Philippe Durand
Lamarche/Ovize
Gonzalo Lebrija
Corinne Marchetti
Aleksandra Mir
Vincent Olinet
Rajak Ohanian
Mika Rottenberg
Henrik Samuelsson
Haim Steinbach
Gérard Traquandi
Wang Du

Green On Red Gallery
26–28 Lombard Street East
Dublin 2, Ireland
T +353 (0) 1 6713414
F +353 (0) 1 6727117
M +353 (0) 87 2454282

info@greenonredgallery.com
www.greenonredgallery.com

STAFF
Jerome O Drisceoil, Mary Cremin,
Mary Conlon

ARTISTS
Gerard Byrne
John Cronin
Paul Doran
Fergus Feehily
John Graham
Patrick Hall
Tom Hunter
Mark Joyce
Conor Kelly
Alice Maher
Fergus Martin
Martin & Hobbs
Niamh McCann
Bea McMahon
Dennis McNulty
Niamh O'Malley
Paper Rad
Bridget Riley
Nigel Rolfe
Corban Walker

Page 64–65
Brian DeGraw, *John Lennon*, 2008
Graphite on paper, 8 × 10 inches

Page 66–67
Scoli Acosta, *Carbon Footprint,* exhibition
view, Gallery Laurent Godin, 2008

Page 68–69
Fergus Feehily, *Untitled,* morning, 24 July 2008
Shadow, dimensions unrecorded

**Greener Pastures
Contemporary Art**
1188 Queen St. West
Toronto, ON, M6J 1J6, Canada
T (416) 535 7100
F (416) 535 9300
M (917) 319 1142

kinekoivic@bellnet.ca
www.greenerpasturesgallery.com

STAFF
Kineko Ivic

ARTISTS
Huma Bhabha
Joe Bradley
Benjamin Butler
Holly Coulis
Andre Ethier
Jason Fox
Dana Frankfort
Daniel Hesidence
Rose Kallal
Derek Mainella
Mike Murphy
Anders Oinonen
Sasha Pierce
Emmy Skensved

**ANDREAS GRIMM
MÜNCHEN / NEW YORK**
Theresienstr. 56/Rgb
80333 München, Germany
T +49 89 38859240
F +49 89 38859241
M +49 174 9742296

530 West 25th Street
New York, NY 10001 USA
T (212) 352 2388
F (212) 352 2389
M (646) 641 6799

info@andreasgrimmgallery.com
www.andreasgrimmgallery.com

STAFF
Andreas Grimm, Martina Tauber,
Jessica Murray, Adam O'Neal,
Ashley Ludwig

ARTISTS
Jonathan Berger
Katarina Burin
Damien Cadio
Nana Dix
Terry Haggerty
Daniel Robert Hunziker
Inez van Lamsweerde & Vinoodh
Matadin
Bjørn Melhus
Thomas Palme
Dennis Scholl
Felix Schramm
Stefan Sandner
Matt Saunders
Katarina Sieverding
Lisa Tan
Cornelius Völker

Guild & Greyshkul
28 Wooster Street
New York, NY 10013, USA
T (212) 625 9224
F (212) 625 0151

info@guildandgreyshkul.com
www.guildandgreyshkul.com

STAFF
Sara VanDerBeek,
Johannes VanDerBeek,
Anya Kielar, Esme Watanabe,
Chelsea Spengemann

ARTISTS
Ernesto Caivano
Anna Conway
Lucas de Giulio
Benjamin Degen
Trenton Duerksen
Valerie Hegarty
Ryan Johnson
Lou Laurita
Devin Leonardi
Aaron Morse
Lisi Raskin
Mariah Robertson
Halsey Rodman
Kirsten Stoltmann
Mateo Tannatt

Page 70–71
Anders Oinonen, *In the Midst*, 2007
Oil on canvas, 40 × 55 inches

Page 72–73
Stefan Sandner, *Untitled*, 2008
Acrylic on canvas, 110 × 79 inches

Page 74–75
Ryan Johnson

Kavi Gupta Gallery
835 West Washington Blvd
Chicago, IL 60607, USA
T (312) 432 0708
F (312) 432 0709
M (312) 399 0007

Spinnereistr. 7
04179 Leipzig, Germany

info@kavigupta.com
www.kavigupta.com

STAFF
Kavi Gupta, Julia Fischbach,
Kristen VanDeventer,
Jennifer Leutner, Daniel Zaretsky

ARTISTS
Scott Anderson
Johanna Billing
Jeff Carter
Susan Giles
Angelina Gualdoni
Danielle Gustafson-Sundell
Hans Hemmert
Jo Jackson
Chris Johanson
Ashley Macomber
Sarah Nesbit
Melanie Schiff
Adam Scott
Claire Sherman
Zak Smith
Tony Tasset
Scott Treleaven

Jack Hanley Gallery
395 Valencia Street
San Francisco, CA 94103, USA
T (415) 522 1623
F (415) 522 1631

136 Watts Street
New York, NY 10013 USA
T (646) 918 6824

info@jackhanley.com
www.jackhanley.com

STAFF
Jack Hanley, Ashley Bellouin,
Ava Jancar

ARTISTS
Tauba Auerbach
Michael Bauer Carter
Ajit Chauhan
Anne Collier
Bjorn Copeland
Simon Evans
Harrell Fletcher
Christopher Garrett
Tamar Halpern
Jo Jackson
Colter Jacobsen
Piotr Janas
Xylor Jane
Chris Johanson
Saskia Leek
Ed Loftus
Camilla Low
Euan MacDonald
Andrew Mania
Alicia McCarthy
Keegan McHargue
Mathieu Mercier
Muntean/Rosenblum

Scott Myles
Shaun O'Dell
Bill Owens
Jon Pylypchuk
Tyson Reeder
Will Rogan
Michael Sailstorfer
Leslie Shows
Alexandre Singh
Hayley Tompkins
Anna Von Mertens
Chris Ware
Erwin Wurm

Page 76–77
Melanie Schiff, *Carson*, 2008
Archival inkjet

Page 78–79
Tauba Auerbach, *STATIC 6*, 2008
C-type print, 60 × 42 inches

Hudson Franklin
508 West 26th Street #318
New York, NY 10001, USA
T (212) 741 1189
M (917) 670 3642

nicole@hudsonfranklin.com
www.hudsonfranklin.com

STAFF
Nicole Francis, John Guida,
Audra Wolowiec

ARTISTS
Michael Bernstein
Jeremy Boyle
Mark Booth
Yolanda del Amo
Martin Esteves
Andreas Fischer
Alice Könitz
Keiko Narahashi
Jamisen Ogg
Arthur Ou
Elizabeth Saveri
Anne Thompson
Philip Vanderhyden
Genevieve Walshe

Hunt Kastner
Kamenicka 22
170 00 Prague 7, Czech Republic
T +420 603 525 294
  +420 777 571 306
F +420 233 378 196

info@huntkastner.com
www.huntkastner.com

STAFF
Katherine Kastner, Camille Hunt

ARTISTS
Zbynek Baladran
Josef Bolf
Viktor Kopasz
Jan J. Kotik
Alena Kotzmannova
Daniel Pitin
Jan Serych
Stepanka Simlova
Jiri Skala
Michaela Thelenova
Jiri Thyn
Tomas Vanek

IBID PROJECTS
21 Vyner Street
London E2 9DG, UK
T +44 (0) 208 983 4355
F +44 (0) 208 980 4605
M +44 (0) 7961 860 705

info@ibidprojects.com
www.ibidprojects.com

STAFF
Magnus Edensvard, Tobias Wagner,
Romilly Eveleigh, Yianni Vassiliou

ARTISTS
David Adamo
Janis Avotinš
Guillermo Caivano
Ross Chisholm
Anthea Hamilton
William Hunt
Christopher Orr
Michael Portnoy
Olivier Richon
Daniel Silver
Anj Smith
Marianne Vitale

Page 80–81
Arthur Ou, *Blue Screen (Equivalence)*, 2008
Pigment print on silver rag paper,
35 × 45 inches

Page 82–83
Jan Serych, *Intelligence Test*, 2008
C-print, dimensions variable

Page 84–85
Marianne Vitale, *The Honesty Parlor's Slits
for Spit Under Habit of Muss* (detail), 2008
Collaged drawing with pen and ink,
17.7 × 24 inches

Jancar Jones Gallery
965 Mission, Suite 120
San Francisco, CA 94103, USA
T (415) 281 3770

info@jancarjones.com
www.jancarjones.com

STAFF
Eric Renehan Jones, Ava Jancar

ARTISTS
Gina Borg
Virginia Holt
Prajakti Jayavant
Bill Jenkins
Chris Lux
Chadwick Rantanen
Sean Talley
Nancy White
Takako Yamaguchi

Parker Jones Gallery
506 Bernard Street
Los Angeles, CA 90012, USA
T (213) 618 6464
F (323) 227 0102

info@parkerjonesgallery.com
www.parkerjonesgallery.com

STAFF
Jasmine Jones

ARTISTS
Heather Brown
Steve Canaday
Gerald Davis
Charles Karubian
Nick Lowe
Ry Rocklen
Phil Wagner

Galerie Juliette Jongma
Gerard Doustraat 128-a
1073 VX Amsterdam,
The Netherlands
T +31 20 463 69 04
F +31 20 463 69 04

info@juliettejongma.com
www.juliettejongma.com

STAFF
Juliette Jongma, Jeanine Hofland

ARTISTS
Alexandra Bachzetsis
Tim Braden
Chris Evans
Melissa Gordon
Frank Hannon
Arjan van Helmond
Kim Hiorthøy
Donna Huddleston
Lisa Oppenheim
Ursula Mayer
Malin Perssons
Pablo Pijnappel
Misha de Ridder
Karen Sargsyan
Guido van der Werve

Page 86–87
Sean Talley, *White and Blue*, 2008
Digital Print, 10 × 14.25 inches

Page 88–89
Phil Wagner, *Untitled (Alternative Healing Institute)*, 2008
Water-based oil paint on linen,
50 × 40 inches

Page 90–91
Arjan van Helmond

Karma International
Richard Wagner Str. 16
8002 Zurich, Switzerland
T + 41 43 535 85 91
M +41 76 327 22 78
   +41 79 457 76 59

info@karmainternational.org
www.karmainternational.org

STAFF
Karolina Dankow,
Marina Leuenberger

ARTISTS
Marlo Pascual
Thea Gvetadze
Pamela Rosenkranz
Latifa Echakhch
Boris Mrkonjic
Chris Lipomi

Galerie Ben Kaufmann
Strausberger Platz 8
10243 Berlin, Germany
T +49 30 4401 04 66
F +49 30 4401 04 65
M +49 17 4317 45 53

mail@benkaufmann.com
www.benkaufmann.com

STAFF
Ben Kaufmann, Rhea Gaardboe Dall

ARTISTS
Bara
Andreas Bunte
Ben Cottrell
Sebastian Dacey
Matthias Dornfeld
Hansjoerg Dobliar
Poul Gernes
Maja Körner
Florian Morlat
Robert Orchardson
Berthold Reiß
Bernd Ribbeck
Claudia Wieser
Alexander Wolff

Rowley Kennerk Gallery
119 N. Peoria St., #3C
Chicago, IL 60607, USA
T (773) 983 0077
F (978) 926 0076

info@rowleykennerk.com
www.rowleykennerk.com

STAFF
Rowley Kennerk,
Michelle Vondiziano,
Mike Fleming

ARTISTS
Matthias Dornfeld
Gaylen Gerber
Molly Zuckerman-Hartung
David Lieske
Florian Morlat
Jordan Wolfson

Page 92–93
Marlo Pascual, *Untitled*, 2006
Digital c-print

Page 94–95
Matthias Dornfeld

Page 96–97
David Lieske, *il mio solo idolo
e la realta (room I)*, 2007
Scanned book page processed to targa
sequenz transferred to 16 mm
13 minutes, dimensions variable

Parisa Kind
Offenbacher Landstr. 11–13
60599 Frankfurt am Main, Germany
T + 49 69 6060 54 38
F + 49 69 1524 70 40
M + 49 157 7574 65 37

info@parisakind.com
www.parisakind.com

STAFF
Parisa Kind

ARTISTS
Lucas Ajemian
Julien Bismuth
Mike Bouchet
Trenton Duerksen
Isabelle Fein
Marcus Gundling
Thilo Heinzmann
Richard Jackson
Kalin Lindena
Bernhard Martin
Olaf Metzel
Dave Miko
Martin Neumaier

Nicole Klagsbrun Gallery
526 W. 26th Street No. 213
New York, NY 10001, USA
T (212) 243 3335
M (212) 243 1059

gallery@nicoleklagsbrun.com
www.nicoleklagsbrun.com

STAFF
Nicole Klagsbrun, Ruth Phaneuf,
Carrie E. A. Scot, Natalie Campbell

ARTISTS
Ryoko Aoki
Jonathan Callan
Beth Campbell
Nancy Davenport
Echo Eggebrecht
Jacob El Hanani
Alona Harpaz
Dennis Hollingsworth
Matthew Day Jackson
Ezra Johnson
Rashid Johnson
Barney Kulok
Rosilene Luduvico
Adam McEwen
Mitzi Pederson
John Pilson
Elaine Reichek
Mika Rottenberg
Peter Schuyff
Dylan Stone
Hiroshi Sugito
Billy Sullivan
Andrzej Zielinsk

Klaus von Nichtssagend Gallery
438 Union Avenue
Brooklyn, NY 11211, USA
T (718) 383 7309

info@klausgallery.com
www.klausgallery.com

STAFF
Rob Hult, Ingrid Bromberg Kennedy,
Sam Wilson

ARTISTS
Graham Anderson
Glen Baldridge
Donna Chung
Alex Dodge
Pamela Jorden
Jonah Koppel
Samuel Lopes
Liz Luisada
Emily Newman
Thomas Øvlisen
Ian Pedigo
Jenny Ping
Rindfleisch | Rapedius
David Scanavino
Teresa Seemann
Barry Stone

Page 98–99
Trenton Duerksen, *Ascetic Train*, 2007
Collage, 27.5 × 38 centimeters

Page 100–101
Rashid Johnson, *run*, 2008
Spray paint on mirror, 53 × 65 inches

Page 102–103
Donna Chung, *Untitled*, 2008
Digital file, 14.25 × 10 inches

Klemm's
Brunnenstr. 7
10119 Berlin, Germany
T +49 30 4050 49 53
F +49 30 4050 49 53
M +49 177 786 7419
   +49 177 214 4395

info@klemms-berlin.com
www.klemms-berlin.com

STAFF
Sebastian Klemm, Silvia Kaske

ARTISTS
Viktoria Binschtok
Gwenneth Boelens
Peggy Buth
Ulrich Gebert
Falk Haberkorn
Sven Johne
Alexej Meschtschanow
Adrian Sauer

KLERKX
Via Massimiano, 25
I-20134 Milan, Italy
T +39 02 2159 77 63
F +39 335 694 4904

info@manuelaklerkx.com
www.manuelaklerkx.com

STAFF
Manuela Klerkx, Gabriella
Bongiovanni, Laura Bottin

ARTISTS
Matt Calderwood
Adam Gillam
Marijn van Kreij
Dacia Manto
Navid Nuur
Jürgen Ots
Ariel Schlesinger
Josef Schulz
Jennifer Tee,
Simone Tosca
Roman Wolgin

Layr Wuestenhagen
Contemporary
An der Huelben 2
1010 Vienna, Austria
T +43 1524 5490
F +43 1523 8422
M +43 660 300 0606

info@layrwuestenhagen.com
www.layrwuestenhagen.com

STAFF
Emanuel Layr, Thomas Wüstenhagen

ARTISTS
Julien Bismuth
Frauke Boggasch
Tillman Kaiser
mahony
Annelies Oberdanner
Nick Oberthaler
Bernhard Resch
Fabian Seiz
Joao Pedro Vale
Andrea Witzmann

Page 104–105
Adrian Sauer, *Komposition #3*, 2008
Digital c-print, diasec, 11.8 × 15.7 inches,
edition 3+1 a.p.

Page 106–107
Marijn van Kreij, *Untitled
(The First TimeÖ, The Last TimeÖ)*, 2007
Acrylic on paper, 2 sheets,
25.6 × 6.9 inches each

Page 108–109
Fabian Seiz, *Always More Less*, 2008
Pencil on paper, 8.25 × 11.7 inches

Kim Light/LightBox
2656 S. La Cienega Blvd
Los Angeles, CA 90034, USA
T (310) 559 1111
F (310) 559 2911

info@kimlightgallery.com
www.kimlightgallery.com

STAFF
Kimberly Light, Alex Couri,
Patrick Marcoux

ARTISTS
Skip Arnold
Keith Boadwee
Simmons & Burke
Kim Dingle
Samantha Fields
Dustin Fosnot
Ry Fyan
Yvette Gellis
Kathy Grayson
Richard Hoblock
Ben Jones
Christina Malbek
Keith Mayerson
Sharon Ryan
Analia Saban
George Stoll
Eric Yahnker

lokal_30
Foksal 17 B/30
Warsaw, 00-372, Poland
T +48 22 425 90 40
F +48 22 615 73 63 ext. 22
M +48 602 13 99 63
　+48 608 29 09 96
　+48 880 13 71 71

lokal30@home.pl
www.lokal30.pl

STAFF
Zuzanna Janin, Agnieszka
Rayzacher, Michal Suchora

ARTISTS
Anna Baumgart
Filip Berendt
Andrzej Cisowski
Zuzanna Janin
Anna Maria Karczmarska
Anna Konik
Piotr Kopik
Tomek Kozak
Maciej Kurak
Jan Mioduszewski
Laura Pawela
Jozef Robakowski
Karolina Zdunek

Linn Lühn
Lindenstrasse 19
50674 Cologne, Germany
T +49 (0) 221 3976 907
M +49 (0)178 4975 888

info@linnluehn.com
www.linnluehn.com

STAFF
Linn Lühn, Julia Bulk

ARTISTS
Florian Baudrexel
Alex Jasch
Matthias Lahme
Linder
Sebastian Ludwig
Christoph Schellberg
Clare Stephenson
Kevin Zucker

Page 110–111
Simmons & Burke, *You Can Live Forever in Paradise on Earth #3* (Detail), 2008
Lightjet print and custom audio software
72.5 × 48.5 inches, edition of 6

Page 112–113
Karolina Zdunek, *Sunken Cities*, 2008
Photograph, 8.25 × 11.8 inches

Page 114–115
Florian Baudrexel, *New Constructivism*, installation view
Bielefelder Kunstverein, Germany, 2007
Infant, 2007, cardboard, dimensions variable
Fomal, 2007, plaster on styrofoam, neopor, 67 × 23 × 32 inches

Andreiana Mihail Gallery
Str. Pandele Tarusanu 4 bis
Bucharest, Romania
T +40 722 650 221
F +40 21 220 3446

info@andreianamihail.com
www.andreianamihail.com

STAFF
Andreiana Mihail

ARTISTS
Tom Chamberlain
Alexandra Croitoru
Adrian Ghenie
Katerina Drzkova
Mihai Iepure Gorski
Ciprian Muresan
Cristi Pogacean
Mona Vatamanu and Florin Tudor

Francesca Minini
Via Massimiano, 25
20134 Milan, Italy
T +39 02 262 4671
   +39 02 2159 6402
   +39 335 7843 543

info@francescaminini.it
www.francescaminini.it

STAFF
Francesca Minini, Paola Caravati,
Elisa Miotti

ARTISTS
Ghada Amer
Matthias Bitzer
Armin Boehm
Alessandro Ceresoli
Paolo Chiasera
Jan De Cock
Simon Dybbroe Møller
Ali Kazma
Deborah Ligorio
Gabriele Picco
Riccardo Previdi
Derek Rowleiei
Francesco Simeti

MISAKO & ROSEN
Kita-otsuka, 3-27-6, 1F,
Toshima-ku, Tokyo 170-0004, Japan
T +81 3 6276 1452
F +81 3 6276 1453

gallery@misakoandrosen.com
www.misakoandrosen.com

STAFF
Misako Rosen, Jeffrey Ian Rosen,
Kanako Aita

ARTISTS
Yuki Okumura
Kazuyuki Takezaki
Nathan Hylden
Naotaka Hiro
Maya Hewitt
Shimon Minamikawa
Miki Mochizuka
Mie Morimoto
Stephen G. Rhodes
Will Rogan

Page 116–117
Ciprian Muresan, *Untitled*, 2008
DVD Pal, 2'

Page 118–119
Paolo Chiasera, *The Following Days*, 2005
DVD, Pal 16/9, color, sound, 5' 11"

Page 120–121
Shimon Minamikawa, *Bikini*, 2008
Acrylic on canvas, 9.5 × 13.2 inches

**Monitor Video
and Contemporary Art**
Via Sforza Cesarini 43A-44
00186 Rome, Italy
T +39 335 5842 365

monitor@monitoronline.org
www.monitoronline.org

STAFF
Paola Capata, Hannah Gruy,
Marta Silvi, Simone Testi

ARTISTS
Francesco Arena
Adam Avikainen
Ra di Martino
Graham Hudson
Ursula Mayer
Robert Orchardson
Alexandre Singh
Antonio Rovaldi
Ian Tweedy
Guido van der Werve
Nico Vascellari
Kostis Velonis
ZimmerFrei

Mother's Tankstation
41–43 Watling Street
Usher's Island
Dublin 8, Ireland
T +35 31 6717 654

gallery@motherstankstation.com
www.motherstankstation.com

STAFF
Finola Jones, Fee McHardy,
Niamh NicGhabhann

ARTISTS
Petri Ala Maunus
Margrét H. Blöndal
Ian Burns
Nina Canell
Kevin Cosgrove
Brendan Earley
Mairead O'hEocha
Atsushi Kaga
Ciaran Murphy
Alan Phelan
Garrett Phelan
David Sherry

Murray Guy
435 West 17 Street
New York, NY 10011, USA
T (212) 463 7372
F (212) 463 7319
M (917) 293 3507

info@murrayguy.com
www.murrayguy.com

STAFF
Janice Guy, Margaret Murray,
Jacob King, Fabiana Viso

ARTISTS
Matthew Buckingham
Francis Cape
Alejandro Cesarco
Patricia Esqivias
Kota Ezawa
Noriko Furunishi
Munro Galloway
Matthew Higgs
An-My Lê
Ann Lislegaard
Barbara Probst
Beat Streuli
Shirley Tse

Page 122–123
Alexandre Singh

Page 124–125
Mairead O'hEocha, *Church Street,
Gorey, Co. Wexford*, 2008
Oil on board, 15.3 × 20 inches

Page 126–127
Ann Lislegaard, *Untitled*, 2008

Museum 52
52 Redchurch Street
London E2 7DP, UK
T +44 20 7366 5571
F +44 20 7739 6707
M +44 79 5853 6764

95 Rivington Street
New York, NY 10002 USA
T (212) 228 3090
F (212) 228 3094
M (917) 604 8348

info@museum52.com
nyc@museum52.com
www.museum52.com

STAFF
Christopher Taylor, Matthew Dipple,
Lucy Chadwick, Liz Jonckheer,
Melissa Emery

ARTISTS
Pierre Ardouvin
Kate Atkin
Sarah Braman
David Brooks
Benjamin Degan
Tom Gallant
Philip Hausmeier
Valerie Hegarty
Shara Hughes
John Issacs
Jacob Robichaux
Stefan Sandner
Frank Selby
Esther Stocker
Anthony Titus
Kon Trubkovich
Stephen Vitiello
Nick Waplington

Myto
Temístocles, 23-2 Chapultepec
Polanco
México, D.F., 11560, México
T +49 (0) 221 3976 907
M +49 (0)178 4975 888

info@mytogallery.com
www.mytogallery.com

STAFF
Gonzalo Méndez, Belén Moro

ARTISTS
Alejandro Almanza Pereda
James Bonachea
Raúl Cordero
Adonis Flores
Yunior Mariño
Ariel Orozco
Marianela Orozco
Fabián Peña
Cecilia Ramírez-Corzo
Nathalie Regard

Neue Alte Brücke
Schöne Aussicht 6
60311 Frankfurt am Main, Germany
T +49 69 17 07 13 52
F +49 69 36 60 94 15
M +49 176 6422 6509

info@neuealtebruecke.com
www.neuealtebruecke.com

STAFF
Mark Dickenson

ARTISTS
Wolfgang Breuer
Adam Chodzko
Simon Fujiwara
Nadira Husain
Morag Keil
Mandla Reuter
Florian Roithmayr

Page 128–129
Jacob Robichaux, *Props*, 2008
Collage on paper, 2 parts,
10 × 7 1/8 inches each

Page 130–131
Raúl Cordero, *Barbitúrico,* 2008
Oil on canvas, 67 × 86.6 inches

Page 132–133
Simon Fujiwara, *Paquito - Egg White
Jack-Off,* 2008
Submitted for print in the magazine
Straight to Hell, Courtesy the artist and
Neue Alte Brücke, Frankfurt am Main

Mihai Nicodim Gallery
944 Chung King Road
Los Angeles, CA 90012, USA
T (213) 621 2786
F (323) 610 3780
M (213) 621 2786

info@nicodimgallery.com
www.nicodimgallery.com

STAFF
Mihai Nicodim, Luana Hildebrandt

ARTISTS
Ciprian Muresan
Adrian Ghenie
Serban Savu
Neal Rock
Tom Chamberlain
Katie Pratt
Jonathan Parsons
Robert Holyhead
Cristian Pogacean

Office Baroque Gallery
Lange Kievitstraat 48
2018 Antwerpen, Belgium
T +32 484 599 228

info@officebaroque.com
www.officebaroque.com

STAFF
Marie Denkens, Wim Peeters

ARTISTS
Becky Beasley
Mathew Cerletty
Tamar Halpern
David Hominal
Owen Land
Davis Rhodes

Overduin and Kite
6693 Sunset Boulevard
Los Angeles, CA 90028, USA
T (323) 464 3600
F (323) 464 3607
M (323) 350 7374

info@overduinandkite.com
www.overduinandkite.com

STAFF
Lisa Overduin, Kristina Kite

ARTISTS
Frank Benson
Merlin Carpenter
Guy de Cointet
Tony Conrad
Barry Johnston
Ree Morton
Scott Olson
Eileen Quinlan
Stephen G. Rhodes
Haim Steinbach

Page 134–135
Ciprian Muresan, *Communism Never Happened*, 2006
Vinyl records, 78.7 × 59 inches, edition of 3+1 a.p

Page 136–137
Davis Rhodes, Studio Image, 2008
Courtesy Office Baroque Gallery

Page 138–139
Barry Johnston, *Untitled*, 2008
Ink and collage on paper, 14.5 × 10

Simon Preston Gallery
301 Broome Street
New York, NY 10002, USA
T (212) 431 1105
F (212) 431 1106
M (212) 365 4495

office@simonprestongallery.com
www.simonprestongallery.com

STAFF
Simon Preston, Giuliano Argenziano

ARTISTS
Michelle Lopez
Jessica Mein
Marco Rios
Kara Tanaka
Josh Tonsfeldt

Ratio 3
1447 Stevenson Street
San Francisco, CA 94103, USA
T (415) 821 3371

gallery@ratio3.com
www.ratio3.com

STAFF
Chris Perez

ARTISTS
Jose Alvarez
Sam Gordon
Robert Gutierrez
Jordan Kantor
Ruth Laskey
Barry McGee
Ryan McGinley
Takeshi Murata
Mitzi Pederson
Ara Peterson
Ben Peterson
Jonathan Runcio

Roebling Hall
606 West 26th Street
New York, NY 10001, USA
T (212) 929 8180
F (212) 929 8182
M (347) 247 9724
  (347) 526 9533

info@roeblinghall.com
www.roeblinghall.com

STAFF
Joel Beck, Bryan "Keppie" Kepple

ARTISTS
Erik Benson
Eve Sussman & Rufus Corporation
David Ellis
John Elliot
Courtney Smith
Lane Twitchell
Christoph Draeger
Bjorn Melhus
Reynold Reynolds

Page 140–141
Kara Tanaka, *Crushed by the Hammer
of the Sun*, 2008
Mechanical sculpture, silk skirt,
91 × 84 × 84 inches

Page 142–143
Rachel Carns

Page 144–145
David Ellis, *OKAY (Still)*, 2008
HD Video on BluRay Disc, 10 Minute Loop

Sister
955 Chung King Road
Los Angeles, CA 90012, USA
T (213) 628 7000
F (213) 628 7010

info@sisterla.com
www.sisterla.com

STAFF
Katie Brennan, James Griffin

ARTISTS
Robert Gutierrez
Adam Helms
Michael Lazarus
Sandeep Mukherjee
Michele O'Marah
Danica Phelps
Davis Rhodes
Amy Sarkisian
Matthew Spiegelman
Jeni Spota
Kirsten Stoltmann
Henry Taylor
Mary Weatherford
John Williams
Spencer Young

Small A Projects
261 Broome Street
New York, NY 10002, USA
T (212) 274 0761
F (212) 274 0756

info@smallaprojects.com
www.smallaprojects.com

STAFF
Laurel Gitlin

ARTISTS
Michael Bise
Dana Dart-McLean
Jessica Jackson Hutchins
Bob Linder
Anissa Mack
Michael Patterson-Carver
Will Rogan
Allyson Vieira

gallery.sora.
1-25-1, Shinkawa, Chuo-ku,
Tokyo, 104-0033, Japan
T +81 (0) 3 5542 3615

info@gallerysora.com
www.gallerysora.com

STAFF
Nahoko Yamaguchi,
Jeffrey Ian Rosen

ARTISTS
Ei Arakawa
Darren Bader
Brian Fahlstrom
Shinpei Kusanagi
Kyoko Ishikawa
Takeshi Murata
Carter Mull
Ara Peterson
Mark Roeder
Keita Suzuki
Naoko Tamura
Charwei Tsai
Jon Widman

Page 146–147
Jeni Spota, *Giotto's Dream,*
For Gaylen (Newlywed version), 2008
Graphite on paper, 10.5 × 11.5 inches

Page 148–149
Anissa Mack, *Untitled,* 2008

Page 150–151
Akihisa Hirata, *gallery.sora.*
perspective, Model photo and computer
rendering, Courtesy of Akihisa Hirata
Architecture Office

Jacky Strenz
Kurt-Schumacher-Str. 2
60311 Frankfurt am Main, Germany
T +49 (0) 69 21 99 98 70
F +49 (0)69 21 99 98 21
M +49 (0)151 11 64 97 37

office@jackystrenz.com
www.jackystrenz.com

STAFF
Jacky Strenz

ARTISTS
Eva Berendes
Markus Ebner
Kevin Hutcheson
Lin May
Jan Wagner

Studio Voltaire
1a Nelson's Row
London SW4 7JR, UK
T + 44 207 622 1294
F + 44 7930 399203

info@studiovoltaire.org
www.studiovoltaire.org

STAFF
Joe Scotland, Sarah McCrory,
Polly Brannan

ARTISTS*
Nairy Baghramian
Simon Bedwell
Nicholas Byrne
Spartacus Chetwynd
Thea Djordjadze
Chris Evans
Ruth Ewan
Alistair Frost
Simone Gilges
Emma Hedditch
Intoart
Nigel Kingsbury
Doreen McPherson
Dawn Mellor
Maria Pask
Elizabeth Price
Thomas Ravens
Matthew Smith
Joanne Tatham and Tom O'Sullivan
Donald Urquhart
Cathy Wilkes

SUNDAY L.E.S.
237 Eldridge Street, South Storefront
New York, NY 10002, USA
T (212) 253 0700

sundayles@gmail.com
www.sundaynyc.com

STAFF
Clayton Sean Horton

ARTISTS
Saul Becker
Michael Berryhill
Paul Doran
Keltie Ferris
Peter Gallo
Joel Gibb
Paul Housley
Molly Larkey
Michael Jones McKean
Asuka Ohsawa

Page 152–153

Markus Ebner, *Lapidar*, 2007
Acrylic on Canvas, 98.4 × 131.2 feet

Page 154–155

Thea Djordjadze, *Possibility, Nansen*, 2007
Plaster, wire, and plastic sculptures on salt
and glitter, Dimensions variable

*Either previously exhibited or project artists
notrepresented by Studio Voltaire

Page 156–157

Keltie Ferris, *Insignia*, 2008
Oil & enamel on canvas, 10 x 14.25 inches

Take Ninagawa
2-12-4 Higashi Azabu
Minatoku, Tokyo 1060044, Japan
T +81 3 5571 5844
F +81 3 5571 5844
M +81 90 9870 5594

info@takeninagawa.com
www.takeninagawa.com

STAFF
Atsuko Ninagawa,
Kazuyuki Takezaki,
Yuria Shinoda, Shizuka Okada

ARTISTS
Dale Berning
Misaki Kawai
Yoriko Kita
Chikara Matsumoto
Shinro Ohtake
Yukiko Suto

Thierry Goldberg Projects
5 Rivington Street
New York, NY 10002, USA
T (212) 967 2260

info@thierrygoldberg.com
www.thierrygoldberg.com

STAFF
Ron Segev, Claire Lemetais

ARTISTS
Keren Cytter
Barbara Ess
Ben Grasso
Jonathan Hartshorn
Swetlana Heger
Khalif Kelly
Jeffar Khaldi
Joyce Kim
I-Ling Eleen Lin

Triple Base
3041 24th Street
San Francisco, CA 94114, USA
T (415) 643 3943

triplebase@gmail.com
www.basebasebase.com

STAFF
Joyce Grimm, Dina Pugh

ARTISTS
Michelle Blade
Todd Bura
Serena Cole
Bryson Gill
Rachel Kaye
Kyle Mock
Jay Nelson
Hilary Pecis

Page 158–159
Shinro Ohtake, *Hiho-Kan I,* 1998
Printed matter and silk screen on paper,
17.75 x 34.5

Page 160–161
Keren Cytter, *Les ruissellements
du Diable*, 2008
Digital video, 10', color, sound

Page 162–163
Kyle Mock, *Undercovers*, 2008
Graphite on paper, 11 × 14 inches

Upstream
Van Ostadestraat 294
1073 TW Amsterdam,
The Netherlands
T +31 (0) 20 428 428 4

info@upstreamgallery.nl
www.upstreamgallery.nl

STAFF
Nieck de Bruijn, Martijn Dijkstra

ARTISTS
Cristain Andersen
Marc Bijl
Katrina Daschner
David Haines
Jeroen Jongeleen
Maartje Korstanje
Jen Liu
Ronald Ophuis
Laura Parner
Dennis Rudolph
Pepo Salazar
Rob Voerman
Daniela Wolfer
Lucy Wood

Van Horn
Beuthstr. 14 / Entrance Schirmerstr.
40211 Dusseldorf, Germany
T +49 211 5008654
F +49 211 5008654
M +49 172 2355557

info@van-horn.net
www.van-horn.net

STAFF
Daniela Steinfeld, Aude Bertrand

ARTISTS
Jan Albers
Andrea Bowers
Vanessa Conte
Georganne Deen
Alexander Esters
Manuel Graf
Katie Holten
Markus Karstiess
Jens Ullrich

Martin van Zomeren
Prinsengracht 276 hs
1019 HJ Amsterdam,
The Netherlands
T +31 20 420 8129
F +31 20 420 8129
M + 31 61 137 0211

contact@gmvz.com
www.gmvz.com

STAFF
Martin van Zomeren, Ayelet Yanai

ARTISTS
Adam Avikainen
Matt Bryans
Matt Calderwood
Stephan Gripp
Assaf Gruber
Martijn Hesseling
Chris Jones
Alexandra Leykauf
Navid Nuur
Wilfredo Prieto
Cornelius Quabeck
Maurice Scheltens
Praneet Soi
Lucy Stein

Page 164–165
Marc Bijl , *Untitled*, 2008

Page 166–167
Alexander Esters, *Urlaub vom
Ueber-Ich (modified)*, 2005
Linocut on paper, 66 × 57.9 inches

Page 168–169
Navid Nuur

Wallspace
619 West 27th Street
New York, NY 10001, USA
T (212) 594 9478
F (212) 594 9805
M (917) 355 9635
  (917) 518 9274

info@wallspacegallery.com
www.wallspacegallery.com

STAFF
Rosie Brooks, Janine Foeller,
Jane Hait

ARTISTS
Ron Amstutz
Walead Beshty
Kate Costello
Shannon Ebner
Martha Friedman
Brad Phillips
Laura Riboli
Helen Verhoeven
Donelle Woolford
Mark Wyse

Galerie Jan Wentrup
Tempelhofer Ufer 22
10963 Berlin, Germany
T +49 30 4849 3600
F +49 30 4849 3601

info@janwentrup.com
www.janwentrup.com

STAFF
Jan Wentrup, Tina Wentrup,
Mika Schmid, Trevor Good

ARTISTS
Pablo Alonso
Cristian Andersen
Marten Frerichs
Axel Geis
Mathew Hale
Gregor Hildebrandt
Michael Kalki
Thomas Kiesewetter
Jen Ray
Wawrzyniec Tokarski

Western Exhibitions
119 N Peoria Street, Suite 2A
Chicago, IL 60607, USA
T (312) 480 8390

scott@westernexhibitions.com
www.westernexhibitions.com

STAFF
Scott Speh, Kate Ruggeri

ARTISTS
Dan Attoe
Jimmy Baker
Carl Baratta
Nicholas Frank
Adriane Herman
Eric Lebofsky
John Neff
Paul Nudd
Melissa Oresky
Miller & Shellabarger
John Parot
Amanda Ross-Ho
Stan Shellabarger
Geoffrey Todd Smith
Ben Stone
Aaron Van Dyke
Pedro Velez
Mark Wagner

Page 170–171
Martha Friedman, *Study
for Release*, 2008
Cast and pigmented rubber,
dimensions variable

Page 172–173
Thomas Kiesewetter, Installation
view at Galerie Jan Wentrup, 2008
Courtesy Galerie Jan Wentrup, Berlin

Page 174–175
Miller & Shellabarger, *Untitled (Grave)*, 2008

White Columns
320 West 13th Street
New York, NY 10014, USA
T (212) 924 4212

info@whitecolumns.org
www.whitecolumns.org

STAFF
Matthew Higgs, Rebecca Gee,
Amie Scally, Ryan Evans

ARTISTS
Dan Asher
Carter
Janice Guy
Tamar Halpern
Ari Marcopoulos
Dan Miller
Donald Mitchell
Aurie Ramirez
Marlo Pascual
William Scott
Berry van Boekel

Workplace Gallery
The Old Post Office
19-21 West Street
Gateshead NE8 1AD, UK
T +44 (0) 191 477 2200
M +44 (0) 7951 8326 71
   +44 (0) 7905 6182 62

info@workplacegallery.co.uk
www.workplacegallery.co.uk

STAFF
Paul Moss, Miles Thurlow

ARTISTS
Tanya Axford
Eric Bainbridge
Darren Banks
Catherine Bertola
Cath Campbell
Joe Clark
Marcus Coates
Jo Coupe
Jennifer Douglas
Peter J Evans
Francis Gomila
Laura Lancaster
Rachel Lancaster
Ant Macari
Paul Merrick
Paul Moss
Ginny Reed
Richard Rigg
Cecilia Stenbom
Matt Stokes
Miles Thurlow
Sarah Walton
Wolfgang Weileder

ZieherSmith
533 West 25th Street
New York, NY 10001, USA
T (212) 229 1088
F (212) 229 1260
M (917) 837 7201

info@ziehersmith.com
www.ziehersmith.com

STAFF
Andrea Smith, Scott Zieher

ARTISTS
Melora Kuhn
Jeff Ladouceur
Wes Lang
Liz Markus
Eddie Martinez
Tucker Nichols
Rachel Owens
Javier Piñón
André Pretorius
Matt Stokes
Chuck Webster
Karin Weiner
Mike Womack

Page 176–177
Dan Miller, detail of *Untitled*, n.d.
Ink on paper, courtesy of the artist
and Creative Growth Art Center,
Oakland, CA

Page 178–179
Marcus Coates, *Dawn Chorus*, 2006
Fourteen screen video installation, 20'

Page 180–181
Mike Womack, *Metronome* (detail), 2008
Mixed media installation, dimensions vary

NADA Member List

Ancient & Modern London
The Apartment Athens
ATM Gallery New York
Massimo Audiello New York
Jeff Bailey Gallery New York
Bellwether New York
Josée Bienvenu Gallery
New York
Branch Gallery Durham
Brown London
Shane Campbell Gallery
Chicago
Canada New York
Cardenas Bellanger Paris
Cerealart Philadelphia
Cherry and Martin
Los Angeles
Cohan and Leslie New York
Lisa Cooley Gallery New York
Country Club Cincinnati
Elizabeth Dee Gallery
New York
ELASTIC Malmö
Eleven Rivington New York
Derek Eller Gallery New York
Evergreene Geneva
Zach Feuer Gallery (LFL)
New York
Foxy Production New York
James Fuentes New York
Sarah Gavlak Projects
West Palm Beach
Mary Goldman Gallery
Los Angeles
Larissa Goldston Gallery
New York
Green On Red Gallery Dublin
Greener Pastures
Contemporary Art Toronto
ANDREAS GRIMM
Munich/New York
Guild & Greyshkul New York
Kavi Gupta Gallery
Chicago/Leipzig
Jack Hanley Gallery
San Francisco/New York

The Happy Lion
Los Angeles
Parker Jones Gallery
Los Angeles
Juliette Jongma Amsterdam
Priska C. Juschka Fine Art
New York
Galerie Ben Kaufmann Berlin
Rowley Kennerk Gallery
Chicago
Nicole Klagsbrun Gallery
New York
Klaus Von Nichtssagend
Brooklyn
Klemm's Berlin
Leo Koenig Inc. New York
KS Art New York
LaMontagne Gallery Boston
Layr Wuestenhagen
Contemporary Vienna
Kim Light/Light Box
Los Angeles
MISAKO & ROSEN Tokyo
Monitor Video & Contemporary
Art Rome
Mark Moore Gallery
Santa Monica
Mother's Tankstation Dublin
Murray Guy New York
Museum 52 London/New York
Myto Mexico City
Nogueras Blanchard
Barcelona
Otero Plassart Los Angeles
Overduin and Kite Los Angeles
Ratio 3 San Francisco
Daniel Reich Gallery New York
Rental New York
Renwick Gallery New York
Ritter/Zamet London
Rivington Arms New York
Roebling Hall New York
Samson Projects Boston
Schroeder Romero New York
Sister Los Angeles
Small A Projects New York

Smith-Stewart New York
SOUTHFIRST: ART Brooklyn
SUNDAY L.E.S. New York
Take Ninagawa Tokyo
Triple Base Gallery
San Francisco
Uplands Gallery Melbourne
Wallspace New York
Western Exhibitions Chicago
Winkleman Gallery New York
Workplace Gallery Gateshead
Zieher Smith New York
Galerie Zink Berlin

A FAMILY BUSINESS SPECIALIZING IN MUSEUM-QUALITY PRINTING.

QuinnEssentials Books & Printing
Outstanding Print Management
Petaluma, California, USA
T +1 707 769 7484
mq@quinnessentials.com
quinnessentials.com

New Art Dealers Alliance
NADA
Art Fair Miami 2008
12.3–12.7

The Ice Palace
1400 North Miami Avenue
Corner of N Miami Avenue and NW 14th Street

Wednesday, Dec 3: 11am – 5pm
Thursday, Dec 4 through Saturday, Dec 6: 11am – 7pm
Sunday, Dec 7: 11am – 4pm
Admission is free and open to the public

www.newartdealers.org
info@newartdealers.org

NADA Art Fair Miami 2008 Catalog

Concept: PictureBox
Art direction and design: Project Projects
Publication assistance: Max Pitegoff, Stephanie Spiegel

Published by PictureBox and New Art Dealers Alliance.
All images copyright 2008 respective creators.
All rights reserved.
First edition: December 2008

ISBN: 978-0-9820947-2-3

Distributed by DAP/Distributed Art Publishers

Printed in Hong Kong through Quinn Essentials
www.quinnessentials.com